The Way We Were . . .

The Way We CAN Be

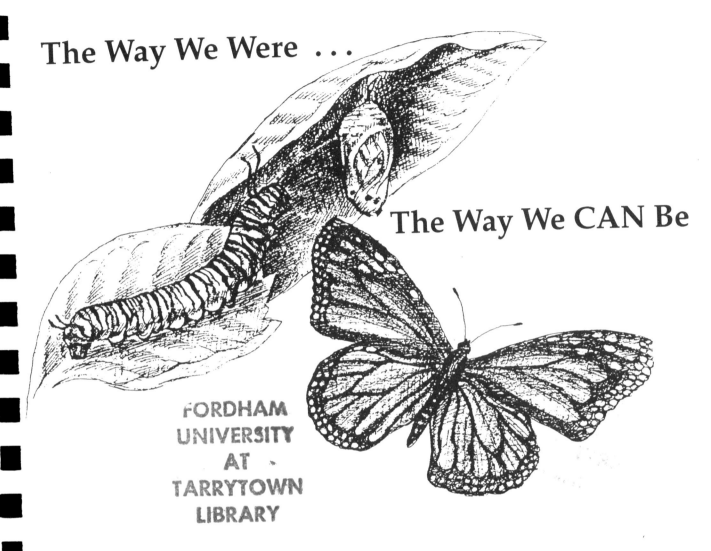

A VISION FOR THE MIDDLE SCHOOL

THROUGH
INTEGRATED THEMATIC INSTRUCTION
SECOND EDITION

by ANN ROSS and KAREN OLSEN

The Way We Were . . . The Way We CAN Be
A VISION FOR THE MIDDLE SCHOOL
THROUGH INTEGRATED THEMATIC INSTRUCTION
Second Edition

Published by Susan Kovalik & Associates

Distributed by Books for Educators
P. O. Box 20525
Village of Oak Creek, Arizona 86341
(602) 284-2389

ISBN-1-878631-05-5 Spiral Bound
ISBN-1-878631-06-3 Library Bound

TABLE OF CONTENTS

Acknowledgements   i
Introduction from the Authors   ii

Chapter

                                                                                    II
I   The Human Brain and How It Learns   1
        Notion 1: Intelligence As a Function of Experience   5
        Notion 2: The Triune Brain—Gatekeeper to Higher Thinking   12
        Notion 3: Seven Intelligences, Not One   15
        Notion 4: The Brain As a Pattern-Seeking Device   20
        Notion 5: Programs—The Basic Unit of Behavior   25
        Notion 6: Impact of Personality   27

II Elements of a Brain-Compatible Environment   35
        Key Elements of a Brain-Compatible Environment   38
        Element 1: Absence of Threat   40
            LIFESKILLS   48
        Element 2: Meaningful Content   52
        Element 3: Choices   56
        Element 4: Adequate Time   59
        Element 5: Enriched Environment   62
        Element 6: Collaboration   64
        Element 7: Immediate Feedback   71
        Element 8: Mastery/Application   76

III The Stuff of Curriculum—Taking a New Look at an Old Issue   77
        A Bit of History   78
        Curriculum: Birthplace of Change   82
            Mismemes in Education   82
        New Memes for Curriculum   90
        Toward a New Meme-Based Curriculum: The Curriculum
            of *Here and Now*   94
            Physical Locations As a Source for Curriculum   95
            Human Issues As a Source for Curriculum   96
        The Gap   104
            The Problem   104
            The Fix   104

IV Curriculum Development—Creating a Yearlong Theme   107
        Step A: Rethink What Students Are to Learn   110
        Step B: Select Physical Locations and Human Issues   110
        Step C: Identify Your Organizing Concept and Rationale   111
        Step D: Select Monthly Components and Weekly Topics   112
        Step E: Dream a Theme Title   114
        Criteria for Evaluating Your Theme   115
        Inside the Mind of a Teacher   116

V   Curriculum Development—Identifying Key Points 123
    Developing Key Points 124
    Characteristics of Good Key Points 129
    Examples of Key Points 130
    Using Key Points 132
    Importance of Using Real World and Multiple Resources ... 132

VI   Curriculum Development—Developing Inquiries 137
    Refining the Essential Content to Be Learned 138
    How to Write Inquiries 139
        Content Tools 139
        Structural Tools 142
        Inquiry Builder Chart 144
    Examples of Inquiries 146
    Criteria for Evaluating Inquiries 148
    How to Use Inquiries 150
    Classroom Management Requirements for Inquiries 151

VII Assessing Competence vs. Grading 155
    Using the Tools at Hand 158
    Setting Standards for Mastery: The "3C's" of Assessment ... 160
    Transitioning to Mastery 161
    Non-traditional Assessment Tools 166
    Tips for Making Traditional Assessment Tools More Brain-
        Compatible 169

VIII Transitions 171
    Model 1: The Single Subject Integration Model 174
    Model 2: Coordinated Model 178
        Two Subjects 179
        Three Subjects 182
        Four Subjects 184
    Model 3: Integrated Core Model 188
    Model 4: Integrated Double Core Model 191
    Model 5: Self-Contained Core Model 193

Appendix A : Characteristics of Young Adolescents 195

Appendix B: Chemistry of Nurturing the Brain 201

Glossary 203

Footnotes 209

ACKNOWLEDGMENTS

This book would not have been possible without the many contributions of the associates and practitioners of Susan Kovalik & Associates—gifted professionals and valued friends. Thank you for sharing who you are as well as your vast professional knowledge and expertise.

We wish to thank those middle and junior high school teachers and administrators who worked with the first edition of this book, especially the participants in The Bay Area Middle School Program funded by the David and Lucile Packard Foundation, and Program Director, Martha Kaufeldt. Their encouragement and comments have greatly enriched this second book, making it an even more valuable guide to the implementation of the ITI model in the middle school.

As is true with most books, their quality and personality are shaped by many hands and minds. Our thanks to Cynthy Black, Karen Kendrick, Kristen McKee, and Jacquelyn Tara for their artistic talents and to Linae Frei who applied her computer graphic skills and artist's eye with great care and precision.

A special thanks goes to Jo Gusman-Anthony, our very special friend and associate. Her special gift with language created the title for this book.

INTRODUCTION FROM THE AUTHORS

The Way We Were . . .The Way We CAN Be is more than a title to the authors. It is a statement—almost a prayer—not only for middle schools but for public education in general and for our nation. We have nearly reached the point of despair for all three; our sense of urgency is nearly overwhelming. It is our intent to convey why we feel such urgency and concern for middle school students (and their teachers and parents), to shake us from our system-induced paralysis, and to galvanize us all into concerted action. We hope, however, we can do so without seeming to disparage or discount the dedication, commitment, and hard work of so many well-intentioned and caring teachers and administrators.

Between us, we have spent nearly half a century in education, wonderful years in which we worked with great zest and conviction that we were among an army of bright, well-intentioned, hard-working educators who were effecting significant change in the "system" for students. To our complete dismay and bitter disappointment, we have had to confess to ourselves that precious little, if anything, has changed about our nation's educational system in over 100 years. Middle school is no exception.

Again, please do not misunderstand us. To say that little has changed in that part of the "system" called middle school during the past 30 years of the middle school movement does not mean that the landscape of middle schools has not been changed. It has. Many schools now feature interdisciplinary team organizations, block scheduling, advisory programs, student activities, the triad of course offerings: academics, electives, and exploratory courses. Further, great strides have been made in gaining awareness of the personal, social, and learning processes of adolescents. And yet, despite these advances, the curriculum of the middle school has remained unchanged and, many believe, has neutralized the accomplishments made in reorganizing and restructuring the middle school.

To understand this progress-without-progress history of the middle school movement, one should read James Beane's book, *A Middle School Curriculum from Rhetoric to Reality*—must reading for anyone working at the middle school level. A courageous book published by the National Middle School Association, it takes an unblinking look at the accomplishments and failures of the 30-year-old middle school movement. On page one, Beane comments:

*"I want to suggest that the work on middle school organization and teaching methods has succeeded partly, **and perhaps mostly,** because it has focused on better ways of transmitting the usual subject matter without questioning that subject matter or the subject area curriculum organization that surrounds it."* He goes on to say that the "absent presence" of the broader curriculum question, *"What ought to be the curriculum of the middle school?"* could be *"partly accounted for by fear that explicitly asking it might just cause a rift in what has mostly been a gentle and friendly reform movement at the middle level."*[1]

Whether from fear or overriding tradition, this "curriculum hole" has undermined the middle school movement for the past 30 years. However, Beane believes, and we hope, that *"As more and more middle school educators work out the organizational reforms and think about early adolescents they will eventually see that organizational 'restructuring' is an incomplete version of reform."*[2] For Beane, even the "new" conceptualization of academics, electives, and core, which is recommended by most middle school leadership documents, is faulty because it is based upon, assumes the basic premises of, and perpetuates the centuries-old conceptualization of the separate subjects—a content based upon an elitist view of what's important to know.

This book is an attempt to make the middle school reform vision more complete by proposing a new view of curriculum and the specifics of how to create such curriculum. It is dedicated to those who see restucturing and reorganizing as insufficient and who have the courage to question both our traditional curriculum at the junior high level and the recommended triad offerings of academics, electives, and exploratory courses for a middle school.

This book also introduces the rather heretical notion that, although middle school students have unique characteristics, they also possess a human brain which operates in ways powerfully similar to that of all fellow human beings, both younger and older. Therefore, we believe that the approach to developing a curriculum appropriate for adolescents should be based as much upon this similarity of human learning as upon the uniquenesses of the adolescent.

Welcome to the world of brain-compatible learning and Integrated Thematic Instruction for the middle school. Welcome to an adventure in becoming "the way we can be."

Ann Ross
Karen D. Olsen

v

THE HUMAN BRAIN
AND HOW IT LEARNS

In 1990, President George Bush proclaimed the final years of the 20th century as the Decade of the Brain. At last, substantial evidence,—how it perceives, processes, and acts upon its natural environment—and information gleaned from the past 20 years of brain research from a number of fields, of how the human brain learns. At last, official acknowledgement that such information should be utilized as the basis for restructuring and school reform efforts. Unfortunately, such recognition is slow in coming within the educational system. Few "reforms" around the country are based upon these new understandings about how learning takes place. Fewer yet are the approaches to curriculum development and instructional strategies designed to implement this new knowledge.

For many, the current brain research findings come as no surprise; the information validates our experience and intuition. Yet, the findings mark a radical departure from the previous foundations of our educational psychology roots; in significant ways, the findings contradict the system's pictures of curriculum and instruction, of the ways that classrooms "oughta be" structured and resourced. Implementation of this information will evoke revolutionary, not evolutionary, change in our nation's public education system.

It is the authors' belief that, although young adolescents have unique intellectual, physical, psychological, social, and moral and ethical development characteristics and needs (see Appendix A), they also possess a human brain which shares more similarities than differences with others of all ages. After 30 years of the middle school movement, information about adolescent uniquenesses is quite well disseminated. However, there is little implementation of current brain research.

This chapter highlights six fundamental notions about how the human brain learns. Included are:

- intelligence as a function of experience
- the triune brain
- seven intelligences, not one
- the brain as a pattern-seeking device
- using what we learn—developing *programs*
- the impact of personality on learning

Chapter II outlines how these notions can be implemented in the classroom and school to create a "brain-compatible"[1] learning environment.

Brain research findings are neither mysterious nor surprising. In fact, it is probably not an overstatement to say that you already know what brain research is telling us. You will find that it rings with your experience. To make the point, gather up what your experience already tells you. Answer the following question for yourself. To find the answers, go back to your preschool years; your elementary school years—in or out of school; your high school days—again, in or out of school; college—in or out of classes; your adult work or play times; yesterday. Let your mind wander freely. Here's the question:

Think back to a time when you
- learned a great deal,
- very quickly,
- had a great time doing it,
- could readily apply it, and
- still vividly remember what you learned.

Take time to jot down the learning event that comes to mind. Mull it around in your mind for a moment. How did you feel as a learner? For example, excited, enthusiastic, empowered? Note your own descriptors

_____

_____.

How did you learn it; what was the "instructional" process? For example, you did it hands-on or trial and error; it was an "experience" that got your juices flowing; you learned it with a friend(s); time was under your control; you received immediate feedback telling you if you were hot or cold? Again, recall and record your own experience so that you can compare your everyday-experience descriptors with brain research findings

_____

_____.

What was the "stuff" you learned; how was it organized; how did it get presented to you? For example, you chose it because it was meaningful to you—it was the "real" version from the real world with all the richness and complexity of the real world—you had to either "get it" (the whole thing) or understand nothing OR you went from piece to piece first and then understood the whole thing? Who chose it? Who shaped it as you went along? What were your own experiences?

_____

_____.

Keep a record of your above responses. If you do, you will soon be treated to the realization that you already know a great deal about what current brain research says about how the human brain works. And your everyday labels will be very useful to you later on as you prepare to make your classroom more "brain-compatible."

More than likely, your responses sounded something like the ones in the following mindmap. If so, you have an inside track on what the brain research of the past fifteen years has been telling us about how the human brain learns.

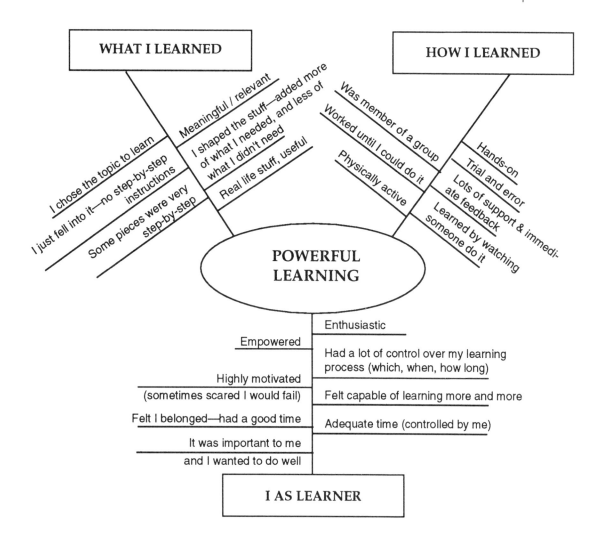

There are several notions from recent brain research regarding how the human brain learns which are fundamental to establishing a theory of learning and which have been corroborated by researchers studying the brain from many different avenues.

These six notions are:

- Intelligence is a function of experience rather than of immutable genetics

- The brain has evolved over millions of years; its three "parts" have different functions among which we "downshift" and "upshift," accounting for sudden and mercurial emotional and mental shifts by young and old alike

- We have not one generic intelligence but at least seven, each of which operates from a different part of our brain

- The mind is a pattern-seeking device; it is not logical or sequential in the way it takes in and makes meaning of input.

- Most information that we use is embedded in programs, a planned sequence to accomplish a purpose or goal; information not embedded in programs is generally unretrievable and thus unusable

- Personality has a significant impact on learning—how we take in information, organize it, make decision about it, and operate with others with it.

NOTION 1:
INTELLIGENCE AS A FUNCTION OF EXPERIENCE

We used to be told that genetics was the great determiner of intelligence: smart mom and smart pop, then smart kiddo; conversely, not-so-smart mom and pop would result in a not-so-smart kid. Work by Marian Diamond, UC Berkeley, Reuven Feurstein in Israel, and many others refute this popularly held credo. Feurstein and his associates have even gone so far as to stipulate that "Genetics is no barrier to learning." If, they claim, you know how the brain learns—what happens physiologically when learning occurs—one can assist a learner to create new "hardware" in the mind to carry new learnings and make quantum jumps in learning outcomes.

Diamond's work with rats and old people (not together!) has helped illustrate what happens inside the brain as the result of stimulation from an enriched environment. In short, when we have an "experience" (an event associated with enthusiasm), the electrical/chemical soup of the mind "wakes up" and neurons react by enlarging and by growing dendrites, nerve fibers which sprout from the neuron and increase in density and in the complexity of their connections.

As the dendrites grow and branch, a single neuron becomes capable of "communicating" with 600,000+ other neurons. This physiological capability to make connections underlies our common sense definitions of intelligence: the ability to see connections between things, observe subtle similarities and differences, and use metaphors that are useful in understanding how things work and how they can be used in new settings or for new purposes. Physiologically, this build-up of dendrites results in a denser brain, a heavier brain; intellectually, this build-up results in capacity for greater intelligence, i.e. problem-solving and/or product producing capability.*

What has all this to do with a classroom teacher? Plenty! An "enriched environment," according to Diamond's work, is associated with changes at the neuronal level in the brain, changes in the number of neurons dedicated to an area of operation, the size of the nuclei of those neurons, and the pattern and qualities of synoptic connections.[2] In loose terms, an enriched environment is one which causes the brain to remain actively engaged with objects and events.

The key question for the classroom teacher here is how to elicit maximum activation of students' brains. What kinds of input—what instructional strategies and materials—will produce maximum dendritic growth and neuron connection? Simply, it is a learning environment which activates not two or three or five senses but all 19 of them.

---

* Recent research suggests that there is a burst of such dendrite growth between age four and six and significantly less thereafter. Yet even these researchers believe that the use of these dendrites through later life is key descriptor as the dendrites continue to alter themselves in response to new information, changes in information, and ways to use information. "Use it or lose it" appears to be an appropriate maxim.

The 19 Senses[3]

SENSE	KIND OF INPUT
Sight	Visible light
Hearing	Vibrations in the air
Touch	Tactile contact
Taste	Chemical molecular
Smell	Olfactory molecular
Balance	Kinesthetic geotropic
Vestibular	Repetitious movement
Temperature	Molecular motion
Pain	Noiception
Eidetic imagery	Neuroelectrical image retention
Magnetic	Ferromagnetic orientation
Infrared	Long electromagnetic waves
Ultraviolet	Short electromagnetic waves
Ionic	Airborne ionic charge
Vomeronasal	Pheromonic sensing
Proximal	Physical closeness
Electrical	Surface charge
Barometric	Atmospheric pressure
Geogravimetric	Sensing mass differences

Consider for a moment an "experiences" you have had which engaged those senses. Each of us, for example, will carry to our deaths vivid images from childhood—"unforgettable" memories—which are replete with minute details perceived and recorded by many senses. For example, at age eight whiling away a lazy summer afternoon with my older brother: engaged in the thoroughly hopeless but intriguing task of attempting to dam up the creek; sunshine on our backs; bare feet scrunching in the pebbly gravel; the tepid, slow moving water with darting minnows disturbed by our rearranging of rocks and shovelfuls of smelly mud; our laughter rippling across the creek; my brother's nearness; his patience with a little sister who "never stayed home like the other girls did" . . . The lessons of that day, the wonder and science of the creek, the beauty of family relationships, will never be forgotten.

Imagine if every school day produced memories of this power! Can the school have such impact on learners? We believe the answer is a resounding "Yes!"

"Yes," if we if our curriculum is focused on here and now (see Chapter III) and "yes" if our instructional strategies utilized *being there* and *immersion*.

© 1992 Susan Kovalik & Associates

See the next page for an illustration of the senses that can be activated by each of the above kinds of instructional approaches. As the illustration makes clear, the easy but uncomfortable answer to our questions is that there is simply no substitute for the real thing—real-life things in real-life contexts. The second and last hand tools provided by the system are wholly inadequate to the task of creating learning of consequence.

The moral to the story when applied to the classroom is that "Dittos don't make dendrites!" That is to say that neither dittos nor the textbook or workbooks create an enriched environment which activates the brain. In other words, every minute spent on what students experience as boring or as "seat work" is a minute spent NOT building intelligence.

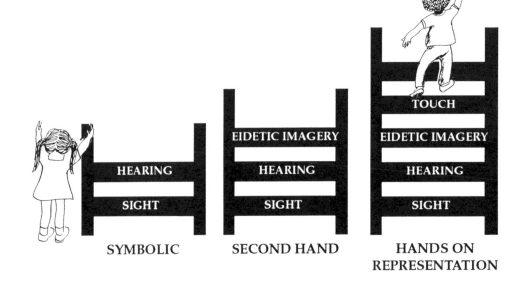

SYMBOLIC

SECOND HAND

HANDS ON
REPRESENTATION

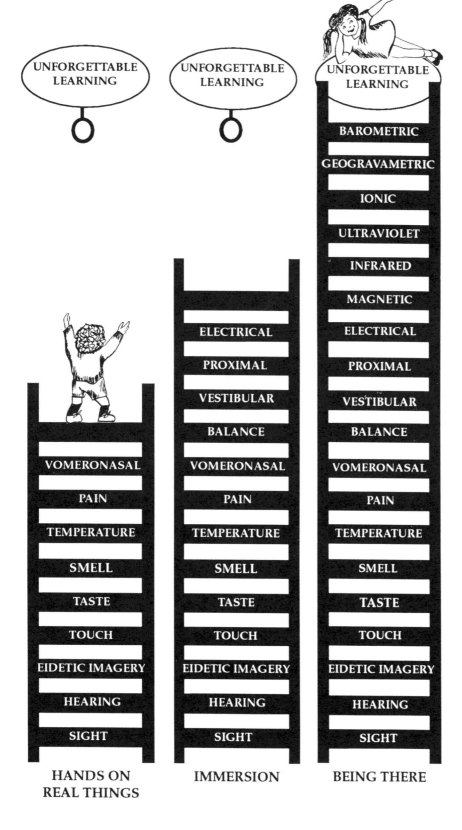

HANDS ON REAL THINGS	IMMERSION	BEING THERE

Column 1 — HANDS ON REAL THINGS:
UNFORGETTABLE LEARNING

VOMERONASAL
PAIN
TEMPERATURE
SMELL
TASTE
TOUCH
EIDETIC IMAGERY
HEARING
SIGHT

Column 2 — IMMERSION:
UNFORGETTABLE LEARNING

ELECTRICAL
PROXIMAL
VESTIBULAR
BALANCE
VOMERONASAL
PAIN
TEMPERATURE
SMELL
TASTE
TOUCH
EIDETIC IMAGERY
HEARING
SIGHT

Column 3 — BEING THERE:
UNFORGETTABLE LEARNING

BAROMETRIC
GEOGRAVAMETRIC
IONIC
ULTRAVIOLET
INFRARED
MAGNETIC
ELECTRICAL
PROXIMAL
VESTIBULAR
BALANCE
VOMERONASAL
PAIN
TEMPERATURE
SMELL
TASTE
TOUCH
EIDETIC IMAGERY
HEARING
SIGHT

9

THE CHALLENGE INCREASES

Jane Healy, in her book *Endangered Minds: Why Children Don't Think*, states that the brain today's children bring to school is different from that which came to school 30 years ago. Accordingly, the curriculum of today's schools needs drastic revision if it is to keep students "actively engaged with objects and events." The nature of the changes which need to be made are characterized by Leslie Hart as he compares the student and curriculum needs of the past to those of today. "The students of those days, in their hours and months out of school, were drenched in exposure to reality. They helped grow and process food, fed and birthed animals, helped maintain machines and build structures, made many necessities, wove and sewed clothing, assisted family manufacturing and business efforts, knew the community and its people intimately. Their input was varied and often oppressively 'real'. **The school could well afford, on balance, to bring them into a once- or twice-removed, symbolic world** (the curriculum and its materials in the school)."[4]

In contrast, **"today's students are starved for exposure to reality,** yet the schools have failed to bring reality inside their walls to offset the loss."[5] The "once- or twice-removed, symbolic world" of school does not constitute an "enriched environment" for the young human mind. Just as 80 percent of reading comprehension hinges on prior knowledge, learning from today's curriculum occurs only for those who bring meaning to the printed page, who bring meaning to the symbols being studied. Most of today's students do not bring sufficient prior experience of the real world with them to the school to allow them to profit from school.[6]

In short, we can no longer assume that the neural networks and connections needed to succeed at reading or writing or dealing in the abstract are in place. The good news about the brain is that it is sufficiently powerful and malleable to take on new learnings at virtually any age.

BRAIN POWER

The plasticity of the brain and its ability to build dendrites and neural connections is dramatically illustrated by Feurstein in his work with multiple-handicapped (genetic and trauma-based) children and adults. His work, has proven that the brain is sufficiently plastic that it can be significantly altered by the nature and kinds of sensory input provided. Key in this process is the "mediation" or assistance of another person to assist the learner to perceive things, and in ways, that they, left to their own processing, would not be able to perceive; this then requires the brain to respond differently and process differently. His model, the "mediated learning" process, is a powerful tool for teachers when working with all learners.[7]

One last comment about experience and its role in developing intelligence is Frank Smith's assertion that learning is incidental, that the mind processes huge gulps of input per minute, only a small portion of which may directly relate to a teacher's intended objective for the lesson or classroom activity at hand. Because the teacher is lecturing does not mean that the brain shuts down its processing of input from the other senses. Other messages are being received. For example, input: "This is a cold, sterile room." Message received: "I'm not welcome here." A campus, dirty and in need of repair gives off clear messages that no one cares. Contrast this to the messages from the environment of Disneyland or EPCOT: "You'll it love here. We've been waiting to serve you. Is there anything more we can do to make your visit a wonderful experience for you?" The environment of the school and classroom virtually bristle with messages to students; many are negative, brain-antagonistic. To enhance learning, all messages to the brain must be brain-compatible.

NOTION 2: THE TRIUNE BRAIN—
GATEKEEPER TO HIGHER THINKING ABILITIES

The human brain is staggeringly complex in its structures, chemistry, electrical signals, and functions. To view it in three basic "chunks" is admittedly a vast oversimplification, yet a useful one. As first theorized by Dr. Paul MacLean, NIMH, Bethesda, Maryland, the brain, evolving over millions of years, can be thought of as three brains in one, each with specific responsibilities essential for human survival and growth, each constantly assessing the needs of the situation at hand to determine what response(s) is most appropriate.

The brain stem—The first brain, over 200 million years old, can be referred to as the reptilian brain. The existence of our species attests to the success of this brain. Always on the alert for life-threatening events, it is the part of the brain we "downshift" to when responding to life-threatening conditions. This downshifting has the effect of shutting off input to the much more slowly processing cerebral cortex and the limbic system. The brain stem has no language. And while this brain sees and responds to visual input, it typically does not store it. Storing things in memory takes time, coming up with a verbal defense takes time, a luxury which the human organism under life-threatening attack cannot afford. Action is needed NOW.

Recall, for example, a near accident. Almost before you are consciously aware of the circumstances, even before you have time to register fear, you find yourself giving the steering wheel a hard yank to the left. Your "old" brain perceived the threat from the car moving into your right rear door and it reacted instantly to preserve your life. Or, in the case of one of the authors, a one inch trickle at the bottom of the ravine becomes an eight foot wall of water. As it hit her car and swung the tail end toward the edge of the rail-less bridge and a fifteen foot drop off, adrenalin exploded through the body and the mind "blanked out." Seconds later, after "coming to," she found herself standing on the opposite side of the ravine, purse in hand (yes!, ladies, her purse!), with no visual memory of how she got out of the car and managed to get through the water without being swept away. These are everyday examples of the "downshifting" of the brain to the brain stem when threat is extreme and considered life-threatening. When operating from the brain stem, the brain perceives but does not take time to record. And there is no language.

When this ancient brain goes to school, it does not shut off. It remains on the alert for any and all threat—real or perceived. And, when triggered, downshifting occurs, shutting down the cerebrum and thus eliminating the possibility of learning multiplication tables, Shakespearean sonnets, or observing for science. The threat from the classroom bully, fear of a low grade, the possibility of public ridicule—all create downshifting out of the cerebrum, the home of academic learning.

The limbic system — The second brain, the old mammalian brain or limbic system, is more than 60 million years old. Home of the emotions we associate with being human—love, hate, jealousy, frustration, anger, fear—this part of the brain has visual memory but language is limited to yells, screams, expletives.

In the classroom, put-downs from classmates or teacher, and even the threat of "not belonging" to one's group is threatening to this "old brain" and is sufficient to create downshifting. While not serious enough to trigger downshifting into the brain stem where we "blank out," such stimuli are more than sufficient to trigger downshifting out of the cerebrum into the turbulent soup of emotions of the limbic system. Again, long division, writing an essay, the checks and balances of our government cannot be processed.

It is important for middle school students to understand the operation of their brains under highly emotional times. Given the raging hormones experienced by middle school students and the social and personal developmental upheavals, it is only a slight overstatement to say that middle school students are downshifted much of their time in school. Examples include a disagreement with their parents upon leaving for school, a fight with their best friend, being slighted by an important other, a zit that just popped out on their chin, boredom with school, or just "being in a funk." And it isn't just negative emotions that downshift the brain. Spring fever, love, joy, awe, and bliss also make us forget forget the "serious side" of learning.

The role of the limbic system is complex and fascinating. According to Ned Hermann, the limbic system, even though considerably smaller than the cerebral hemispheres, "plays an enormous role in our functioning. If blood supply is a significant indication of importance, then it is worth noting that the limbic system has one of the richest blood supplies in the entire body. And no wonder! The limbic system regulates eating, drinking, sleeping, waking, body temperature, chemical balances such as blood sugar, heart rate, blood pressure, hormones, sex, and emotions. It's also the focus of pleasure, punishment, hunger, thirst, aggression, and rage."[8] Recent research also suggests that the limbic system is a gatekeeper or switching device. Its functions include:

- converting information that the brain receives into appropriate modes for processing, constantly checking information relayed to the brain by the senses and comparing it to past experience.

- directing information to the appropriate memory storage areas of the brain. This function is needed because memories are not stored in one specific place, but rather are distributed throughout the brain in the areas functionally associated with the nature of the memory to be stored. Words, numbers, and visual images, for example, are stored in areas associated with the language center, the calculation center, and the visual cortex, respectively.

- transferring information transfer from short-term to long-term memory.[9]

13

The cerebral cortex — The third brain, the new mammalian brain or cerebrum, has been with us for only a few million years. In evolutionary terms, a very new item indeed. The cerebral cortex is a multi-modal, multi-path processor of thousands of bits of information arriving via the 19 senses per minute. Given the volume of such information, it understandably is the slowest of the three levels of the brain. The cerebral cortex can think, solve problems, analyze, create, synthesize and handle a multitude of other complicated tasks. It is the part of the brain that students must be in if learning is to take place. Consequently, the first step toward brain-compatibility in the classroom is creating an environment with an absence of threat. Without the the necessary preconditions for remaining upshifted into the cerebral cortex, all other instructional efforts by a teacher could be a waste of time.

This is the home of academic learning. This is the part of our brain which handles language, symbols, and images for learning Shakespeare, exploring the complexities of science, studying ancient history, or contemplating the issues and problems of the future.

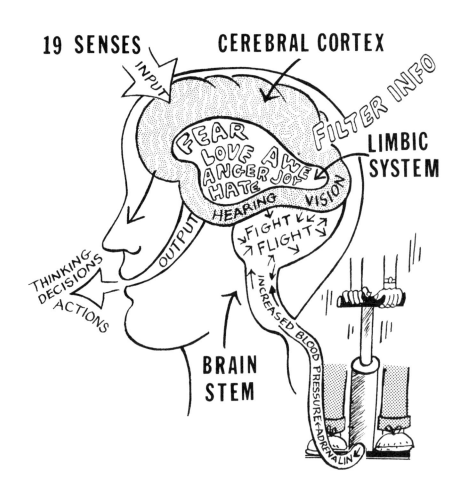

(Illustration from *ITI: The Model* by Susan J. Kovalik, 1992.)

NOTION 3: SEVEN INTELLIGENCES, NOT ONE

Intelligence is typically thought of as a general characteristic, that is, an I.Q. of 140 is indicative of an all-around smart person, that intelligence is a general capacity which every human possesses to a greater or lesser extent which, for the most part, is set at birth by genetics. Not true!

A neurobiological perspective of recent brain research suggests a view of intelligence that is markedly at odds with the "educational psychology" view of intelligence from years gone by or, for that matter, the view generally held in this society, i.e., intelligence is a thing granted in ample or meagre amounts at birth, after which it is relatively unchangeable.

Howard Gardner in his book, *Frames of Mind: Theory of Multiple Intelligences* suggests that we each have seven intelligences (at least). By intelligence he means "problem-solving and/or producing products, producing capability that is valued across all cultures."[10] What a nice definition! Nothing airy fairy here, just a practical look at human potential and behavior regardless of culture.

Gardner theorizes that each of these intelligences is relatively independent of the other, with its own timetable for development and peak growth. On the other hand, "only the blend of intelligences in an intact individual makes possible the solving of problems and the creation of products of significance."[11] And, very importantly, an individual's intellectual gifts in one area, e.g., logical-mathematical, cannot be inferred from an individual's skills in language, music, or interpersonal understandings.[12]

Each of the seven intelligences operates from a different part of the brain. Thus, schools should have as their mission the development of as many areas of the brain as possible in order to, in effect, create 21st century Renaissance citizens. Gardner's seven intelligences help point the way to the what's and how-to's of curriculum designed to move us toward the elusive "maximum development" of each student. In contrast, **today's typical curriculum only addresses two of the seven intelligences**.

To grasp the power of Gardner's theory of multiple intelligences, one must make a distinction between how students take in information (the modalities of visual, auditory, tactile, and kinesthetic) vs. how students process information inside their brains in order to first make meaning of the input and then to act upon the world with it. Remember that these seven intelligences are sets of problem-solving skills, not merely gateways through which information passes to reach the brain. *Do not equate modalities with these intelligences.*

According to Gardner, intelligence "entails a set of problem-solving skills, enabling the individual to resolve genuine problems or difficulties that he or she encounters and, when appropriate, to create an effective product; it also entails the potential for finding or creating problems, thereby laying the groundwork for the acquisition of new knowledge."[13]

The following brief descriptions of the seven intelligences are excerpted from *Frames of Mind*. They provide curriculum designers and classroom teachers alike with beginning outlines for restructuring.

LOGICAL-MATHEMATICAL INTELLIGENCE
(left hemisphere but also front and back of both sides of the brain)

This intelligence is the home of science and math. The core function is the confrontation with the world of objects—ordering and reordering them and assessing their quantity; comprehending numerical symbols, appreciating the meaning of signs referring to numerical operations, understanding the underlying quantities and operations themselves.

This intelligence appears early and the most productive work is done by age 40 if not by age 30. The basis for all logical-mathematical forms of intelligence spring from the handling of objects; later these become internalized ("done in one's head"). One proceeds from objects to statements, from actions to the relations among actions, from the real of the sensorimotor to the realm of pure abstraction—ultimately to the heights of logic and science.

The classical description of the development of this intelligence is that of Jean Piaget; his work remains an extremely accurate description of this intelligence but it does not describe development of the other six intelligences.

LINGUISTIC INTELLIGENCE
(predominantly left hemisphere—temporal and frontal)

Linguistic competence is the most widely and most democratically shared across the human species. While all of us are not poets, "one could not hope to proceed with any efficacy in the world without considerable command of phonology, syntax, semantics, and pragmatics."[14] Thus, this intelligence has striking importance in human society.

The core operations of language used with special clarity include sensitivity to the following: the meaning of words; the order among words, e.g., capacity to follow rules of grammar, and, on carefully selected occasions, to violate them; the sounds, rhythms, inflections and meters of words; and the different functions of language—its potential to excite, convince, stimulate, convey information, or simply to please.

The major uses of linguistic intelligence:

- rhetorical aspects—the ability to use language to convince other individuals of a course of action
- mnemonic potential of language—the capacity to use this tool to help one remember information

- role in explanation—much of teaching and learning occurs through language, oral and written

- potential of language to explain its own activities—the ability to use language to reflect upon language, to engage in "meta-linguistic" analysis

To state the obvious here, success in our public education system, as it is currently conceived and operated, requires that every student arrive at school in the morning functioning at a very high level of linguistic intelligence, an expectation that is unwarranted, patently unfair to students, and disastrous. Current brain research makes clear that there are many ways of knowing, of taking in information about the world. The most powerful of these is not through reading or lecture but rather through full involvement of the 19 senses with the real world or what Dr. Larry Lowery, Lawrence Hall of Science, University of California, Berkeley, refers to as "firsthand"[15] information, that which can be experienced directly by our senses. (See *being there* and *immersion*, p. 7.)

SPATIAL INTELLIGENCE
(right hemisphere)

The core operation of spatial intelligence here is the ability to image, the capacities to perceive the visual world accurately, to perform transformations and modifications upon one's initial perceptions, and to be able to re-create aspects of one's visual experience, even in the absence of relevant physical stimuli. This intelligence should be arrayed against, and be considered equal in importance to, linguistic intelligence. Loosely put, the mind's link to language is through pictures, not sound. Linguistic and spatial intelligences are the principal sources of storage and solution.

It is important to note that spatial intelligence should not be equated with the visual sensory modality. Even people who are blind from birth can develop spatial intelligence without direct access to the visual world. The problem-solving function of the spatial intelligence is the processing of information received, not just the avenue for bringing in information. Spatial intelligence is a collection of related skills. The images produced in the brain are helpful aids to thinking; some researchers have gone much farther, considering visual and spatial imagery as a primary source of thought. (An excellent resource book is *Visualizing and Verbalizing for Language Comprehension and Thinking* by Nanci Bell.)

A keenly developed spatial intelligence is not only an invaluable asset in our daily lives but is essential for understanding the application of what is learned in school, particularly in areas where the elements are abstract and unseen (microscopic in size or such invisible physical science areas such as the forces of gravity, electricity/magnets, etc.).

Examples of imaging as a primary source of thought are Darwin and the "tree of life," Freud and the unconscious as submerged like an iceberg, and John Dalton's view of the atom as a tiny solar system. For many of the world's famous scientists, their most fundamental insights were derived from spatial models rather than from mathematical lines of reasoning. Albert Einstein once commented: "The words of the language, as they are written and spoken, do not play any role in my mechanisms of thought. The psychical entities which seem to serve as elements in thought are certain signs and more or less clear images which can be voluntarily reproduced or combined. . . . The above mentioned elements are, in my case, of visual and some muscular type."[16]

BODILY-KINESTHETIC INTELLIGENCE
(tendency for left hemisphere dominance—in right-handed people)

Characteristic of this intelligence is the ability to use one's body in highly differentiated and skilled ways for expressive as well as goal-directed purposes (e.g., a mime, actor, athlete, construction worker, fisherman, or gourmet chef) plus the capacity to work skillfully with objects, both those that involve the fine motor movements of one's bodily motions and capacity to handle objects skillfully.

As Piaget described sensorimotor development, progress is from simplest reflexes (e.g., sucking and looking) to behavioral acts that fall increasingly under the control of environmental variation and individual intention.

Involving the body in any learning event increases the neural activity of the brain, increases the flow of adrenalin (which aids transfer from short-term memory to long-term memory) and involves another area of the gray matter of the brain in processing and storing learnings, thus providing "additional hooks" for recalling information for later use.

MUSICAL INTELLIGENCE
(right hemisphere)

This intelligence is the earliest to appear. Core functions include pitch (melody), rhythm, timbre (tone), and pattern.

While the most autonomous of the intelligences, students who are unusually high in musical intelligence but relatively low in linguistic intelligence will use their musical intelligence skills to "translate" language into musical components from which they can absorb the content or message. For example, the students whose body begins to jive and tap the instant the teacher begins to speak, stopping the second the teacher stops talking, restarting with the next burst of speech, all in rhythm with the teacher's words. Content in rhyme can be readily absorbed by these students while the same information in an uninspiring lecture or in the stilted prose of a textbook can be completely indigestible. Monotone speakers have particularly deadening effects for the high musical students.

INTRA-AND INTERPERSONAL INTELLIGENCES

While the forms of spatial or bodily-kinesthetic intelligence are readily identified and compared across diverse cultures, the varieties of personal intelligence prove more distinctive, less comparable, perhaps even unknowable to someone from a different society. Also, the patterns of development and of breakdown in the personal intelligences turn out to be far more varied than in the other intelligences; and there is an especially wide range of end states.

Intrapersonal—examination and knowledge of one's own feelings or "sense of self"—the balance struck by every individual and every culture between the prompting of "inner feelings" and the pressures of "other persons"

The core capacity of intrapersonal intelligence is access to one's own feeling life—one's range of affects or emotions: the capacity instantly to effect discrimination among these feelings and, eventually, to label them, to enmesh them in symbolic codes, to draw upon them as a means of understanding and guiding one's behavior. At its advanced level, intrapersonal knowledge allows one to detect and to symbolize complex and highly differentiated sets of feelings, e.g., the novelist who can write introspectively about feelings, the patient (or therapist) who comes to attain a deep knowledge of his own feeling life, the wise elder who draws upon his own wealth of inner experiences in order to advise members of his community.

Interpersonal—looks outward, toward behavior, feelings, and motivations of others

The core capacity of interpersonal intelligence is the ability to notice and make distinctions among other individuals and, in particular, among their moods, temperaments, motivations, and intentions.

In an advanced form, interpersonal knowledge permits a skilled adult to read the intentions and desires—even when those have been hidden—of many other individuals and, potentially, to act upon this knowledge, e.g., by influencing a group of disparate individuals to behave along desired lines. We see highly developed forms of interpersonal intelligence in political and religious leaders (a Mahatma Gandhi or a John Fitzgerald Kennedy), in skilled parents and teachers, and in individuals enrolled in the helping professions, be they therapists, counselors, or concerned friends.

NOTION 4:
THE BRAIN AS A PATTERN-SEEKING DEVICE

Recent brain research; has shattered our previous ideas about how learning takes place and new definitions of learning are emerging. Most notably the awareness of the human brain has a phenomenal penchant for seeking and detecting patterns. In his book, *Human Brain and Human Learning*, Hart stipulates that "no part of the human mind is naturally logical"[17] while it is learning (as distinguished from its ability to use information already learned in a "logical" or sequential way if the situation so requires). Instead, the brain learns by sifting through massive amounts of input, processing thousands of bits of information per minute arriving through the 19 senses. Obviously, and fortunately, this information is processed in a multi-path, multi-modal way—far outstripping the most sophisticated version of computer artificial intelligence to date. The simultaneity of its processing makes patterns obvious when processing (however speedy) along one avenue at a time would produce no ah-ha's whatsoever. Imagine if the brain processed only one set of information at a time, e.g., first vision, then hearing, then bodily-kinesthetic, etc. Like the three blind men, recognizing an elephant would, at best, be an extremely time consuming and laborious task.

As the brain attempts to make sense out of the chaos which surrounds each of us, it constantly searches for patterns that can impose meaning on the input received. Its "aha's" arise from detection of a pattern or patterns. This pattern detection propensity is seen in the operation of each of the senses. The ear registers every sound wave within its perceivable frequency but it attends only to those which provide a meaningful pattern. Sounds of traffic or workshop chatter is ignored and only the presenter's voice is "tuned in" or noted as a pattern to attend to. Similarly, the eye "recognizes" a chair be it a three-legged milking stool, a church pew bench, part of a student desk, a log in the forest when we are tired, or the more common no-frills chair at the kitchen table.

Hart identifies six major categories of patterns to which the brain attempts to attach meaning.[18]

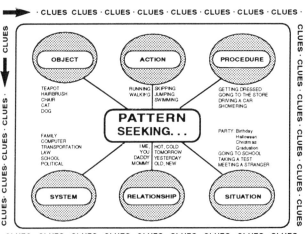

Hart, author of *Human Brain and Human Learning*, defines pattern as:

"An entity, such as an object, action, procedure, situation, relationship or SYSTEM, which may be recognized by substantial consistency in the CLUES it presents to a brain, which is a pattern-detecting apparatus. The more powerful a brain, the more complex, finer, and subtle patterns it can detect. Except for certain SPECIES WISDOM patterns, each human must learn to recognize the patterns of all matters dealt with, storing the LEARNING in the brain. Pattern recognition tells what is being dealt with, permitting selection of the most appropriate PROGRAM in brain storage to deal with it. The brain tolerates much variation in patterns (we recognize the letter "*a*" in many shapes, sizes, colors, etc.) because it operates on the basis of PROBABILITY, not on digital or logical principles. Recognition of PATTERNS accounts largely for what is called insight, and facilitates transfer of learning to new situations or needs, which may be called creativity."[19]

From the time we are born until we die, the brain takes in these patterns as they present themselves, sorting and categorizing down in an attempt to make sense out of our complex world. Learning takes place when the brain sorts out patterns using past experiences to make sense out of input the brain receives.

This pattern-detecting aspect of the brain can be clearly seen in the brain's mastery of one of its biggest accomplishments: learning the mother language. Watch mothers just home from the hospital with their newborns (or even listen to them talk to their child in utero!). Mothers know how to teach language. They do not "dumb down" their language to the infant to single syllable communications. Instead, mothers discuss the everyday happenings of life and share their hopes and dreams for their little one—"When you grow up, you'll go to Harvard and become an astronaut. You'd like that very much, I think. Very, very exciting occupation." "Oops, in 30 minutes your father comes home from work; we'd better get dinner started. Let's see, mother's milk for you and hmmm . . . oh, oh, I forgot to buy something for the main course tonight. Be sweet and charming, little one, when Daddy comes through the door!" Another night of macaroni and cheese won't go over well!

Such a barrage of sounds coming at the child in real-life fashion would at first seem a hopeless environment in which to master language—an environment giving input to the child which can accurately be described as **rich, random, even chaotic.**[20] As educators, we have been carefully and logically taught that such an environment would make the task of learning a language impossible. Consequently, we teach English as a second language logically and carefully, "This is a pen. What is this? This is a _____ ." Unfortunately, the human brain does not learn well from such logical, tidy, greatly restricted input because it is so antagonistic to the brain.

Why antagonistic? Because such approaches rob the brain of its natural sources and kinds of "food for thought," thereby eclipsing its natural—and thus most powerful—way of operating. To repeat Hart's words, learning is "the extraction, from confusion, of meaningful patterns." In real life settings, says Hart, information comes at the learner "in a way that can best be described as rich, random, and even chaotic." Over the millenniums, the brain has perfected learning within such an environment.

Stripping a learning situation of its real-life richness robs the child's mind of the possibility of perceiving patterns and thus making sense of what is in front of him/her. Ironically, we do this consistently with Chapter 1 students. If they are slow, conventional wisdom has dictated that the task be broken into smaller and smaller pieces. We've now achieved pieces that are so small and so "easy"—only one item to focus on—that there is no longer any pattern to perceive. Consequently, Chapter 1 students with their finely chopped, over-simplified diet, "don't get it" which confirms to us that they are "slow." However, most Chapter 1 students are adept learners from real-world in-put. They come to us having learned their mother tongue and a wide range of skills for coping with life.

The amazing flexibility of the brain in its pattern-seeking is apparent in its ability to recognize the pattern of the letter "*a*"; we recognize it amid an amazing range of fonts, sizes, shapes, positions. This speed and flexibility can occur because the brain naturally works on a *probabilistic* basis. The brain does not add up, for example, all the parts of a cat until all parts are perceived and accounted for: four legs, a tail, fur, meows, purrs, etc. Rather the mind "jumps to the conclusion" that the pattern "cat" applies when only one or a few characteristics have been noted. While this jumping to conclusions sometimes gets us in trouble, it is crucial to rapid completion of myriad actions minute by minute. The rapid reader, for example, does not see every letter before deciding what the word is. Context clues or the mere outline of the word are used, in probabilistic fashion, to jump to the rapid conclusion that it was an elephant that came crashing through the brush.

In the example of our infant learning its mother tongue, language pours around the child for hours and hours a day. The more input, the more readily the child learns. The first patterns perceived are those that are most meaningful – the child's name and then the name of mom and dad. Patterns are at first quite gross, i.e., "Dadda" means any man in trousers. As the snickers erupt, the child's mind is alerted to a problem with the pattern and, over time, with continued rich input, the patterns become more and more refined until, finally, the educated adult ends up with a vocabulary of 10,000 plus words with subtle shades of meaning and used with considerable precision.

The entire structure of language is based on pattern. Plurals mostly end in *s* except for mouses, mooses, fishes, etc. Past tense generally ends with *ed* except when it doesn't. Gerunds are a real thrill for most children; when the "ing verb" pattern is first grasped by children, everything is jumping, leaping, hitting, running, etc., for several days until another "pattern" of language is discovered.

Much of our difficulty in teaching comes from our rather sloppy handling of input and output processing. This is quite understandable: we cannot observe the goings-on inside a child's mind, we can only observe behaviors—what a child does with what he/she knows. While understandable, it has caused us to make "logical" assumptions about learning which are false.

Input — stimulates initial processing of sensory data to arrive at meaning or understanding of something. Processing of input is not logical or sequential but rather multipath, multi-model as the brain seeks to identify a pattern that will give meaning.

Output, or use of what is learned—behavior during which student uses, applies or puts into action what has been learned. Output is often very logical and sequential. (Using or acting upon what one knows is discussed on later pages under the term "programs.")

Pattern-seeking is the brain's way of striving to extract meaning from its surroundings based upon the thousands of bits of input pouring into the brain each minute through the 19 senses. And, very importantly, **what is one learner's pattern is another learner's hodgepodge**. This is to say, we cannot predict what any one particular child will perceive as a pattern because so much depends upon prior knowledge and the existing neural networking of the brain used to process the input. A common mistake of the public schools is stripping down the input to a small amount of "stuff" so the "right" answer seems inescapable. **This does not work**.

In short, the mind is genetically designed to learn from the natural complexities of the natural world. To the extent that schools oversimplify, or make logical, or restrict the world's natural complexity is the extent to which schools inhibit the natural workings of the mind and restrict a student's ability to learn. Input from the real world can best be described as "rich, random, even chaotic." Logical, sequential curricula delivered in logical ways are highly brain-antagonistic. Comments Hart, "Perhaps there is no idea about human learning harder to accept for people familiar with classroom schools than this: that the ideal of neat, orderly, closely planned, sequentially logical teaching will, in practice with young students, guarantee severe learning failure for most."[21]

This pattern-seeking penchant of the brain is in diametric opposition to the underpinning of our tradition curriculum—its structure and content. A look at our current curriculum reflect several erroneous suppositions: small, isolated pieces automatically add up to large pictures of real life; small, isolate pieces provide focus for the brain, making it easier to learn, especially for slow or limited ability students; study of "subjects" explains the world to students; all students learn effectively through lecture, reading, and completing paper/pencil assignments.

Instead, this pattern-seeking capacity of the mind, plus the notion of multiple intelligences, suggests that we begin with real life (as the students experience it) and provide a conceptual not factoid base (see Chapter III for a discussion of curriculum).

NOTION 5:
PROGRAMS—THE BASIC UNIT OF BEHAVIOR

The behavior of our fellow human beings (and of ourselves) has long been one of life's greater mysteries. Behavior—its building blocks, why specific building blocks are chosen at any one moment in time—must be understood if we are to create schools which foster real learning.

According to Hart, the key to understanding behavior is "the realization that we act very largely by programs . . . a fixed sequence for accomplishing some intended objective." In other words, to carry on activities, one must constantly select a program from among those stored in the brain and implement it—put it to use.[22]

Hart defines a program as:

"A sequence of steps or actions, intended to achieve some GOAL, which once built is stored in the brain and "run off" repeatedly whenever need to achieve the same goal is perceived by the person. A program may be short, for example giving a nod to indicate "yes," or long, as in playing a piece on the piano which requires thousands of steps, or raising a crop of wheat over many months. A long program usually involves a series of shorter subprograms, and many parallel variations that permit choice to meet conditions of use. Many such programs are needed, for instance to open different kinds of doors by pushing, pulling, turning, actuating, etc. Language requires many thousands of programs, to utter each word, type it, write it in longhand, print it, etc. Frequently used programs acquire an "automatic" quality: they can be used, once selected, without thinking, as when one puts on a shirt. Typically, a program is CONSCIOUSLY selected, then run off at a subconscious level. . . . In general, humans operate by selecting and implementing programs one after another throughout waking hours."[23]

The basic cycle in using programs is:

- **Evaluate** the situation or need (detect and identify the pattern or patterns)
- **Select** the most appropriate program from those stored
- **Implement** the program

For many people, this is no doubt a surprisingly active view of learning—learning as measured by action, not by paper and pencil tests. Hart, in fact, defines learning as "the acquisition of useful programs." Further, information that does not become part of a program is usually unretrievable. For example, recall your sophomore college days and the traditional western civilization class. The characteristics of this stunning experience: yearlong, 99.9 percent lecture, and an enormously fat textbook. For the mid-term and final exams, you used the ubiquitous blue book. Weeks later when the blue book was graded and returned, you glanced inside. To your total shock, there were paragraphs of stuff you didn't even recognize—never heard of it before! A classic example of information which never became part of a program and, thus, is unretrievable and often even unrecognizable. In other words, most information that we *use* is embedded in programs; the corollary is: information which is not used is also not retrievable and, truth be told, was probably never "learned" in the first place. Thus, "covering information" is a colossal waste of time for both students and teachers.

The implications for the classroom of the 21st century are obvious—we need to do less and do it better and more in-depth, giving students time to "use" the information again and again in varying settings until the information is recallable in a usable form, i.e., a behavior, a *program*.

The first step in the learning process is, as we have seen, detecting pattern. Once a situation has been analyzed, and if action is required, the brain scans its repertoire of stored programs, selecting the one that is most appropriate or calling forth two or more and using them in fresh combinations. Such capacity seems to underlie what we call creativity.[24]

It should be noted that subskills and programs are not identical and have little in common. A program, while it can be enormously complex, such as driving a car, is a sequence for accomplishing some end—a goal, objective, or outcome—an end with meaning to the learner. Subskills such as the blend *ch* or the short *i* are not a sequence for accomplishing some end; they are experienced as isolated, fragmented pieces. In contrast, the program or end goal to be attained is the act of reading.

Successful implementation of programs are their own reward, accompanied by feelings of accomplishment and increased satisfaction. Aborting a program that doesn't work is emotionally unsettling and disturbing; frequent aborting of non-working programs decreases our sense of confidence in self.[25]

One last point: one's stock of patterns and programs "reflects experience much more than something called intelligence."[26]

A complete definition of learning is twofold: first, the identification of patterns and assignment of meaning to them and, second, developing a program to use what is learned. Learning involves pattern detection and program development.

NOTION 6: IMPACT OF PERSONALITY

Personality preferences or temperament strongly impacts the learning process, affecting how the learner takes in information, how he/she organizes during learning and when applying learnings, decision-making (one of the most important decisions to be made by the learner is "I want to learn this"), and orientation to other learners (which greatly affects collaborative processes). A useful framework for looking at these processes is described in *Please Understand Me: Character and Temperament Types* by David Keirsey and Marilyn Bates whose work is based upon that of Carl Jung and the team of Meyers and Briggs.

TAKING IN INFORMATION[27]

Knowing how students, and we ourselves, take in information is critical. Differences in this area are at the root of most friction and exasperation and, occasionally, the complete inability to get along with people—family, friends, co-workers, students. If information received isn't accurate or is not what the speaker intended . . .well, relationships will be difficult.

It is important to note here that this concept describes the internal "wiring" of the mind—how it works when it acquires sensory input and munches it about. This is different from the issue of how one acquires information—the modalities of visual, hearing, kinesthetic, and tactile. It is also different from the seven intelligences. **Examined here is what the preferred form of data as it is being gathered.** The two extremes are sensing and intuiting.

TAKE IN

SENSING——————————————————————INTUITIVE

details, concrete   INFORMATION   wholes, theory,
                                                hunches, future

K   C   AP   AN   E   S

Sensors learn by dealing with the concrete—what can be seen, heard, touched or otherwise experienced. They learn by gathering details, collecting them one after the other and fitting them together until they snap into place, into a pattern that makes sense. This is much like putting together a puzzle with isolated, seemingly unrelated pieces and working toward an understanding of how they fit together. Most of us are this kind of learner—75 percent of the population. This learner learns best by being allowed to interact with the real world, not textbooks which are an abstraction about the real world and so fragmented that the pieces "never add up." These learners need additional time to manipulate information, to ferret out its relevance, to practice its applications so that the nature of the parts to the whole is clear and becomes one unified whole.

In contrast, "intuitors" are sometimes referred to as the "big W" people — whole notion. They prefer to begin with the "big picture"—a framework or theory to give meaning to the pieces and then they make up the details. Using the puzzle analogy, they feel they must first start with the outside frame and the picture on the box lid—a structure for handling/giving meaning to all the pieces. This is in contrast to those who don't bother with what the whole picture is but select out all red pieces or all pieces for the house, etc. These learners are also the "what if" people, preferring to deal with the possible rather than the details of actuality; they deal in hunches and the future. Often they are very impatient with details. Reaching an understanding of the nature of the parts to the unified whole is a faster process for the intuitor.

However, it is important to note that **the end result for both sensors and intuitors is the same—a full understanding of the concept and the particulars. Only the route differs.**

Applications — The implications here for curriculum in a brain-compatible classroom are critically important when designing instructional settings and processes for students to experience. When comparing and organizing, the sensor generally tends to work with smaller pieces. On first glance, our traditional curriculum would seem ideal for this students—small pieces for learners who prefer pieces. Unfortunately, the pieces of the curriculum, e.g., 847 skills for reading, are so small that they don't "add up," they don't evoke meaning.

Further exacerbating the situation, information is typically presented via "second hand" sources or, even worse, via symbolic sources, thus making learning nigh on impossible. It is therefore not surprising to find that, of those students who drop out of school prior to completing the 8th grade, **99.6** percent of them are sensors. A truly shocking statistic! What the typical curriculum does not assist the sensor to develop is a sense of how the pieces of the curriculum and their world come together to help answer the question, "What's it all about, Alfie?"

So, what's the solution? Curriculum redesign to provide conceptual rather than factoid key points to be learned plus redesign of instructional activities. Note, for example, the effect of using Bloom's taxonomy. The letters below the line in the previous graphic illustrate the approximate nature of "pieces to wholes" curriculum for students at each level of Bloom's Taxonomy: K=knowledge, C=comprehension, AP=application, AN=analysis, E=evaluation, S=synthesis.

DECISION-MAKING[28]

Given the centrality of working toward independence/interdependence and taking one's own decisions and the need for choice in the curriculum, decision-making is a very significant issue for the young adolescents and all who work with them. The scale described by Keirsey and Bates examines what people value as they weigh the facts, events, circumstances, and their own thoughts and feelings, in order to make a decision.

DECISION-

FEELING————————————————————————THINKING

subjective, empathetic   **MAKING**   objective, logical

Those at the "feeling" end of the scale strongly value how the decision will affect others, more so than the logic or principle(s) of the factors involved. As a consequence, their decisions tend to be quite subjective and empathetic. For example, if a "feeling" policeman stopped a car for rolling through a stop sign enroute to the hospital delivery room, he would likely conclude that, under the circumstances, allowing the nervous young father and expectant mother with labor pains to get to the hospital as quickly as possible is more important than applying consequences for the stop sign infraction. He might even decide to provide an escort to the hospital.

The "thinking" decision-makers value the objective, logical elements of a decision. If the principle is "x" then the choice of "y" is obvious, inescapable and not to be distorted by extraneous circumstances or reactions of the people involved. Thus, a "thinking" policeman observing the running of the stop sign would likely reach the conclusion that labor pains do not necessarily signal imminent birth and, besides, the safety of others as well as the mother-to-be and child is of paramount importance and the nervous husband should receive a ticket AND be monitored for several blocks to ensure that he doesn't speed or run another stop sign.

It is not difficult to imagine the reactions of these students to rules, homework assignments, discipline measures, and so forth. For example, some students will react to the procedures not being followed properly regardless of the circumstances or seeming fairness, "A rule is a rule." Others will react to the nature of the issue, the circumstances, perceived fairness, regardless of the procedures or rules. Needless to say, groupwork goes much more smoothly for students and teacher if students are taught this information about decision-making early in the year as part of group development and LIFESKILLS (see page 48 for a list of the LIFESKILLS).

Applications — Decision-making is a skill so fundamental to success in life that it hardly needs restating. This information about temperament and decision-making should be shared with students. Give your students a gift, give them the temperament survey and let them read abut themselves. Include observations of temperament in debriefing from cooperative learning exercises.

Lifestyle—not as in living high on the hog but rather how we like our life to unfold—refers to how people like to organize their lives. On one end of the scale are people who live life by judging—not in the sense of good or bad but rather by decree or judgement, e.g., in Camelot, by decree of the king, it only snows between certain hours during certain months of the year.

LIFESTYLE

JUDGING————————————————————————PERCEIVING

organized, closure, priorities   open, flexible, spontaneous

"Judgers" are described as organized, makers (and doers!) of to-do lists, people who set and work toward priorities, and who are adamant about closure and nailing down loose ends. The judging person is the one to announce in a loud voice during a meeting, "Well, what's the decision here? We've wasted 25 minutes and no decision has been made! For heaven's sake, let's stop the jawing and make a decision here!" Ambiguity is intolerable, closure (even if the decision is a bad one) is highly valued. Also, judgers do not like surprises in their world. They plan carefully to make things run smoothly and predictably.

Perceivers, on the other hand, literally "perceive" their environment, take in new information, perceive the essence of the new moment minute-by-minute and respond to the "right now" situation. Forget the to-do lists and last week's priorities. The moment is now! Perceivers are frequently described as open, flexible, spontaneous (and those are the nice words to describe them! Colleagues who are in supervisory or close teaming roles often use other, not-so-kind descriptors!). For example, deadline, for a perceiver, means "It's almost time to start." A loose end, not a problem; it's never too late to rethink an issue or change one's course of action. Ambiguity? No worries. Handle things as they come up; just improvise a little. Got a fire to put out, a crisis to handle? Here is your person! Spontaneity is the hallmark of the perceiver.

Applications — For the judger and perceiver to work together—as team teachers or as students in a cooperative learning group—is assuredly a strain. Imagine traveling together . . . the judging person is likely to insist upon arriving at the airport at least an hour in advance, pre-paid ticket with pre-assigned seating designation in hand. In contrast, the perceiver is likely to cut arrival time down to the very last minute—no ticket and, not unlikely, no reservation. He/she is the last passenger to enter the plane, giving a slight leap to clear the widening gap as the jetway is withdrawn.

ORIENTATION TO SELF AND OTHERS[30]

Extroversion and introversion are two commonly known qualities. Much of the folk wisdom about them is accurate enough to be useful. Not so well known, however, is the energy flow that occurs.

ORIENTATION

EXTROVERSION————————————————————INTROVERSION

gains energy from
being with others

loses energy being
with others

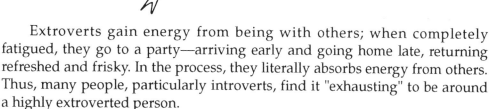

Extroverts gain energy from being with others; when completely fatigued, they go to a party—arriving early and going home late, returning refreshed and frisky. In the process, they literally absorbs energy from others. Thus, many people, particularly introverts, find it "exhausting" to be around a highly extroverted person.

Introverts, on the other hand, lose energy when around other people. When tired, a party or any grouping of people is the last place introverts want to go. They instead prefer to go off to a quiet place alone and re-energize from the inside out. It is important to note, however, that just because introversion is the preferred orientation, it does not follow that the introvert cannot behave like an extrovert. Many introverts can socialize and dramatize along with the best of the extroverts. Many have jobs that require a high degree of extrovertive behavior. Being an introvert merely means that the energy cost is very high, the basis for "burn-out" for many.

Applications — The structure of junior highs, with their fast-paced changing from class to class and interaction with 150+ students and many teachers, is incredibly draining for introvertive students, and their teachers. Add a little friction between personalities, pressure to perform, etc., and the school day becomes a horror for an introvert.

The implications for teachers are quite obvious. Either gear down or gear up but "match" your energy flow with that of individual students and, with groups, vary the nature of the activities to best fit introverts at times and extroverts at others. For example, a steady diet of cooperative learning assignments is as deadly as an unvarying lecture.

FURTHER IMPLICATIONS

This model of viewing the impact of personality on learning is well researched and the statistics are fascinating, even mindblowing. For example, although 38 percent of the general population are sensor-perceivers in the way they take in information and their lifestyle (SP), only 2 percent of teachers are that temperament type. On the other hand, 56 percent of teachers (compared to only 38 percent in the population at large) are sensor-judgers (SJ).[31] Thus, it is rare for SP students to ever have an SP teacher, someone who understands them. On the other hand, SJ students have many teachers whose temperament matches theirs; school is a relatively comfortable experience for them.

Most shocking of all, 75-90 percent of at-risk students are SP personalities. They are not "drop outs," they are push outs." The system is simply too structured, too rigid, too boring, too oppressive. While an SJ student has less than a 25 percent chance of becoming a dropout, an SP student has more than a **200** percent chance of becoming a casualty of the system.

ELEMENTS OF A BRAIN-COMPATIBLE ENVIRONMENT

The Integrated Thematic Instruction (ITI) model is a way of conceptualizing and orchestrating a brain-compatible learning environment. It is a model for implementing the best of what we know from brain research and its implications for curriculum development and teaching strategies. Its outcomes: quantum leaps in student achievement and a lifelong love of learning.

The model, developed by Susan Kovalik and continually updated by Susan and her associates, is based upon the overlapping of three areas:

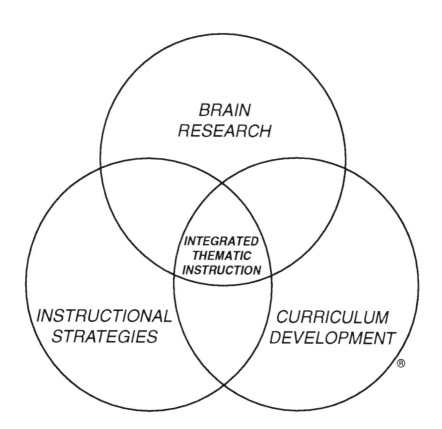

ELEMENTS OF A
BRAIN-
COMPATIBLE
ENVIRONMENT

Within the focal point of these three circles lives the best of curriculum, instruction, and how students learn—a dynamic coming together which empowers both students and teachers. It is here that the isolated, severely fragmented descriptions of instructional strategies and curriculum come to life. It is here, not in the pages of district scope and sequences, state mandates, or textbooks, that the essence of our civilization is passed along and the future of our high tech world is prepared for.

If teaching were not so human an enterprise, undoubtedly it would be much easier. And, whether you consider teaching an art or a science or a combination of both, the range of needed professional and personal skills is enormous. The diagram on the next page depicts the elements of a brain-compatible learning environment which must be maintained at all times if the brain is to continue operating in the cerebral cortex so that powerful learning can occur. **Absence of even one of the brain-compatible elements destroys the brain-compatible nature of the learning environment.**

BUILDING BLOCKS OF ITI

FOR STUDENTS
Key elements of
a brain-compatible environment:

- absence of threat
- meaningful content
- choices
- adequate time
- enriched environment
- collaboration
- immediate feedback
- mastery

TO BUILD THIS ENVIRONMENT FOR STUDENTS, TEACHERS MUST:

CURRICULUM DEVELOPMENT

- create a yearlong theme with monthly components and weekly topics
- identify key points
- develop inquiries using Gardner's Seven Intelligences and Bloom's Taxonomy
- create real world closures and opportunities for social and political action
- develop research skills and the ability to apply new knowledge/skills
- practice lifelong learning
- increase knowledge of the curriculum content
- be aware of the essence of the basic skills and how to teach them without dependence upon textbooks

INSTRUCTIONAL STRATEGIES

- develop effective direct instruction balanced with ability to guide learning
- pose questioning strategies that support acquisition of natural knowledge
- orchestrate collaboration
- improve ability to image
- maintain effective classroom leadership and management
- use multiple resources

The elements of a brain-compatible environment and how to implement them in the classroom are discussed in this chapter. Curriculum development is discussed in Chapter III; instructional strategies are discussed in Chapter VIII.

KEY ELEMENTS
OF A BRAIN-COMPATIBLE ENVIRONMENT

Although the basic notions about how the human brain works outlined in the first chapter have been known for 20 years, the information has yet to filter down through the educational system into the classroom. This is unfortunate because it is in our own best interests that we begin to apply it in our schools. Not only does student achievement skyrocket in a brain-compatible environment, but implementation of brain-compatible elements could save us from the whiplash of the pendulum swings that plague our profession—phonics to look-say and back again, math drill vs. new math, grammar vs. fluency of expression, open space vs. the square box, departmentalized vs. self-contained. The best news for teachers is that the research of the past 20 years—a confluence of many fields from ever more sophisticated medical and research technology—continues to reinforce the basic findings. We now have the best information on how the brain learns in our history and, happily, it rings true with our experience, both personal and professional.

The term "brain-compatible" was coined by Leslie A. Hart in his book *Human Brain and Human Learning*.

". . . today we have the knowledge to design brain-fitting, *brain-compatible* instructional settings and procedures. The 'compatible' concept may startle us, simply because we are not used to it in education. All around us are hand-compatible tools and machines and keyboards designed to fit the hand. We are not apt to think of them in that light, because it does not occur to us that anyone would bring out some device to be used by human hands without being sure that the nature of hands was considered. A keyboard machine or musical instrument that called for eight fingers on each hand would draw instant ridicule. Yet we force millions of children into schools that have never seriously studied the nature and functioning of the human brain, and which not surprisingly prove actively brain-antagonistic. We know less than we might and will; but we already know amply enough, I contend, to bring about instructional environments that, being compatible, will produce huge gains in learning."[1]

When we think about it, the human brain is enormously powerful and inventive. If it weren't, our species would not have survived. The concept of a brain-compatible learning environment simply suggests that we should create schooling environments which would allow the brain to work as it naturally—and, therefore, most powerfully—works, rather than asking it to adapt itself to a new, foreign mode of operation, one that is awkward and less effective. We would like to suggest to you that, although print is omnipresent in our lives in America, it is a fairly recent invention for the human brain. The evolutionary success of the human brain is its ability to make meaning of and act upon the natural world. In contrast, the human brain has to learn how to go about learning to read, write, and perform mathematics. We argue in this book that **schools should begin where the human mind is prepared to begin—the real world—and utilize print as a follow-up, not a lead-in to learning.**

KEY ELEMENTS OF A BRAIN-COMPATIBLE ENVIRONMENT

ABSENCE OF THREAT
BRAIN-COMPATIBLE ELEMENT 1

Eliminating threat—real or perceived—must be a teacher's first consideration. If the environment is not free of threat, students cannot stay "upshifted" out of the limbic system into the cerebral cortex. Again, brain research is clear—no academic learning can occur when the brain is downshifted. Period. This begins with creating a classroom environment free of threat **between teacher and students** and **among students**. (It is important to note, however, that the environment of the school at large also spills over into the classroom. Creating a threat-free environment requires that teachers work together to alter the entire school environment.)

In structuring the context for teacher-student and student-student interactions, there are three important areas of classroom operation. The teacher controls all three:

- relationship
- classroom leadership
- classroom management

Each of these three factors are discussed here at some length.

RELATIONSHIP

The quality and nature of the relationship between the teacher and his/her students is the keystone for all else in the classroom. If students do not feel they have a relationship with their teacher, they have nothing to gain or lose by their behavior in the classroom. The classroom becomes just one more social context in which they feel disconnected, uninvolved.

Developing a Sense of Group

A wonderfully useful tool for developing relationship in a group is the work of Jeanne Gibbs, *TRIBES: A Process for Understanding Social Development and Cooperative Learning*. Gibbs outlines three conditions necessary to group development and a sense of trust: **inclusion, influence, and affection**.

These three aspects of relationship must be present between the teacher and each and every student present because, if a teacher excludes even one student from his/her relationship with the class, the students feel that the teacher cannot be fully trusted to maintain a relationship with the others. The possibility of being the one rejected or of being party to an act of exclusion is a powerful threat to anyone, but especially so to the middle school age student.

Social Skills

Perhaps the best model of being in and maintaining a relationship with others and the social actions that nurture relationships is to consider the classroom as your living room, your students as neighbors and friends. What a different place the classroom would be!

If you were to invite neighbors to your home, how would you go about it? Remember, you never get a second chance to make a first impression. So, prior to the beginning of school, every student should receive a phone call or postcard from their teachers inviting them to their new class and giving them information about the year (semester) theme, etc. Tell them that you are looking forward to the year. (This kind of greeting is extremely difficult to do if your school is still completely departmentalized and you have 150 students on your roster. There are large and small reasons for moving to teaming as quickly as possible, not the least of which is reducing the number of students with whom an individual teacher interacts.)

As your students arrive on the first day of school, greet them at the door, introduce yourself, exchange a word of welcome with them, establish eye contact, and share a personal observation, e.g., "Welcome to our classroom. I'm excited about your being in this class."

As you would at a sit-down dinner, invite them to find their name tag and their personal copy of the student handbook for your classroom (which includes, among other things, your theme, components, and topics for the year/semester theme); tell them what they can do to settle in and feel comfortable. Your level of preparation says that you care, you can be counted on to be consistent, and you expect learning to take place, today and every day! Activities to create a sense of group and relationship should begin immediately.

In relationships, consistency is essential. On each and every day meet and greet students at the door by name. ("Glad you're back today, Jack; hope you're feeling better this morning.") This is your chance to connect with each student, to reaffirm your relationship with them, to start their day off right. Have soft music on to set the tone. Each and every day be prepared as you would be for guests. Again, preparation says you care. You can be depended upon to maintain the relationship, create the space for learning, and be ready for interacting with them every time they see you.

Remember, you are modeling. And what you want to model for students is not the indifference of a large bureaucracy but skills for life, the adult interaction skills for successful living.

CLASSROOM LEADERSHIP

Your leadership style and procedures in the classroom are a major means of sculpting teacher-student interactions. It is worth taking a moment to consider both the style and substance of your leadership. Are you so spontaneous that students are forever anxious and feeling off-balance? Or so predictable that they're bored? Or so in need of controlling situations that the classroom is your domain with no room for ownership by students? You must demonstrate yourself worthy of being trusted before you can ask your students to be trustworthy.

Four Elements of Classroom Leadership

According to Pat Belvel of TCI (Training and Consulting Institute), good classroom leadership consists of four elements:

- **powerful curriculum** is planned and ready to go—meaningful, useful, relevant, with opportunities to be creative and emotionally engaged

- the **prerequisites** are in place—teacher and students are in **relationship** with each other as are students with students

- the **parameters** are clear at all times—general and specific ground rules, procedures, and directions

- **participation** is expected and nurtured (students are actively engaged and on task; direct instruction provides for student involvement)[2]

How to develop powerful curriculum is discussed in Chapters V through VII. The prerequisite—relationship—must be worked at daily, at both group and individual levels, as discussed earlier. How to set parameters and nurture participation are key issues to a teacher's classroom leadership; they are discussed here.

Setting parameters is another means of guaranteeing understanding, consistency, and personal responsibility. By posting in clear terms the steps necessary to do particular activities in the classroom, you eliminate most discipline issues before they start. Two essential parameters are:

- directions— the specific how-tos to carry out a task or assignment
- procedures—the guidelines for social interaction

Both directions and procedures should be written down and posted in a location that students can easily see and refer to as needed while they work, or they should be included in the students' binders.

Directions for the assignment must be clear in content and procedure. Students must understand both what they are to do and how to go about doing it. Common mistakes here are the assumption that students understand the content of the assignment, e.g., they know how to do long division. On non-ditto, more creative assignments, it may not be clear to the students how to proceed.

Procedures are the accompanying social and personal behaviors that provide the context for doing the assignment or task. For example: when you enter the room in the morning, greet as many classmates as possible and share something that already made you happy this morning. "You may talk and share your findings at step two, but not before"; "If you want to share with a partner, move to the exploratory center"; or, "Talking is allowed but only in pairs. You may move to any place in the classroom you wish so long as you don't interfere with another person's work."

The most common pitfall when giving procedures is assuming that students know what behaviors are appropriate and when. Many students don't know the desired behaviors, or their idea of what is appropriate may not match the teacher's. According to Pat Belvel, **misbehavior is a result of lack of knowledge of the right behaviors or too much of the wrong behaviors rather than deviance of behavior.**[3] This suggests that "discipline" is more properly a teaching task (teaching which behaviors are appropriate when), rather than measuring out punishment. Your gift to your students is to teach them guidelines for behavior which will be appropriate throughout their lives, guidelines which will serve them well regardless of the pathways their adult lives follow.

The Lifelong Guidelines used in an ITI classroom are:

- trustworthiness
- truthfulness
- no put-downs
- active listening
- personal best

These five guidelines are the source of leadership in the classroom and constitute the only ITI "rules" for "discipline."

Lifelong Guidelines

Trustworthiness — In the brain-compatible classroom, trustworthiness is an essential underpinning of a sense of relationship between teacher and student as well as among students. And, as in real life, trustworthiness is earned—earned by the teacher and by each student in the room. Teacher behavior sets the model and becomes the basis for leadership in

Note: For our discussion of leadership and management, we are using the definitions of Stephen Covey, author of *The Seven Habits of Highly Effective People: Powerful Lessons in Personal Change* and *Principle-Centered Leadership*: one manages things, not people; one provides leadership to people.

the classroom. What one does—motives and intentions, attitudes and behaviors—is ever so much more compelling than words or philosophy.

A sense of trustworthiness is also enhanced when expectations of performance (behavior and academic) have been clearly stated and are upheld by the teacher in a positive tone, **with consistency.** It is imperative that a teacher's "discipline" program be a consistent and thoroughly integrated part of his/her classroom leadership and be brain-compatible, an important part of which is creating and maintaining trustworthiness. The teacher must extend the belief that each student is trustworthy until that student proves otherwise. It is important for students to understand that the teacher will trust them until that trust has been violated. If teachers are modeling trustworthiness, their students may feel more inclined to trust the teacher. Students must be able to count on the teacher to be just, fair, giving consequences that fit the situation. In return, teachers need the trust of their students. In contrast, many discipline approaches are highly inappropriate in an ITI classroom; in theory and practice, they are brain-antagonistic.

Also, students carry considerable responsibility in establishing a sense of trustworthiness as well. They, too, must model what it looks like, sounds like, and feels like to be worthy of trust. In so doing, they develop a **habit of mind** that will serve them well as adults. However, in schools which are inconsistent in expectations and standards, or where students may arrive at school under less than ideal situations (due either to community or family situations), students must learn how to handle frustrations and unpleasantness rather than "dumping" it on the next person as it was "dumped" on them; this is a very tough habit of mind to break (or perhaps they don't know any other way of dealing with it).

Truthfulness — Once trust is in place, it is safe for students to be truthful. Students need to know that the teacher will be honest and truthful with them. In turn, the teacher should "trust" the students to be honest and truthful, handling the consequences of untruth while continuing to put out the expectation of integrity until students rise to the standards.

As with each of the Lifelong Guidelines, being truthful is best taught through consistent modeling. Being truthful yet tactful, respectful, and appropriate is a lifelong challenge. Through modeling, the teacher creates an atmosphere in which truth can flourish and grow. Insisting that students are truthful will help them learn to be responsible for their decisions and their lives.

Role-playing classroom and campus situations involving truth and untruths followed by class discussions will help students understand the importance of being truthful.

Active Listening — Students and teachers need to be heard. A great line from Arthur Miller's play, *Death of a Salesman*, emphasizes this point. "Man's greatest need . . . a need greater than hunger, sex, or thirst . . . is to leave a thumbprint somewhere on the world." Being heard—having someone really get our intended message—is a wonderful way to leave a thumbprint on the world. It is much more socially positive than graffiti, more satisfying to the soul.

The Chinese symbol for listening provides a powerful definition of active listening: listening with the ears, eyes, heart (intending to get what the speaker means), and doing so with undivided attention.

YOU

EYES

EARS

UNDIVIDED
ATTENTION

HEART

Chinese verb, "TO LISTEN"   Source: TRIBES Training

It is important to learn how to be an audience. Everyone needs to understand the importance of listening to what others have to say; it is a fundamental building block for building a sense of inclusion and influence in groups. Thus, whenever anyone is giving a presentation, answering a question, or teaching a lesson, all listeners' eyes and ears are directed toward the speaker and they listen with the **intention** of understanding what the speaker has to say.

It may go without saying, but perhaps deserves a footnote, that if a speaker expects active listening from his/her audience, the speaker in return is obligated to speak with care—well-chosen words, careful of the listener's time, demonstrating that communication is a two-way street, not a one-way lecture.

No Put-downs — Put-downs are akin to a mental bomb in the classroom. They shatter trust, undermine truthfulness, undercut active listening by shutting down listening with the heart, and are the antithesis to personal best. They are guaranteed to cause the recipient to downshift out of his/her cerebral cortex. Middle school age students (and, all too often, some of their teachers) excel in the art of putting down others. However, if learning is to be nurtured in the classroom, if the environment is to be brain-compatible, put-downs must be eliminated—completely and totally.

What is a put-down? A put-down is a way of saying, "I am better than you, richer than you, smarter than you, have more options than you." The goal is to shine the spotlight on the speaker and allow him to control the behavior of those around him by undermining the relationship between/among people, sidetracking the real issues at hand, promoting the speaker by creating a laugh at someone else's expense. Put-downs can be words, tone of voice, gestures, or deeds. Teachers and students need to learn how to handle put-downs, how to prevent them from controlling their lives.

The first step in eliminating put-downs is to spend some time brainstorming about what constitutes a put-down. A good introduction to put-downs is to watch a short clip from a current television situation comedy and count the number of put-downs. Discussing reasons why put-downs can be harmful and brainstorming put-downs that have made students feel unhappy or uncomfortable brings it home. Don't be surprised, however, to find that put-downs are so pervasive that students are unconscious of the way put-downs are used.

In middle schools particularly, it is important to discuss the major causes of most fights, the root of which can often be traced back to one put-down or several put-downs which then escalated out of control. Letting students know that teachers and other adults need their help in stopping the unconscious use of put-downs is also an important part of the process to get rid of them in the classroom and on the entire school campus. Whenever teachers use a put-down, they should expect students to call it to their attention.

Another tool in the campaign to stamp out put-downs is to stress the positive things students do by referring to the LIFESKILLS which assist students to do their personal best at all times (see page 48). Because these skills are needed to succeed in life, they help us move beyond the usual affirmation-type statements, which are often bondage statements, e.g., "I like the way you did . . .," to a more powerful modeling of values and life skills for students, i.e., "Marty is being *responsible* by putting his materials in his binder in an organized way."

The Lifelong Guidelines should be displayed in a highly visible place in the classroom. You can then refer to them whenever a situation occurs in which one or more of the guidelines have been violated. It serves as an important reminder for teachers as well as students.

Eliminating put-downs is a critical step toward a threat-free environment for the brain and is essential to prevent frequent downshifting. Thus, the negative aspects of students' (and teachers') lives must be left outside the four walls. It is the job of the teacher to impress upon the students the necessity of being in a classroom where all students strive to be the best they can be. The classroom must be free from threat and embarrassment so that all students are willing to take risks. Teachers must make the classroom a place where the students want to come, a place where they feel certain that they will be able to experience success.

Personal Best — Modeling personal best and expecting it of each and every student is perhaps a teacher's biggest leadership challenge. If you succeed, student growth—academic, personal, and social—will occur in quantum leaps.

Although few situations in the real world seem to expect personal best performance, operating at one's personal best is the source of zest and high self-esteem in life. It generates both intrinsic and extrinsic rewards. Perhaps the most precious gift a teacher can give to students (and to him/herself) is experience in living fully. This would appear to be a well-kept secret. It is important for students to know that nothing short of personal best is acceptable. This applies to classwork as well as class behavior, because it is from doing one's best that one develops pride in self and the willingness to set high standards and expectations for the rest of one's life.

This guideline to live by cannot be taken lightly because it demands that teachers model their personal best at all times. The old adage, "Do as I say, not as I do," is not appropriate in an ITI classroom. Interestingly, despite the sophistication of current brain research, one of the the major findings is terribly homespun: *children learn what (they see) others do.* Your "doing" your personal best is perhaps your most important leadership tool.

As students look around them—at home, in school, and out in the community—role models of personal best may be difficult to find. Thus, teachers must model personal best not only academically when they teach students the importance of mastering concepts and what it means to be a lifelong learner but also in social and personal realms as well. Encouraging students to be responsible for their decisions, school work, and their behavior will help them develop positive attitudes about the importance of doing their personal best.

What is personal best? And who decides? The following list of LIFESKILLS is a beginning definition distilled out of the American dream and psyche. There may be others that you would want to add, some you would concentrate upon more than others because of grade level or the nature of your class. We suggest these for the ITI classroom; they are readily understandable by students and, when in operation in the classroom, they provide parameters which improve learning on all levels—academic, social, and personal.

LIFESKILLS

INTEGRITY: To be honest and sincere and of sound moral principle

INITIATIVE: To do something because it needs to be done

FLEXIBILITY: The ability to alter plans when necessary

PERSEVERANCE: To continue in spite of difficulties

ORGANIZATION: To plan, arrange, and implement in an orderly way;
to keep things in an orderly, readily-usable way

SENSE OF HUMOR: To laugh and be playful without hurting others

EFFORT: To try your hardest

COMMON SENSE: To use good judgment

PROBLEM-SOLVING: To seek solutions in difficult situations and
everyday problems

RESPONSIBILITY: To respond when appropriate, to be accountable
for your actions

PATIENCE: To wait calmly for someone or something

FRIENDSHIP: To make and keep a friend through mutual trust and
caring

CURIOSITY: A desire to learn or know about one's world

COOPERATION: To work together toward a common goal or purpose

CARING: To feel concern for others

The purpose of this list is to provide parameters which help students evaluate their own performances—to guide them individually and in groups to an understanding of the human dimensions that we can exercise towards ourselves and others.

The LIFESKILLS are easy to use in the classroom—merely label examples of behavior that occur in the classroom: "Team A was using the LIFESKILL of cooperation so well that they have completed their project. All the members agree it's a better job than if each had done it by themselves." "Bill took responsibility for himself by moving to a part of the room where he could complete his assignment." "Class, your patience while waiting for me is to be commended. Thank you."

Notice that we have dropped the "I" statement that many of us were taught to exercise in our classroom management class. "I (the teacher) like the way so and so is doing such and such." "I feel . . . , I notice . . . , I'm angry because . . . ." These comments too often send the message that pleasing the teacher is the primary goal for behavior; they easily become "bondage statements" which shift the locus of control from internal to external, from self-discipline to efforts to please the teacher. Our concern is that individuals become responsible for themselves and know what that looks like, sounds like, and how to do it.

The LIFESKILLS and the Lifelong Guidelines are examples of mental parameters in a classroom. By posting them and using them daily they can become your silent partners in creating an environment of trust.

Administrative note: If change in classrooms and schools is to occur, "absence of threat" must be a condition of the adult environment Just as teachers must remove threat from the classroom for students, administrators must remove threat from the schools for teachers. Willingness to risk is necessary if significant change is to occur and willingness to risk is possible only if there is a high degree of trust.

A trusting environment demands consistency and forethought. A number of key issues surrounding the teacher are critical. First, are the Lifelong Guidelines in operation at the adult level—among and between teachers, administration, parents, and community?

Second, do teacher and administration have the knowledge they need in terms of brain research, content, skills, instructional methodologies, in change processes and interpersonal skills?

Third, have staff been given the support and tools necessary to succeed?

CLASSROOM MANAGEMENT

Time

A key management issue is how teachers use and value time—theirs and their students'. In the ITI model, direct instruction should be limited to not more than 11–16 minutes of direct instruction by the teacher per hour. "Hogging" speaking time sends out a multiplicity of messages, all of which undermine relationship, trust (a shared sense of influence as well as inclusion), and trustworthiness (you can trust me as teacher to make the best use of your learning time). Use a video camera, place on wide-angle lens, and leave it on for the entire class period; give yourself direct feedback on how your style of presenting comes through to others—tone of voice, eye contact with the audience, clarity of thought, responsiveness to different learners, the classic criteria of a speaker and of a teacher.

Curriculum

The most important area of management in the ITI classroom is curriculum—creating your year theme, identifying what is most important for students to know, developing inquiries, gathering resources, using the real world as teaching material rather than printed material. How you handle these tasks and orchestrate them for students is the heart and soul of the ITI brain-compatible learning environment. Chapters IV through V describe these areas in detail.

Letting Your Room Speak For You

Much about classroom management is common sense . . . letting the real world seep into the classroom. For example, just as our homes get their most thorough cleaning and careful attention to detail when company is coming, the classroom must be inviting—clean yet not sterile or institutionally mechanical, rich without being cluttered, focused without being regimented. The classroom speaks to your students as they come through the door. What message will they receive?

Functionally, the room must offer areas for specific purposes, such as a work area for groups and for individual quiet time, a place for materials, area for a resource center, teacher space, work space for students (group and individual), an area for direct instruction, and spaces for personal belongings. There should be order and symmetry, allowing for movement and organized flow within the room. This should not be a "junior" high school/college classroom, a place where lectures are administered. This should be a space for interactive and active learning.

Even the walls should speak about the content students will experience this year. The yearlong theme should occupy one whole wall—be colorful, easy to read, and as three-dimensional as possible. Skills and concepts should be clearly stated so that all may know what is expected in this class this year.

Guidelines for creating trust in the classroom:

- insist that students leave the language and attitudes of the street and situation comedies at the door; create the classroom as a place where fellow human beings are included, respected, and cared about

- honor students as important human beings worth knowing; let them know that you value your relationship with them

- do group-building activities regularly, at least once a week throughout the year (intensely at the beginning of the year until trust has been created)

- don't assume students come with social skills and LIFESKILLS; teach them to the students

- through consistent offering of meaningful (to the students) curriculum, develop the expectation that if you're offering it, it is worthy of students' time and careful consideration. Such an expectation is the best possible "anticipatory set"

MEANINGFUL CONTENT
BRAIN-COMPATIBLE ELEMENT 2

Critical questions to ask when examining the issue of meaningfulness for students are:

- Why do we go to school?

- What does it mean to live in the Age of Information? What is the purpose and impact of "the textbook" in such an era?

- Are we really in a post-literate society? (How many teachers on your staff read at least two nonfiction books a month?)

- If television is the primary means of communication, are we teaching our students to be critical audiences?

- If our economy is undergoing a massive reorganization, are we preparing students to be problem-solvers of personal and societal issues and effective decision-makers (starting with their own lives)?

- And . . . just what should the end product of 13 years of public education look like anyway?

The pursuit of answers to these questions leads to a discussion of meaningfulness, an analysis of our curriculum content, and, eventually, to the inescapable admission that the content of our current curriculum is, for the most part, meaningless in its content and boring in its delivery. Yet, curriculum content has remained virtually unchanged for over 100 years. If you don't believe it, go to an antique store and pick up some old textbooks. The foreword to the teacher in the Silver-Burdett series of 1897 reads like the reading series of 1992—teach reading through literature, etc. Try a 60-year-old science text . . . it recommends teaching through hands-on strategies the same content that our 1992 science textbooks suggest teaching through hands-on. Sound familiar?

The sad and weary truth is that our curriculum models go back even beyond Prussia to the medieval university established by the church. Students attempting to prepare themselves for life in the 21st century need and deserve much better from us. (See Chapter III for a discussion of curriculum, its origins, and history.)

How would one describe meaningful content? That's a tricky question for an educator because, in fact, it is not the educator's question to answer. Just as beauty is in the eye of the beholder, so is meaningfulness determined by the learner. And yet, it is worth answering because meaningful content is the most powerful brain-compatible element. It digs deeply into the learner's pool of intrinsic motivation and provides focus for the ever active brain, thus harnessing the brain's attention and channeling its power. Fortunately, we can do a better job than ever before of surmising what the learner beholds and how he/she processes learning now when we look to recent brain research.

Although what constitutes "meaningfulness" is unique to each learner, there are several factors which contribute significantly to making something meaningful. From the learner's perspective, meaningfulness occurs when content:

- is of/from real life, the natural world around us
- connects to prior experience
- is significant to membership in a "learning club" in which the learner holds full membership
- is age-appropriate and thus understandable
- is rich enough to allow for pattern-seeking as a means of identifying/creating meaning
- can be used within the life of the learner (now or in the very near future)

The brain's requirement that content be meaningful clashes head-on with our current curriculum and textbooks—most of which is trivialized, fragmentary, and confusing. The brain cannot remember what it was confused about—only that it was confused. Thus, our fondness for the notion of spiral curriculum is unwarranted. The brain does not store bits and pieces of stuff which it could not understand. The brain stores what it perceives as meaningful and useful. Concepts are not viruses. "Exposing" or "introducing" students to a concept if understanding and mastery don't occur is a waste of student and teacher time. There is nothing to build upon the following year; worse, a negative attitude toward the topic and/or a loss of self-esteem is likely to have occurred.

It is a thoroughly mistaken notion that learners must be motivated to learn. What nonsense! The will and desire to make sense of the everyday world about us is innate to humans. As Paul Messier points out in his article, "The Brain: Research Findings Undergirding Innovative Brain-Based Learning Models,"[4] the brain is a self-congratulator, i.e., the significant "rewards" for learning are intrinsic. When we find ourselves resorting to external rewards such as M & M's, smiley face stickers, student of the month award programs, etc., we must recognize that we have failed to provide meaningful content for students to learn and therefore must bribe them to stick to the task.

Frank Smith, in *Insult to Intelligence: The Bureaucratic Invasion of Our Classrooms*, makes the point that when meaning is reached, "learning" occurs automatically and simultaneously.[5]

The learner is always asking, What does this situation/information mean to me? How can I use it? How does it affect me now and in my future? "Making sense of the everyday world in relation to ourselves, our needs (physical, emotional, mental), and motivations (interests and need for fun in our lives) is our greatest concern and motivator."[6] According to Hart, "How much is learned by rote is a direct function of time and effort. But when the learning is meaningful we learn much faster and without effort."[7]

From the teacher's perspective, meaningfulness is planned for in two ways: 1) in the selecting and organizing of the content of curriculum, and 2) in the choice of the instructional strategies used to engage students in the content of what is to be learned (concepts and skills).

The purpose of the yearlong/semester-long theme is to focus upon the students' world and their relationship to it. The theme takes the content of state and district curriculum guidelines and frames it in locations, events, and situations which are directly experienceable by students or which can be richly simulated. (See Chapter III for an in-depth discussion of selecting, organizing, and integrating curriculum.)

In selecting instructional strategies to make the learning come alive, the teacher uses **C.U.E.** as a planning guideline—which instructional strategies would make this direct instruction *creative, useful*, and/or provide an *emotional bridge*?

Creative — What would make the learning of this direct instruction creative and thus memorable? For example, putting the concept or skill to song, any form of music (individual or group), writing a poem, expressing the ideas through an art form such as sculpture or painting, dance, drama, fantasy, use of rhythm or rhyme, building something (a tangible, real something from the stuff found in real life), or inventing.

Useful — What would make this learning useful to the learner, relevant to their world (as they perceive it)? When the learner perceives information as useful to them, it is logged into the brain under several "addresses," one for each way in which the learner believes it will be useful; concepts and skills are thus more easily retrieved later on and more easily built upon during future learnings. Two foolproof techniques are to build upon prior real life experiences of students and to provide real life experiences for students which engage all 19 senses and place them in a "doing" role.

Emotional — What would provide an emotional bridge between the learner and the information, what would create sufficient epinephrine to carry the learning from short-term memory to long-term memory? How can humor or an element of fun be injected here, a bit of laughter? Or whimsy or fantasy? What other emotions are innate to this particular learning; how can I accentuate them so that students have an opportunity to experience "the world in which they live." Positive emotions allow the brain to remain upshifted into the cerebral cortex and alert the brain to something worth learning; the chemicals produced by emotions speed the growth of dendrites and help transfer learnings from short-term memory to long-term memory.

Guidelines for building in meaningfulness include:

- curriculum which
  - is age-appropriate, comprehensible by the student given his/her stage of brain growth
  - does not assume/require experiences which the student does not have
  - excites the interest of both student and teacher

- instructional strategies which
  - involve firsthand interaction with the real world
  - meet the C.U.E. criteria

CHOICES
BRAIN-COMPATIBLE ELEMENT 3

If the reader is counting the ways in which our antique school system is brain-antagonistic rather than brain-compatible, then you have recognized that its biggest crime is its assembly line sameness. The unspoken paradigm underlying the current system is that all students learn the same. Yet, it is plainly and painfully clear that all students do NOT learn the same. Parents know that, and so does every teacher. But the system seems to be impervious to truth and reality.

Thus, we put age-mates together (in spite of the fact that age is one of the least powerful predictors of what a child's learning needs and processes will be), we make all students read the same textbooks, do the same pages in the workbooks, receive the same curriculum year by year. Even if we track students, all that alters is the time of year or year that they hit a particular textbook; in the end, algebra is algebra, world history is world history, science is science.

Webster defines choice as "the act or power of choosing, the thing chosen, alternative, preference, the best."

The definition of "power of choosing" is wonderfully descriptive because it pinpoints the essential characteristic of the lifelong learner. "Preference" acknowledges what brain research tells us over and over again: that every brain is different and, therefore, each individual learner has preferred ways of learning which that individual knows to be more effective and reliable for him/her.

If Hart is on target, if Healy's worldwide research is accurate, then the question "Should we or should we not provide students choice" is not even a question. Of course we should! And politically, the issue appears to have been decided on the national level—both the Democratic and Republican parties included choice within the public school in their platforms for the 1992 elections.

Choice isn't just for students . . . teachers should also be allowed choice when selecting how best to go about providing a brain-compatible environment—choice of theme, resource materials, activities, and projects. This is not to say that every teacher selects what content to teach—that decision must be made schoolwide. The issue of choice is an issue of how to best teach that content to one's students in ways consistent with how the human brain learns.

According to recent brain research, choice is critical because it:

- increases the likelihood that the learner will be able to detect similarity to or relationships between new information/situation and existing patterns and programs in their brain (meaningful content)

- provides a variety of input and thus a variety of possible patterns to recognize (brain as pattern-seeker)

- prevents downshifting as a result of stress or frustration due to boredom or failure (triune brain)

- allows the learner to select, organize, and experience input in preferred ways resulting in more learning. As illustrated by Jung, Meyers-Briggs, and Keirsey-Bates, personality preferences with which we are born affect ways of taking in information (details vs. theory), lifestyle (highly organized vs. spontaneous), orientation to others (extrovert vs. introvert)

- leads to high interest which increases epinephrine (a necessary chemical in the brain to shift learnings from short-term to long-term memory)

- allows the learner to steer his/her own ship and establish the appropriate level of challenge (controlled risk)

- allows the learner to utilize tools/materials/situations which would be most effective in individual problem-solving (seven intelligences)

- allows the learner to build independence as a learner by providing ample opportunity to create or select learning processes and situations which are meaningful for the learner and, in so doing, build confidence and competence

To some, however, the idea of offering choices to students (and teachers) may seem like warmed-over "Do your own thing" from the '60's, that somehow offering alternatives is antithetical to high standards or the notion of "core" curriculum, with its expectations for all. Some might believe that having choices is fluff or, more to the point, that it runs against the grain of our Prussian schooling roots and Puritan ethic: one can't just go around doing what one wants all the time—learning is serious business and therefore should be expected to hurt a little.

The truth is that offering choices is essential if one's goal is mastery and application of skills, concepts and the creation of lifelong learners who possess a passion for learning.

According to Smith, thinking is made easy and effective when two fundamental requirements are met: 1) we understand what we are thinking about, and 2) the brain itself is in charge, in control of its own affairs, going about its own business.[8] Smith goes on to say that "Thinking becomes difficult and inefficient when the brain loses control, when what we try to think about is contrived rather than an integral part of whatever we would otherwise be engaged in at the moment. . . . Contrived thinking of this kind goes against the predominant tendency of thought; in effect, it throws the brain out of gear. Something that in less forced circumstances might be thought about with ease becomes an obstacle, a blurred focus of contrary purposes, aggravated often by frustration and irritation. The brain is no longer in charge. And the most difficult kind of thinking is that which is imposed on us by someone else . . ."[9]

Curriculum planning typically begins with identifying what is to be learned (see Chapter III), which usually defines a common core of concepts and skills all students are to learn. Learning to speak and write standard English is, for example, not an item of choice for an educated person. However, choice begins with the teacher's planning of interactions with the world that students need in order to "learn" the important material. Such action and real world-oriented work of students, called "inquiries," are the heart and soul of the ITI classroom (see Chapter VI). The seven intelligences provide a true range of choice for students and are the operational means of integrating subjects and skills into an understandable whole.

Guidelines for providing choice:

- the choices should be genuine and truly varied (see childhood's why and wherefores, seven intelligences, levels of Bloom's Taxonomy in Chapter VI)

- each choice should do the job of moving students toward mastery of the identified key points; they are not a collection of unrelated "fun" activities or trivial pursuits

- whenever possible build in playfulness; remember C.U.E.

- the choices offered to students should immerse them in real life and *being there* and *immersion* experiences to the extent possible

ADEQUATE TIME
BRAIN-COMPATIBLE ELEMENT 4

It was Albert Einstein who said that man invented the concept of time and has spent the rest of his life being controlled by it! It seems all the more true today when technology has literally added 20 percent to our work week, mainly because we take on larger and larger undertakings due to the fabled promise of assistance from our technological helpers—computers, fax machines, cellular telephones, and instantaneous worldwide communication.

In addition, knowledge continues to accumulate daily at an ever-expanding rate. As it does so, it is more essential than ever that we constantly reevaluate what we "believe" students should know in order to become contributing members of society. Too often I hear history teachers say they never get past World War II, leaving me to wonder when we will be willing to drop the details of past events, trotted out in chronological sequence, and instead look to the important concepts represented by the events. Perhaps then we could better understand our present and face our future with greater confidence.

Finding the confidence to handle this deluge of information is not an easy task. As Richard Wurman notes: "Information anxiety is produced by the ever-widening gap between what we understand and what we think we should understand. It is the black hole between data and knowledge, and it happens when information doesn't tell us what we want or need to know."[10]

So how can we assist students? One of the greatest gifts we can give them is adequate time to sort through the welter of input, to establish the meaning of it all, and to apply what is learned to their lives.

To understand the power of this brain-compatible element, it might be helpful to apply it to our own lives first. For example, how many of us would sit down to complete our income taxes on a short weekend, knowing that the task will take at least three to four days of uninterrupted work? Or how many of us are eager to take a two-hour task out of our in-basket when we don't have a two-hour time block and we know that, with interruptions, it will end up taking us six hours? Answer: a very rare few.

Lack of completion, time wasted in "figuring out where we were" on the last round, frustration and disappointment having to drop something just when we were "getting into it"—these are all side effects of inadequate time and the rigid time schedule in classrooms. High school and departmentalized junior highs build this violation into their very core; elementary schools which have, in theory, more flexibility, cast it away with schedules that read: 8:30-9:30 reading; 9:30-10:00 spelling; 10:00-10:15 recess; 10:15-11:00 math, etc. Elementary schools also violate student and teacher need for adequate time.

Recall that the brain is a meaning seeker. Think back to the incredible attention spans young children have when engaged in something that has meaning to them. Think back to the frustration that occurs when there is a rush to complete and time runs out before the task is completed. Think back to the satisfaction that comes from doing a job well from beginning to end. Think back to the enjoyment of time to "go with the flow" while learning something new, the pep and energy that comes from confidence in succeeding if we just "stick with it."

In short, we know from our own experience that lack of adequate time is a killer; it inhibits comprehensive understanding and mastery. In terms of brain research, the anxiety and frustration trigger downshifting (triune brain) and spawns shoddy work, low standards, and, eventually, apathy.

Adequate time is needed to get the job of learning done well, to accomplish mastery (the ability to use the concept/skill in real life settings), to fully understand the connections among prior learnings and learnings yet to come. Using fragments of time—20 minutes for this, 40 minutes for that—is the ideal way to guarantee a low degree of meaningfulness and high failure rates. Using uninterrupted time to allow students full concentration is the ultimate gift, e.g., a two-hour block, all morning or even an entire day devoted to a major concept and its application to real life. Learning should be more than covering the material, it should be understanding and applying the material and building *mental programs* for future use.

Guidelines for providing adequate time:

- eliminate "regular schedules" with their specified time blocks

- make yourself slow down, plan at the conceptual rather than factoid level; this will give you less to do so it can be done more thoroughly—to the level of application to the learner's world

- build in time for "opportunities to manipulate information" and apply what is learned in real world settings before you move on to the next time block

- don't be afraid to allow a lesson to take on a life of its own, to take advantage of the so-called "teachable moment" and open the windows of opportunity* when children are truly engaged. Their interests and excitement will take them on side excursions, adventures into the land of personal responsibility and growth: "What's this to me? What's it good for?" Learning to learn, learning how to steer one's own learning takes time

---

*This should not be confused with child-centered curriculum which is often characterized as curriculum put together by having the children decide what they're going to learn. In the ITI model the teacher is responsible for the basic curriculum decisions about what students are to learn (framed by the district/state curriculum guidelines); students can and should be involved in shaping the what and how it is to be learned.

The implications for the classroom of the 21st century are obvious—we need to do less and do it better and more in-depth, giving students time to "use" the information again and again in varying settings until the information is recallable in a usable form, i.e., as a behavior, a *mental program*.

BRAIN-
COMPATIBLE
ELEMENT 4

**ADEQUATE
TIME**

ENRICHED ENVIRONMENT
BRAIN-COMPATIBLE ELEMENT 5

Think of your favorite restaurant, vacation site, thinking space at home, favorite memories from your childhood . . . which locations and situations come to mind? Describe them to yourself—the sights and sounds, the feelings, the intangible impressions . . . the thoughts.

It should not come as a surprise that what you describe reflects awareness of input that draws from all 19 senses. An enriched environment is one which awakens the entire nervous system, one which is stimulating, curiosity feeding, capable of answering many questions and engendering more, a setting which is alive with resources and reflective of real life, an environment bursting with non-print materials such as experts in their fields discussing samples of the real McCoy.

In contrast, the typical classroom is barren, sterile, unpleasant in its institutionality, and greatly restrictive in its input to the nervous system. Classically, classroom input consists almost entirely of print and lecture. Perhaps the most pernicious aspect of our current curriculum and related materials—textbooks, workbooks, skill packs, dittos, etc.—is their poverty of input and their artificiality. As noted earlier, the brain is always in search of meaning. The detection of *patterns* (identification of elements related in a way that has meaning to the perceiver) and the development of *mental programs* through application and use of knowledge and skills in real life contexts depends heavily upon a learning environment being rich and real life like. Remember, the brain is designed to learn from the complexities of real life.[11] The artificial simplicities of textbooks and "seatwork" are highly brain-antagonistic. (For discussion of the physiology of learning, see Chapter I.)

When creating an enriched environment, it is important to keep in mind the extent and kind of the experiences with the *natural world* that your students bring with them to school. The key here is to balance that experience, not replicate it. For example, if students come to you long on TV, videos, Sesame Street, and secondhand sources (books and pictures), then the classroom must provide the REAL stuff—not books about, videos about, pictures about, replicas of, models of, but the real thing!

Guidelines for creating an enriched environment:

- immerse students in reality; use *"being there"* experiences and sources

- next, and only after all available firsthand resources have been exhausted, use only those secondhand items which allow for hands-on learning

- books and print materials, videos and pictures are to be used as supplementary extensions of what is taught through firsthand resources

- each class should have a current set of *World Book Encyclopedia* (the organization and graphics are superb!)—technology, computer, laser disc, etc.

- a healthy environment[12]

- no clutter; avoid distraction and overstimulation

- change bulletin boards and displays frequently; always stay current with what is being studied at the moment. Put away the old except for a few items (e.g., the mindmap for the component) which will jog recall

- consider not purchasing class sets of textbooks (buy only a few for teacher resource) and spend the money on firsthand materials for students and inservice for teachers

COLLABORATION
BRAIN-COMPATIBLE ELEMENT 6

The history of the United States has been the enshrining of individualism—the spirit of Frank Sinatra's "My Way." In schools, students work alone at their work, no sharing (no cheating), no talking (learning occurs when everything is quiet), competition (get graded on the bell curve). And while such a picture fits Hollywood's notion of how the West was won, it belies the reality of day-to-day living in the 1990's. The pioneers relied heavily on each other for their very existence. And today, real work of significance (landing a man on the moon, designing the user-friendly mouse for computers) is also a collaborative venture. In short, our schools, with their Prussian ancestry, are out of step with the real world.

In 1989, the U.S. Department of Labor released its commission report entitled, *Investing In People.* An entire chapter is devoted to what education needs to do in order to improve the quality of the American work force. This is one of their observations:

> "Business can make additional contributions by providing schools with the information that they need to develop course content and instructional methods that meet the current and emerging needs of the work place. Increasingly, employees will have to work in cooperative groups, be able to make decisions about production problems and processes, and develop the ability to acquire new skills and behavior on the job. We urge schools to adjust their instructional methods to match more closely the situation students will later face in the work place."

The requisite skills for running one's own business—a farm, a home, being an inventor or a businessman (even as a shoeshine boy or delivering papers)—were and have always been problem-solving, decision-making, and the ability to communicate with peers and adults. However, with the growth of huge, multi-national corporations and large bureaucracies, a significant portion of the population are now employees, not entrepreneurs. Significant numbers of children are now growing up in homes where the work of the parents or other adults is not known to the child and the standards of successful business (drive to master skills and provide quality customer service) are rarely practiced with a sense of consequence to the survival of the business or to one's personal reputation in the community.

In addition, there is great generational segmentation in our society—great rifts in understanding and appreciation between retired citizens, youth, and the working adult. The school, with its rigid age-gradedness, reinforces this sense of segmentation and is out of step with the needs of today's students and society. Segregation by age is an enormous mistake.

Teaching students the skills to successfully collaborate in the classroom will assist them in becoming effective members of society as adults.

Another, and more powerful, rationale for collaboration comes from brain research. Hart talks about the need for great quantities of input to the brain; Smith stipulates that a learner needs "much opportunity to manipulate information."[13] According to both authors, one teacher armed with uniform textbooks facing a classroom of 30 brains, each with very different ways of learning, is insufficient to the task. Collaboration, cooperative learning, students teaching each other and providing a sounding board for each other is an essential element in a brain-compatible learning environment.

What Is Collaboration? — The choice of the word "collaboration" rather than cooperation or cooperative learning is deliberate here. As defined in *Webster's* dictionary, collaboration means **"to work in association with, to work with another."** Collaboration means working together toward a common goal. The common goal in an ITI classroom is achievement of mastery and competence of skills and knowledge that have application in the real world, not a short-term goal of completing a worksheet or assignment.

In the ITI model, it is irrelevant which approach to collaboration a teacher may choose, so long as the end result is achieved. In other words, collaboration is a desired end, the means may vary. Our favorite resources are *Designing Groupwork: Strategies for the Heterogeneous Classroom* by Elizabeth Cohen and *TRIBES: A Process for Social Development and Cooperative Learning* by Jeanne Gibbs.

Designing Groupwork provides a clear analysis of the peer social norms which a teacher must alter if low status students are to succeed, plus some how-tos for multi-ability classrooms and for bilingual classrooms. *TRIBES* is a wonderfully practical book with lots of ready-to-go activities for developing a sense of group, the prerequisite qualities being inclusion, influence, and affection.

STRUCTURING EFFECTIVE COLLABORATION

Structuring effective collaboration in the classroom involves two areas: the design of the curriculum and flexible grouping of students for different purposes.

Curriculum Design

Cohen points out that collaboration, or "groupwork," is the appropriate vehicle for achieving outcomes in three areas: cognitive or intellectual goals, social goals, and for solving common classroom problems.

Cognitive Goals

Collaboration is especially powerful in promoting conceptual learning, practice with creative problem-solving, the learning of language, and the improvement of oral communication. In contrast, Cohen points out that putting groups together for other cognitive tasks such as the infamous seat-work ditto is a complete waste of time. Student response to such assignments is quite predictable: let the smartest kid do it and then everyone else copies.[14]

ITI inquiries developed for collaborative work must be designed with care. Two criteria to follow: 1) the outcome should be something that even the most capable student can't do alone, and thus everyone's contribution is needed, and 2) it should be engaging, reflective of real life.

Social Goals

In real life, each of us is a member of many groups: family, extended family, close friends, peer acquaintances, neighbors, fellow workers, clients, car pools. The contribution to our learning from each group is different and greatly enriched by the diversity in ages, experience, and points of view. If we could only belong to one group, our learning would be severely restricted. So it is in the classroom. An enormous mistake in the system is segregating students by age. True brain-compatibility in the classroom will not be achieved until multi-aged grouping of students occurs (a minimum of three years) and there is frequent interaction with experts.

The truth is that we live our lives in groups and much of the satisfaction (and dissatisfaction) in our lives comes from our level of success at being group members. According to Brady, "most personal needs are met, most problems are solved, most public goals are attained by *organized collective action*."[15] Yet nowhere do we get formal training in how to be successful group members. If our parents did not have those skills to pass on to us, we have to resort to trial and error; the pain level for failure is high, the time line for learning long.

We owe it to our students, and to ourselves, to learn how to be successful group members. Therefore, we need to develop curriculum which uncovers the concepts and skills of group membership. The content focus for the first two to three weeks of the school year should be the nature of groups, group development, how to be a group member and understanding one's own learning processes.

The basic building blocks for collaboration in an ITI classroom are the Lifelong Guidelines described on pages 43 to 49: trustworthiness, truthfulness, active listening, no put-downs, and the LIFESKILLS that assist one in doing one's personal best.

In our move to collaboration, behaviors need to be modeled and labeled for others to see what the Lifelong Guidelines and LIFESKILLS really look like, sound like, feel like, and how they affect the outcomes we achieve.

Again, one of the best resources we have found to build the necessary inclusion, influence, and affection between individuals is *TRIBES*.* The premises upon which the TRIBES Program is based are:

- Children who maintain long-term membership in supportive classroom peer groups will improve in self-image, behave more responsibly, and increase their academic achievement
- Teachers will spend less time managing student behavior problems and have more time for creative teaching
- Schools, organized into the TRIBES system, will create a positive climate for learning
- Parents will report a carry-over of positive statements and attitudes from their children into the home environment[15]

Flexible Student Grouping

Among the lessons needed to operate effectively in a group is the willingness to be flexible, patient, and to believe that cooperation is beneficial to the whole as well as to each member of the group. If this is firmly in place and applied daily, students will not have difficulty moving from group to group in the classroom or in real life.

As mentioned above, learning in real life settings occurs through a multitude of groups. It is probably not too great an exaggeration to say that the difference between a country cousin and a city slicker, between a parochial perspective and a world view, is the number and variety of learning groups encountered in life. Similarly, assignment in school to a one collaborative learning group for the year is restrictive. For maximum brain-compatibility, we recommend using at least three groupings: family, skill, and interest.

The Family Group — This is the basic membership group through which students learn how to be group members, handle most conceptual learning inquiries, write in their journals, and record the daily agenda. In the true sense of family, the family group is the context in which students come together daily, checking in, asking for advice, getting assistance, and generally "touching base."

Family groups should be heterogeneous and multi-aged; the ideal size is four to five students. The family group meets daily.

---

* *TRIBES* is an eminently practical book, containing more than a hundred pages of activities which can be used as is or adapted to incorporate content from subjects being studied. Also, many of the activities can be used with adults. We recommend that group-building activities be built into each staff meeting and that the entire staff consider being trained as a group in the TRIBES process.

Skill Groups — Skill groups operate "as needed" on a short-term, ad hoc basis. No one is assigned but, as the need comes up, the teacher will form a group to give an assortment of opportunities for studying specific skills or concepts. Students shift from group to group as mastery is attained.

Groups can (and should) vary throughout the day depending on what is to be learned; most do not last more than a week or two weeks maximum.

Interest Groups — Like skill groups, interest groups are short-term, ad hoc, very spontaneous. They are appropriate when creating projects, doing specific inquiries, planning a closure, working on research, or sharing common interest regarding a long-term project. They change from day to day, week to week. They are very loosely knit, largely autonomous; their success requires a high degree of cooperation by each member and high commitment to the task at hand.

Care should be given to see that membership, whenever the groups are established by self-selection, is done with content in mind rather than merely current friendship. This can usually be done by simply restating the criteria for the groups' formation—they are *work* committees.

The above group structures are used for organizing all students around learning tasks. Yet another group, the work group, involves only a few students at a time.

The Work Group

The above group structures are used for organizing all students around learning tasks. Yet another kind of group, the work group, involves only a few students at a time. The work group is a practical response to the teacher's need to get the business of the day accomplished for the classroom. These groups may be for the moment, the day, the week, the month. Because such a group usually consists of not more than two or three students and results in tangible, easily measured results, it provides a good opportunity for developing leadership skills. Examples include cleaning cages, setting up a display, making a bulletin board, improving skills, or working on a project.

The work group is also a vehicle for an individual student when he/she needs to accomplish a personal task. Just as adults understand who to contact when they need to undertake a specific project, students learn to choose the partner needed for a specific activity. Listing the specific tasks with the needed skills on a bulletin board or job list assists students in selecting a partner who would best assist in getting the job done well and on time. Similarly, having a chart inside each student's binder listing the student's talents and added space to write the date when the talents have been tapped helps students focus on who they are becoming and what they have to offer others and the world. The important lesson here is that we all have very specific areas in which we are competent and are willing to assist others. Commitment to contribute to one's community, not just take, is an essential value to teach all students in a democratic society.

The Committee of One

One of the common mistakes in implementing collaboration is the assumption that if a little is good, then lots must be really terrific. Under this mistaken notion, teachers attempt to have students in groups all day long, day after day. This is brain-antagonistic for three reasons: first, the sameness is boring. Second, group environments are not the best context for some assignments and tasks. Third, the classroom should nurture development of intrapersonal intelligence and provide quiet time for introverts as well as develop group skills.

A Touch of Common Sense

Don't be rigid in your scheduling of group work. Be flexible. Choose collaboration, whole class work, individual work, pairs, or other configurations **based on what is the most appropriate vehicle for the moment**. The bottom line is common sense. Don't get tied into something that is unworkable and chaotic. Always be willing to discuss with the students the effectiveness of the working arrangement.

Collaboration as a structure is not an end in itself. It exists for three reasons:

- manipulation of information substantially increases when collaborating
- helping students learn group skills is essential to success in life
- when a group context is the best vehicle for carrying out a particular activity or inquiry

Most importantly, collaboration is not just a tool for the classroom, it is a way of life—a philosophy and a system of values.

Outcomes of Working in Group Settings

During the early stages of implementing collaboration, it is not unusual to panic about the amount of time it takes: "When will I ever get to my subject content? I can't afford to delay getting to what my principal expects me to be teaching." The pressure to give it up will become extreme. Just know that those before you had the same worries. And you, as they, will discover that, once the family groups have developed a sense of group and learned

69

the skills of working together, cognitive learning is speeded up enormously. Students will learn far more—in breadth and depth—once they have handled the social and personal issues in the classroom. This is especially true during the personal and social upheaval of adolescence.

Work habits and skills learned through working in groups include the LIFESKILLS plus the following:

- thoughtfulness—assisting others when it is needed
- follow through—knowing the rest of the group is depending on you
- respect—being able to act in a way that allows others the confidence to do their best
- creativity—seeing new ways to solve problems and enhance projects
- planning—learning how to structure an activity within a time frame
- leadership and followership—learning when and how to lead and when and how to follow others' leadership

Guidelines for encouraging collaboration

- the information processed during collaboration must be meaningful from the learner's point of view and provide real life problems to be solved, not contrived worksheet exercises

- if students have low peer status, teachers must make every effort to *alter their social standing* within their group(s) and in the class as a whole in order to prevent the pygmalion effect from shutting down their learning

- it is important to make a distinction between two or more students sharing the same assignment together vs. true collaboration in which there is a sense of group built and maintained by attention to process and development of requisite group and social skills

IMMEDIATE FEEDBACK
BRAIN-COMPATIBLE ELEMENT 7

Immediate feedback is essential to the accurate and speedy building of *mental programs* (see discussion of *program* building and information storage and retrieval, key concepts in learning, Chapter I). In all learning environments except the school, immediate feedback is present in abundance. Consider, for example, when children first begin to talk. Each time they say something incorrectly we immediately give them the correct word, usage, pronunciation. Imagine letting all their mistakes pile up during the week and correcting them on Friday!

Or, think back to the time you learned to drive a car. Feedback was instantaneous and continuous. If you returned home with no dents and no tickets, your parents knew you had a fairly successful time! Similarly, when learning to play a game or sport or hobby, feedback is built in, immediate, and continuous. In such cases, either the learning materials or the conditions themselves provided the immediate feedback, or your "teacher" or fellow adventurer interpreted your approximation toward mastery. This is a far cry from the classroom setting with the often asked question, "Is this right, teacher?" "Teacher, is this the way it's supposed to turn out?"

Smith, in *Insult to Intelligence: The Bureaucratic Invasion of Our Classrooms*, states that learning does not require coercion or irrelevant reward. Learning is its own reward. The feedback that we have succeeded at a learning task produces a burst of fire from neurotransmitters, producing a "chemical high" that is readily observable in the spark in a child's eye as the "Aha" registers.

In contrast, each of us has personal experiences with learning when the feedback was confusing, either because it came after the fact or because it was inappropriate to what we were doing or thinking at the time. Examples abound. Many among us experience the frustration of fumbling over the spelling of a particular word and our two choices are always the same two, the same incorrect version vs. the correct. We are never sure which is which. Or, confusion over percentages and how (and when) to use which formula. One of the author's upper grade teachers was a bit vague on mathematics in general and percentages in particular. As a result, she rarely taught percentages but, when she did, she taught it differently each time—correctly this time and incorrectly another. As a consequence, her aging student to this day experiences confusion with anything beyond computation of sales tax. Time is wasted, first making up a similar problem with a known answer and then inserting the numbers at hand.

These are examples of having built a *program* incorrectly. And, contrary to popular belief, the hardest thing the brain does is forget something it has learned (as distinguished from forgetting something it never learned in the first place or which never was meaningful . . . which occurs for 80 percent of the students on the bell curve who stopped just short of mastery, of building a *program*). If you doubt that forgetting is difficult, talk with a Vietnam vet who still experiences flashbacks, or think back to your own reoccurring nightmares that replay a horrible experience. When we say **"I taught it but the students forgot it,"** what is really so is that **"I taught it but students never learned it."** Feedback (and usually adequate time) was insufficient for the student to develop a correct *program*.

The importance of immediate feedback to the student, then, is obvious. **Feedback, accurate and immediate, is needed at the time the learner is building his/her *mental program*** to ensure that the *program* is accurate and to help speed up the building of a *program(s)*. *(Program building is such a critical concept, we recommend you re-read pages 25 to 26 in Chapter I before proceeding here.)* Yet, in a classroom with desks in rows, giving feedback is difficult and time consuming. Add to that the burden of departmentalization and a student load of 150 or more per day and it becomes almost impossible to provide immediate feedback.

So what are the implications for middle school? Simply, vast restructuring is needed. Changes in structure, curriculum, instructional strategies and materials, and in how we schedule and use time.

Change the Curriculum

Shift the starting point of your curriculum content from disciplines to the need to understand the real world: locations, events, settings. "Disciplines" are an artifact of Western man's way of talking about his world. They are a classic example of the parts not adding up to the whole. Instead, start with the whole, i.e., the real world, and slice off a chewable piece.

The real world has a great deal of built-in feedback for learners; in fact, it is the best form of immediate feedback because feedback is almost always built into the learning event itself. Such firsthand feedback from *"being there"* in a real world setting is instantaneous and more intrinsic—and thus more powerful—than feedback from an outside source, the teacher or the answer sheet for the workbook or SRA Reading Kit.

(For a full discussion of changes needed in curriculum, see Chapter III.)

Change the Instructional Materials

The best learning environments are those in which the materials and events themselves provide the feedback, e.g., driving a car, riding a horse, hitting a curve ball, building a model bridge, sewing a dress. These are settings which allow learners to sit in the driver's seat, able to judge for themselves whether they have mastered something or not, which allows them to direct their own learning.

This is a far cry from the typical activities and materials of the traditional school. Few worksheets or dittos provide feedback of a self-correcting kind. As a consequence, children feel rudderless, confused, and powerless. Hardly the characteristics of a lifelong learner.

Change the Structure:
Increase the Number of "Teachers"

Remember the one-room, little red schoolhouse? The eight or ten or twenty children, all of different ages—grades 1-8 or even 1-12? What were the advantages? An older, more experienced student was always there to help, support, point out the obvious, and otherwise act as a teacher or mentor to the younger children. Compare that to thirty lower tracked students with one teacher. Where does the immediate feedback come from? How many of the students receive timely, sufficient feedback from the teacher during each activity? During an entire day? Given the arithmetic of it all, each student on average will get less than two minutes of personalized feedback a day. At the instant when they are trying to make sense out of the learning, where can they get feedback to see if they are correct? Certainly not from fellow students who are also struggling with the same task.

If we want greater learning, we must increase the number and availability of "teachers" who have sufficient mastery to provide accurate feedback to the fledgling learner. This is easily done by eliminating tracking and creating heterogeneous classes of students representing a wide range of experiences and expertise. Multi-age grouping of students also deserves consideration.

For all "teachers" (adult and student), reduce the number of interactions during the day by lengthening the time any one group is together.

Change the Structure:
Change How We Schedule and Use Time

Currently, teachers do 90 percent of the talking and students have little time for "doing." To build in immediate feedback, the ratio of doing and being talked at must be reversed. Inquiries which ask for action by applying what is being learned to the real world are the perfect vehicle.

Second, our teachers are encouraged to limit their direct instruction to not more than 16 minutes an hour. Three reasons for this guideline are:

- it demands that the teacher absolutely knows what it is he/she wants to convey to the students (a clear, concise, succinct, this-is-what's-most-important-to-know lesson)

- the remainder of the time (hour, morning) is spent circulating among the students giving them immediate feedback on the activity structured by their chosen (or assigned) inquiry. (See Chapter VI for a discussion of inquiries.) This is a time for re-teaching, for further explanation, and discussion one-on-one

- it provides an opportunity for the teacher to immediately assess the effectiveness of the direct instruction and the subsequent assignment

Again, unlearning something incorrectly stored in the brain is much more difficult than learning it right the first time. It is imperative to stop a student if he/she is on the wrong track and building an incorrect *program*.

Eliminate Delayed Feedback

If one understands the nature of *program-building*, one cannot escape reaching the conclusion that, in most cases, it is a waste of teacher time to grade papers overnight (and at longer intervals). The only exception is long-term, comprehensive projects which are multi-step. For students to do a page of algebra problems incorrectly as a follow-up to the in-class lesson and not be told whether it is right or wrong until the next day is meaningless feedback for *program building*. The student has already logged in the incorrect *program*. To add further damage, send the student home with more algebra problems for homework while the instruction is still fresh in his/her head (which, of course, it may very well not be) . . . more incorrect practice, more incorrect *programs* in the brain.

So, our best advice to you is to stop grading papers overnight! For the teacher, the implications are enormously freeing. What a time saver, what a burden to unload! Imagine what terrific curriculum could be planned during the time traditionally set aside each day for grading papers with letter grades, smiley faces, etc. And, more importantly, what fun teaching could be!

Guidelines for providing immediate feedback:

- stop grading papers overnight! Structure group work so that feedback is provided to each participant on a wide range of issues, e.g., ways of structuring/going about work, LIFESKILLS needed and used, different but successful ways that would de-liver the same end vs. those which don't work and why, plus the content—what it is and how to use it. When working properly, most of this feedback can be built into the activity, often from fel-low students, thus reducing the pull and drag on the teacher

- utilize the two basic tenets behind the authentic assessment movement: assess what is of value (not just what's easy to assess) and make sure that the product utilized for assessment is a prod-uct that has worth to the student in and of itself

- help students sensitize themselves to the feedback built into the real world and to the voice in the back of their heads (their own feedback mechanism as self-directed learners); help them develop confidence in their own ability to provide themselves feedback, a necessary capability for lifelong learners

- change your curriculum and materials. Start with real life content and use real life resources and events. When firsthand assignments are given to cooperative work groups, giving individual (and group) feedback is a much easier task

- don't overlook or underestimate the power and value of peer feedback

MASTERY/COMPETENCE
BRAIN-COMPATIBLE ELEMENT 8

One of the greatest frustrations for teachers is "I taught them but they didn't learn." Somewhere along the corridors of time, our educational system has shifted its focus from learning to teaching. For example, teacher evaluation forms typically require the observer to take copious notes on what the teacher does, i.e., on *teaching*. Any teacher who does not do a formal lesson consisting of directed instruction, but instead orchestrates *learning* through other means, will likely not "score" well. We have inherited a "sage on the stage" rather than a "guide on the side" tradition.

Another pernicious tradition in education is the acceptance of the bell curve—acceptance that mastery* by only 20 percent of the class is an acceptable outcome for all the billions we spend on education. And, make no mistake, brain research makes it quite clear that, if meaning has not been reached, there is nothing for the brain to remember except confusion and, quite possibly, distaste for the topic or even the entire subject area ("I hate science" is an all too commonplace reaction from students and adults alike). **Brain research does not substantiate our devotion to the spiral curriculum notion.** *The brain cannot build on bits and pieces that were meaningless at the time they were encountered.*

From a teacher's perspective, mastery/competence is built into a student's day through both curriculum planning and instructional strategies. (For a full discussion of mastery/competence, see Chapter IX.)

CONCLUDING NOTES

As a conceptual model for teaching, Integrated Thematic Instruction provides a structure which will "hook" all the parts and pieces of "good teaching" you have experimented with over the years. In a new and holistic context, you will see your "old" skills, knowledge, and "new" visions come together into a synergistic, amazingly powerful whole.

---

* As used here, mastery is defined as having arrived at an understanding of and ability to apply—in real world settings—the concept or skill being learned.

III

THE STUFF OF CURRICULUM —
TAKING A NEW LOOK AT AN OLD ISSUE

*"But I'm coming to believe that all of us are ghosts. . . .
It's not just what we inherit from our mothers and fathers.
It's also the shadows of dead ideas and opinions and convictions. They're no longer alive, but they grip us all the same,
and hold on to us against our will. All I have to do is open the
newspaper to see ghosts hovering between the lines. They are
haunting the whole country, those stubborn phantoms—so many of them, so thick,
they're like an impenetrable dark mist. And here we are, all of us, so abjectly terrified of the light."*
Henrick Ibsen, *Ghosts*

If we may paraphrase Ibsen, all we have to do is open the school door to
see the ghosts hovering between the lines of our textbooks. They are haunting the entire campus—classrooms, hallways, gymnasium, playing fields,
offices, and parking lots. The Ghosts of Tradition lie heavily about our shoul-
ders, dragging on our every step.

In its battle with these ghosts, every school feels that it is alone and
unique, that its struggle to improve, to implement the middle school reform
agenda is incomparably difficult due to innumerable idiosyncrasies of the culture and history of its staff, students, and community. The players feel over-
whelmed by the immensity and complexity of the job of true reform. We feel
in the grip of dead ideas and opinions and convictions from which we seem
unable to free ourselves. And the impenetrable dark mist closes in on us.

We have lived in this dark mist for many decades of school reform. Even
the middle school reform movement of the past 30 years has been unable to
shake it. Why? Why have we been unable to shake the ghosts of tradition? Is
there, as Ibsen's analogy suggests, a light that we are terrified to move into?
Jim Beane, and others including the authors, say yes. According to Beane, the
light that terrifies us is asking the hard question about curriculum: "What
ought to be the curriculum of the middle school?" which has not been
addressed during the past three decades years of the middle school movement. Our refusal to do so, says Beane, "could partly be accounted for by fear
that explicitly asking it might just cause a rift in what has mostly been a gentle and friendly reform movement at the middle level."[1]

Carrying his point yet further, Beane comments, "I want to suggest that
the work on middle school organization and teaching methods has succeeded
partly, and perhaps mostly, because it has focused on better ways of transmitting the usual subject matter without questioning that subject matter or the

77

subject area curriculum organization that surrounds it."[2] He goes on to say that we are suffering from the "absent presence" of the broader curriculum question, "What is worth teaching?" According to Beane, our unwillingness to confront the actual content of our subject based curriculum, to reconceptualize what is important for students to know and be able to do as they prepare for life in the 21st century, is stealing the middle school movement's success, nullifying its results.

WHAT students are asked to learn, not HOW it is packaged and taught are the central issues (although vast improvements are needed in this as well). Little, beyond a general watering down, has changed in the curriculum required by state frameworks and district and school scope and sequences in more than 100 years. Students in social studies classes still study the names of famous explorers and the lands they discovered. In science, students study fragmented science concepts in one area of science such as physical science without any attempt to show how all sciences are integrated and cannot be separated, except in textbooks. Math teachers still teach the same math concepts and use the strategies of rote memorization and endless pages of practice problems. English/language arts teachers are still having students learn the parts of speech and diagram sentences as a route to becoming proficient writers.

How can this be so? How is it that the curriculum for a country so dynamic and fast changing as the United States of America, whose elder citizens have seen transportation evolve from the horse and buggy of their childhood to travel to the moon and back and even beyond and other equally stupendous changes . . . how is it that our school system has clung to the old so tenaciously? This question deserves exploration. Until we understand why our schools—elementary and high school (and their "junior" look-alike versions)—have remained virtually unchanged in over 100 years, we can never hope to succeed at school reform. Accordingly, we must understand our curricular and instructional history or, as so often noted, we will be doomed to repeat it.

A BIT OF HISTORY

The history of curriculum for the American public school system is akin to the *World According to Garp*. Like the popular novel of the early 80's, it reads with a grim surrealism, a truly startling degree of distortion of real life and the problems and events which are the stuff of adult life. The following events illustrate a Garpian picture of our educational roots:

1806 - 1819 — In response to its humiliating defeat to Napoleon in 1806, Prussia institutes changes in educational system. Three premises of teacher training in Prussia are: the state is sovereign, the only true parent of children; intellectual training is not the purpose of state schooling, obedience and subordination are; and, the schoolroom and the workplace shall be dumbed down into simplified fragments that anyone, however dull, can memorize and operate.[3] By 1819, Prussia demonstrates first laboratory of compulsory schooling (as distinguished from "educating"). Military fortunes turn sharply upward. New schooling system considered a major element in success.

1838 — the first real comprehensive high school opens in Philadelphia, initially offering three different curricula: the "principal" course, a classical course, and an "English" course (two-year program). Within a few years, the latter two courses disappeared, the "principal" course remained. The subjects of the principal course included modern languages, English, mathematics, social studies, sciences, drawing, and religion. As Barbara Benham Tye comments, "with the exception of religion, no longer taught in our public schools, the principal curriculum offered in 1839 bears a striking resemblance to the general education courses which still, in the late 1900's, form the core of American high school education."[4]

1840 — Horace Mann, in search of a model that will help sell the notion of free universal education, travels to Europe. The Prussian system, highly organized in a militaristic style, class-and-grade system, "a system that reduced human beings during their malleable years to reliable machine parts, human machinery dependent upon the state for its mission and purpose."[5] Attractive to the industrialist mind, the instructional processes and the very structure of the Prussian system look like a factory, considered ideal for processing waves of immigrants. However, the curriculum content remains relatively unchanged, dating back from the early church—the catechism of one right answer within categories of learning delineated in the medieval universities, the birthplace of "disciplines."

1883 — first manual arts high school opens in Baltimore, immediately popular, the idea spreads rapidly. However, the stronger trend is the comprehensive high schools. Before the turn of the century, manual arts and the comprehensive high school are put under one roof. This becomes "the" model for high schools in America.[6]

1890 - 1920 — public school enrollment doubles every decade; educators worry that the new enrollees are less able because they come increasingly from lower-class and immigrant homes. "Like other Americans, many educators took for granted that the immigrants were intellectually inferior, that they came from racially—which is to say genetically—poorer stock than resident white Americans."[7] It thus seems reasonable to conclude that high schools would have to revise their offerings radically in order to cope with the newcomers. By the early 1930s the resultant "reforms" are firmly in place. One essential change is differentiated curriculum, the invention of a few broad academic avenues within the high schools—curriculum tracks—that are tied to preparation for work, the precursors of today's tracking system. "Those students who seemed cut out for higher education and the leadership responsibilities of the professions would enroll in an academic track; they would concentrate on such areas as languages, literature, and science. Those whose futures seemed to hold office work or lower management would enroll in a commercial curriculum; their studies would focus on accounting, clerical methods, and similar matters. Those who seemed likely to move from school to labor in the trades and manufacturing would enroll in one or another vocational program; they would take such courses as drafting or machine work. And those who had no evident destiny, or seemed incapable of settling on one, would enroll in a general curriculum that offered a smattering of studies in a variety of fields.[8] This "new order" is summarized by one school administrator as: "We can picture the educational system as having a very important function as a selection agency, a means of selecting the men of best intelligence from the deficient and mediocre."[9] This structure is basically the one in existence now, one reflective of a deep pessimism about the American people and about the possibility of political democracy.

Circa 1900 — regional accrediting associations are formed by colleges and universities which, in setting college entrance requirements, have the power to determine high school curriculum for those preparing for college. No comparable organizations have been created to influence/lead development of curriculum for non-college bound. By default, curriculum for college bound students holds sway.[10]

1900 — American schools are described as "predominantly formal and traditional. Many pupils understandably felt that schoolwork had little or no relationship to their lives. They saw no connection between school learning and out-of-school experiences and interests. The same academic diet, day after day, resulted in a loss of appetite for education. The average and below average child, in particular, found the heavily academic character of the work tedious and difficult. Poor readers were severely and continuously handicapped, because the school program was almost exclusively based on the printed word. At the ninth grade, the opening of the high school years, the content became still more academic and the method still more formal. Suddenly, the student was confronted with many teachers instructing him in the formal subjects that almost exclusively made up the high school program. The result was often failure. The outcome of failure was often withdrawal. The very ones who dropped out were the ones least prepared to succeed in an increasingly complex and competitive society."[11]

1907-1911 — three influential dropout studies reveal a high dropout rate beyond fifth grade. "Only slightly more than one in three students who entered public school even reached ninth grade and only approximately one in ten completed high school. About one-third of the school children of the time were retained at one time or another while they were in school and about one in six children at any grade was a repeater in that grade." Many reasons are given for dropouts and retentions, among them "illness, late entrance, low intelligence, irregular attendance, and lack of family support for schooling. However, there can be no doubt that the poor quality of the school program, itself, was a major contributor."[12]

Early 1900's — the American junior high school is created. Its purpose: to create an alternative to the academic nature of high school As described in the famous report, *Cardinal Principles of Secondary Education*, developed by the Commission on the Reorganization of Secondary Education in 1918, "junior period emphasis should be place upon the attempt to help the pupil explore his own aptitudes and to make at least provisional choice of the kinds of work to which he shall devote himself." Further, "there should be a gradual introduction of departmental instruction, some choice of subjects under guidance, promotion by subjects, provocational courses, and a social organization that calls for the initiative and develops the sense of personal responsibility for the welfare of the group."[13] The idea is highly popular and spreads quickly across the United States. Almost as quickly, the original purpose is lost and the junior high school becomes a "junior" version of the comprehensive high school structured in and changeless since 1838.[14]

1920's – 1980's — major, nationwide attempts to alter the nature of high schools and their Prussian and medieval university roots, a continuation of what Seymour Sarason calls "the predictable failure of public school reform." In 1972, the Rand Corporation issues report for the President's Commission on School Finance. Known as the "Averch Report," it summarizes its findings as follows: "We are saying that research has found nothing that consistently and unambiguously makes a difference in student outcomes" and that ". . . substantial improvement in educational outcomes can be obtained only through a vastly different form of education."[15] A similar conclusion is reached by Christopher Jencks and others: "We can see no evidence that either school administrators or educational experts know how to raise test scores, even when they have vast resources at their disposal."[16]

1990's — general consensus that American high schools have changed little in over 140 years, particularly in the area of curriculum. The same is true for their look-alike junior versions. The middle school movement, in its attempt to remake junior highs, admits it has failed to adequately address the issue of curriculum—"What should students learn?" Curriculum is still tied to medieval university roots.[17]

CURRICULUM: BIRTHPLACE OF CHANGE

It is the authors' belief, and one concurred with by many observers of failed reform efforts over the past 70 years*, that the reason such reform efforts have failed is primarily because we have never abandoned our notions about "disciplines" and the belief that the purpose of schooling is mastery of identified content based upon a world view forged during the middle ages, a time of limited understanding of our world. It therefore should not surprise us that students have difficulty seeing the relevance of what they are studying to their lives. As 20th century life has pulled ahead of us, with all its multiple and complex changes in daily living, we continue to give our students curriculum content of a bygone era rather than for surviving and thriving in daily life in the 21st century.

MISMEMES IN EDUCATION

So, let us ask ourselves again, how is it that our schools have remained unchanged for over a hundred years? How can so many well-intentioned (and well financed) reform movements come and go without leaving even the smallest permanent dent?

A useful metaphor for examining this queer blindness is that of "memes," a neologism invented by Richard Dawkins. Dawkins, while emphasizing the importance of genes to cells, argues that memes exercise the same kind of control in the mind. It is memes, not genes, that have been shaping the force of our culture. Building on Dawkins' discussion of memes, Richard Bergland, in his book *Fabric of Mind*[18] makes the following comments: "The genetic distinction of Beethoven or Einstein is lost in three or four generations; their splendid genes, once poured into the extraordinarily large vat of the human genetic pool, are lost forever. But the memes of Beethoven and Einstein, their good ideas, are passed from one generation to another and have an eternal significance. All animals are gene dependent. But the evolution of our culture, of our civilization, is meme dependent."

"Genes are body shapers, actually cell shapers, which may infect the cell; once inside, they cause it to 'selfishly' replicate more and more identical genes. Memes, Dawkins contends, are mind shapers, which pass from brain to brain like an infectious virus. Not all of the ideas that pass from one brain to another brain, however, are good ideas; some are mistakes. These I call 'mismemes'."[19]

---

* We recommend the following books as "must read" analyses of what ails the American public school system and the schooling it provides: *What's Worth Teaching? Selecting, Organizing, and Integrating Knowledge* by Marion Brady; *A Middle School Curriculum from Rhetoric to Reality* by James Beane; and *The Predictable Failure of Public School Reform* by Seymour Sarason.

The power of mismemes is well illustrated by the following two stories.[20] Originated with the Pythagoreans, given the ring of authority by Plato, two powerful mismemes shaped scientific thinking for two centuries. One was the idea of the universe as a perfect sphere centered around the earth and the stars moving in perfect circles. No other mismeme has had the impact of this false notion. Although Copernicus knew for certain in 1510 that the sun, not the earth, was the center of our universe, he dared not publish his discovery. Thirty years later, the book was published in the year of this death, 1543. Nearly a century later, Galileo supported Copernicus but was forced by the church to recant his support of Copernicus in 1633 because : ". . . it had been notified to me that the said doctrine was contrary to Holy Scripture." Thus, "the circular movement that Plato gave to the stars took on a scientific, philosophical, and religious significance that held thoughtful people in intellectual chains for 1,900 years."[21] **

Plato's belief in the perfect sphere led him to another strongly held mismeme—the perfect sphere must be the residence of "the divinest part of us." Thus, the brain (located in the spherical skull) must be the source of genetic material for new life; ergo, the brain was a gland that produced semen.

Two centuries later, Leonardo da Vinci's anatomical drawing illustrates a continuous pathway that could carry sperm from the brain, through the spinal cord, and through a fictitious tube into the penis of a copulating male and into the female vagina. This in spite of Leonardo's extraordinary powers of observation. Despite what he saw, he altered his drawings to reflect the anatomical beliefs of the church.

"This mismeme gave the female brain no role at all and regarded women only as flower pots for male seeds. The acceptance of this paradigm led to the exclusion of women from the governance of academic, religious, and governmental institutions for 2,000 years or longer. This is perhaps the best evidence that the form of our culture and our civilization can be shaped—or misshaped—by the scientific views concerning the brain."[22]

You may be laughing now . . . "How quaint," you say. Downright silly of them. The church no longer controls thought in our society. In the year 1992 we are a society of free thinkers. Think again. Education is enormously tradition-bound. Recent findings of psychology and sociology have created but the thinnest of veneers over centuries-old curriculum structures and content, changing our rationales but not the substance. Issues of tradition are

---

** "The trial and condemnation of Galileo by the Inquisition has long been recognized as one of the watersheds in Western intellectual history. Three hundred and fifty years later the Galileo affair still haunts us and remains the subject of controversy. According to Maurice Finocchiaro, author of *The Galileo Affair: A Documentary History*," the questions it raises involved the nature of science and religion, their relationship to politics and society, individual freedom, institutional authority, and the conflict between conservation and innovation."[19] Not until 1978 did the church agree to formally study the issue and consider exonerating Galileo and then it took 13 years to formally acknowledge their errors. Tradition dies hard.

not easily changed. For example, official apology and retraction of Galileo's condemnation for views that clashed with biblical verses and pontifical interpretations did not occur until October, 1992, and that after 13 years of study. Along similar lines, when will the hue and cry for "Back to Basics" be re-examined?

Mismeme 1:
All Students Learn the Same

Let us dig into a parallel example in education. How about the mismeme "All students learn the same."—patently wrong, you say? Flatly contradicted both by recent brain research, personal experience, and common sense. Yes, we agree. But . . . look at the very structure of our schools. Same textbook for all, students of the same age grouped together or, even more dramatically, tracked so that they can be treated alike, same instructional procedures for all students (the time of year may vary). The only possible explanation for such structures and practices is a belief—the mismeme—that all students learn the same—take the same amount of time to learn the same amount of content, process it in the say way.

Mismeme 2:
Yesterday's Curriculum Is Good Enough for Today

"If it was good enough for Grandpa, it's good enough for Tommy," goes the maxim. Not so. To each his time. In the 1920's, only 20 percent of the population graduated from high school. And today, that same 20 percent finds ready success in our secondary schools; 80 percent do not.[23]

Our old notions of what is important to learn remain embedded in structures set during the days of the medieval universities. The study of the natural world was part of a course in philosophy until the quantity of known facts grew too large, at which point it became a separate course. When natural science became too big to study all in one clump, it was broken down into biology, physics, and alchemy. When biology got too big, it was broken down into zoology and botany. And these structures remain with us.

This piecemeal, patchwork stuff—arms' length from a modern world view of knowledge—leaves students unprepared for our fast-paced world. Not only does it get in the way of understanding the interconnectedness and interrelationship of critical issues such as pollution, global economy, and overpopulation of the planet but it simply does not match adult living and experiences. Jobs called biologist or physicist are now almost extinct. Today's occupations are microbiologist, biochemist, biophysicist, nuclear physicist, etc. Such titles are more than a reflection of specialization, they speak of a degree of integration needed to address real problems of the real world.

In similar fashion, in the area of history/social studies, it is no longer possible to study European history or history of the Far East as a backdrop for understanding one's community. Further, studying Vietnam or China will not necessarily enable students to predict the cultural beliefs and values of the Vietnamtown or Chinatown within one's own city. Nor did the study of history of the former USSR allow us to predict the rapid disintegration of the communist empire. **Classical education is backward-looking**; study of the past through old perspectives will not enable one to anticipate and handle day-to-day living in the future. Only study of the present, with the past as a reference (not a beginning) point, will prepare students to handle the future.

Mismeme 3:
Words Create Knowledge

Every culture has its maxim that describes mankind's experience with teaching its young. The Chinese voice it best: "Tell me, I forget; show me, I remember; involve me, I understand." In the United States we are so sure of this that we have an idiom which attempts to divert attention from the power of the truth statement: "Do what I say, not what I do." In the staff development world, our research tells us that we learn and retain:[24]

10 percent of what we hear
15 percent of what we see
20 percent of what we both see and hear
40 percent of what we discuss
80 percent of what we experience directly or practice doing
90 per cent of what we attempt to teach others.[23]

Piaget's work 70 years ago reached the same empirical conclusions and recent brain research substantiates the fact that learning occurs best when it begins with the concrete, then moves to the symbolic, and lastly to the abstract. Traditional secondary curriculum and instruction, to the contrary, typically begins with the abstract or symbolic and hopes that students might intuit how it applies to the concrete, real world.

And yet, despite all the axioms of our language, and those from other cultures around the world, despite research within our own educational community, despite the brain research described in Chapter I, despite our direct experience as parents, secondary education continues to cling to the tradition of lecture as the primary medium to convey knowledge.

Truly, we know better and it is time to make our actions bespeak what we know.

Mismeme 4:
Acquisition of Knowledge and Skills Is the Goal of Education

Acquisition of knowledge and skill is wholly inadequate as a goal for education in the 1990's. First, it carries with it the implication that knowledge can be quantitatively measured by the pound like a commodity on a dry good shelf, purchased by the uniform currency of "seatwork." Second, in our "Age of Information," an era of exponential expansion of knowledge, particularly in science and technology, and rapidly changing macroevents such as the fall of communism, it is a cruel joke to send students out into the real world believing that what they have squirreled away in their knapsacks will be sufficient to the challenges they will face.

Our national goal for public education ought to be learning how to learn from a dizzying array of sources and formats and mastery in applying what is learned. Definitions from *Webster's* dictionary are useful here; they have the correct denotations and connotations.

Mastery: "act of mastery; state of having control over something; superiority in competition; victory; eminent skill or thorough knowledge"

Application: "the act of applying or putting to use"

Mismeme 5:
Textbooks Equal Curriculum and Instruction

For most Americans, textbooks are *the* symbol of education. As Brady comments: "Some measure of their perceived importance is indicated by the action and attitudes of our society related to them. Parents demand that they be brought home from school. Many teachers won't start classes without them. Academic departments will adopt new textbooks and then spend weeks reorganizing courses, as if the change in books had somehow altered the field of study. Administrators sometimes think that all books for a class should be the same, and that all classes using textbooks should be on approximately the same page on the same day. Elaborate and expensive procedures are devised to select them. Angry crowds sometimes burn them and, not infrequently, the courts are asked to make judgments about them. Obviously, textbooks are thought to be very important."[25] How rare! We have obviously confused the tools of schooling with educating and education.

More than a mismeme, Brady suggests that "traditional textbooks are a major, perhaps *the* major obstacle to the achievement of educational excellence."[26] Yet like Galileo's stipulation that the sun, not the earth, is the center of the universe, this criticism of textbooks will seem to many to be nothing less than heresy. As Brady says, "It's acceptable to find fault with textbooks, to criticize the uninspired writing, the 'dumbing down' of vocabulary, the concern for comprehensiveness at the expense of depth and clarity, spiraling cost, the usual several years' lag behind current knowledge, the dreary sameness stemming from publishers' attempts to duplicate the current best-seller. But to suggest that, in most disciplines, the textbooks actually stand in the way of major educational improvement is to risk being labeled as too eccentric to be taken seriously."[27] Yet the authors firmly believe that textbooks, and their organization of content from "disciplines," is the tack that nails one shoe of school reform to the floor, limiting vision and action to a small circle, one already explored, already proven ineffective, and deadening for students.

According to Brady, textbooks offer students only a "kind of residue of a discipline,"[28] a compilation of decades or centuries of thought, argument, exploration, criticism, organizing, and reorganizing. The result is but a thin gruel of what Beane calls "prethought thoughts." Brady identifies two problems with textbooks: 1) the assumption that what's basically a reference book is a proper tool for instruction—which it is not; and 2) because the content of the conventional expository text is primarily a compendium of conclusions, all significant thinking has already been done. "It's very much like giving the student a vast crossword puzzle with all the blanks filled in. There's nothing left to do except perhaps memorize it—a task not likely to generate enthusiasm or sharpen the intellect."[29]

According to Brady, textbooks should be used as a primary instructional tool only when it is impossible to touch the real thing, or its tangible residue.[30] And, of course, "filling in the blanks" should be eliminated entirely.

Mismeme 6:
Changing Organizational Structure Equals Middle School Reform

It is our belief that the primary cause of failure of secondary school reform over the past four decades is that, although the structure of our secondary schools is unworkable and crushing, structure is but a symptom or expression of a view of curriculum that is wrong-headed and brain antagonistic. We will not succeed at transforming our schools until the stuff, the content, that we peddle is age-appropriate and of the real world. To use an analogy, changing structure but leaving the curriculum content the same is akin to rearranging the deck chairs on the Titanic.

The first step in middle school reform should be to rethink the nature and content of curriculum in light of what we now know about how the human brain learns. Unfortunately, most state and national curriculum leadership documents are not terribly useful for this task as they have not thought through the brain research and used it as a foundation for their recommendations. Once done, however, instructional strategies will begin to shift without effort, after which structural changes will occur almost automatically.

Mismeme 7:
An Interdisciplinary Approach Is a Sufficient Goal

We believe that reform efforts which seek interdisciplinary studies are an extension of a mismeme and are thus an inappropriate and inadequate goal for middle schools to pursue. They are an extension of a mistaken belief that disciplines are an accurate and useful way of viewing life in the 1990's. Simply stated, disciplines are neither accurate nor useful as a lens through which to view real life. Pursuit of interdisciplinary study traps teachers. With pin-feathers clipped short, they struggle to take wing, gerrymandering their calendar so that like or related topics from one department can be taught the same week as related topics of another department. And then, of course, there is the stretching to dig up real life examples in order to make the textbooks less boring.

We are suggesting here that the interdisciplinary curriculum options currently defined by the interdisciplinary curriculum movement, shown below, are inadequate.

Continuum of Options for Content Design[31]

Discipline Based	Parallel Disciplines	Multi-disciplinary	Inter-disciplinary Units/Courses	Integrated Day	Complete Program

The fundamental issue here is that the content of our traditional curriculum—however it is organized and delivered—is an inadequate goal for middle schools. Marion Brady describes this dilemma best: "The disciplines, with or without the lines between them, have their uses, but as a foundation for general education they are fundamentally unsound. No matter how we play with them, they will always yield a curriculum that:

- ignores some of the most important aspects of reality
- tells us nothing about the relative significance of various kinds of knowledge
- fails to provide a comprehensive conceptual structure for organizing knowledge
- implies that reality is fragmented rather than systemic
- makes the disciplines themselves the primary focus of instruction rather than the reality they were created to model
- provides no systematic tools for pursuing the basic educational task—exploring conceptual relationships
- leads us to think that the central task of learning is storing and recalling rather than processing information

"And, because of the centrality of the curriculum to the whole of the educational process, its inadequacies affect not only what goes on in students' heads but discipline, evaluation, the design of schools, student motivation, the kinds of people attracted to teaching—everything."[32]

How much easier it would be to start on the other end of the looking glass, i.e., begin with real life and study it as it presents itself in one's community and as it has meaning to the learner. As Hart has noted, "The brain is designed to learn from natural complexity."[33] The real world around us is simultaneously a manifestation of science, history, social studies, math, communication (oral, written, visual), etc. As mentioned, in the real world, there are few occupations such as "biologist," "chemist," "mathematician," or even "historian" (one is an expert on Russia, a field which attempts to provide a relevant view based upon international relations, economics, sociology, anthropology, and so forth.).

Studying by disciplines distorts our view of reality, making us blind to much around us, overly aware of other aspects, insensitive to the state of interrelatedness in which we live. If we are to bring middle school education into the 21st century, we must break free of the old paradigm of subject disciplines and base ourselves in reality, in making meaning and applying what we know in the here and now.

NEW MEMES FOR CURRICULUM

Life in the 21st century and the ITI model demand new memes for middle school curriculum, memes which are consistent with brain research and the intellectual, physical, psychological, social, moral and ethical development needs and characteristics of the middle school age student. To solve the "curriculum hole" problem for middle schools, we need new memes or foundational premises. We suggest the following:

- **The purpose of public education is the perpetuation of democracy**

- **Life is the best curriculum for adolescents**

- **Learning is a personal affair**

- **The curriculum for the 21st century must be based on reality, not on "disciplines" and textbooks**

- **Curriculum at the middle school level should consist entirely of concepts, skills, and attitudes/values which students can experience through *being there* and *immersion***

- **Instructional strategies should provide students choices which allow for their unique ways of learning**

- **Curriculum should be framed so as to eliminate lecture**

- **Assessment should be reality-based**

NEW MEME 1: THE PURPOSE OF EDUCATION

We accept Carl Glickman's statement that "the only purpose of universal education in a democracy is to enable citizens to productively engage in democratic life"[34] as a given. Yet nothing about our secondary education system and its parts models democracy or provides opportunities to practice democracy in both big and little ways. With few exceptions, our schools share the same authoritarian, autocratic practices as their Prussian roots. Unfortunately, and unbelievably, America's public schools are top-down affairs—a "do what you're told" experience for students and staff.

Secondary schools, including middle schools, should operate under a democratic charter, a modified version of our federal—state—local government structure, replete with constitution, legislatures, courts, and executive branches. Democracy is not a set of words, it is a set of daily actions premised upon a philosophy of the inherent dignity and worth of each individual.

Also at odds with democracy, is the content of curriculum which does little to assist students to understand the reality of here and now, an understanding that is desperately needed in the voting booth. In short, the purpose of education should be expanding our sense of reality—to be able to perceive and understand our complex world (see discussion of the study of reality starting on page 94.

NEW MEME 2:
LIFE IS THE BEST CURRICULUM FOR ADOLESCENT'S

To repeat that middle schools are not "junior highs" is to state the illusive obvious. If we believe that statement, then we must call into question at least 80 percent of the curriculum content of middle schools. Little of it, outside of counseling and advisory meetings, has anything at all to do with the "developmental tasks of adolescents" or their "unique characteristics." (See Appendix A.)

The new curriculum for middle schools is a radical one: **the special qualities of adolescence should dictate not only HOW middle school students learn but, more importantly, WHAT they learn.** That is to say that the most important content for students is an explanation of what they are experiencing—their physical maturation, social relationships, development of an independent self, and intellectual interests and levels. In our opinion, ancient history, required by the state curriculum frameworks for sixth grade, should be put on the shelf.

NEW MEME 3: LEARNING IS A PERSONAL AFFAIR

That every brain is unique, having its own way of gathering information, extracting meaning, processing, storing, and using what is learned, is firmly and irrefutably established by recent brain research. Therefore, curriculum must be personalizable—for and by individual students. Choices for students must be built into the curriculum in order for students to steer their own course between too difficult (thus resulting in failure), and too easy (thus resulting in boredom),[35] and to better engage the entire brain and the seven intelligences. (See Chapters I and II for an extended discussion of brain research and its implications in the classroom.)

There must also be a range of choice for teachers. Curriculum simply cannot be made teacher proof—that has been repeatedly proven. Thus, developing curriculum scope and sequences which are overly prescriptive is, first of all, futile as management tools and, second, suffocating and stifling for teachers in the classroom. The balance to be struck here is quite delicate. For the students' sake, there must be schoolwide agreement among teachers regarding what is to be studied and when, in order to prevent repetition and gaps for students. Yet, detailed prescriptions are counter productive. In our opinion, a one-page outline of concepts developed by each teacher or team is about the right level of detail to serve as a schoolwide planning guide. More detailed planning then occurs teacher by teacher.

NEW MEME CURRICULUM MUST BE REALITY-BASED

The curriculum of the 21st century must be based in reality, not in "disciplines" and textbooks. We believe the only way to achieve that goal is to teach students about real life—not life in America of 30 years ago, but **now**; not the life of the disappearing cowboy of the Wild West, but **here** in one's neighborhood—the street where one's house sits, as well as the neighborhood of a world economy. **The here and now of real life in the 1990's.**

While we often argue that reality, like beauty, is in the eye of the beholder, we defined reality as the slice of life directly experienceable by middle school students at, around, or through their school's location or outreach capacity.

For purposes of curriculum building, Beane suggests focusing on the intersecting of personal concerns and social concerns. Brady speaks to a formal model for the study of the concept of culture as the most powerful tool. Both are discussed later under Here and Now Curriculum.

NEW MEME 5: CURRICULUM THROUGH *BEING THERE*

Curriculum at the middle school level should consist entirely of concepts, skills, and attitudes/values which students can experience through being there and immersion. The rationale for curriculum which allows students to "be there" is undergirded by brain research—what happens to the physiology of the brain when all 19 senses are activated—and by the characteristics of the middle school student who thrives on active learning and interaction with peers and important others. (See Chapter I, page 6, and characteristics of the middle school age student, Appendix A.)

NEW MEME 6: CHOICE BUILDS IN POWER

Sameness and uniformity are killers for students and staff. On the other hand, choice opens doors to alternative ways of learning and expressing what is learned, to greater commitment to a task as personally meaningful, to higher motivation to persist on tasks, and many other pluses.

Most importantly, it allows the learner to sit in the driver's seat—experiencing both freedom to be oneself and the responsibility of becoming one's own person, capable and contributing. Like a muscle, lifelong learning is developed only through use.

NEW MEME 7: CURRICULUM SHOULD BE FRAMED SO AS TO ELIMINATE LECTURE

Traditional curriculum consists primarily of factoid statements—statement of facts, dates, definitions, rules which are divorced from a larger context of meaning. From the students' point of view, they are things to be memorized but provide no grasp on understanding the world around them or in their future. Instead, curriculum should be stated in conceptual terms, bottom lines which assist students in understanding events around them and into the future. Furthermore, instructional strategies must include collaboration and much opportunity to apply and practice using what is being learned

In ITI classrooms, the rule of thumb is to limit teacher presentation, lecture, to not more than 11-16 minutes per hour. This is essential for several reasons. The importance of this meme stems from our earlier discussion about how the human brain learns, especially the program-building processing of the mind. Recall that information that we use is embedded in programs; conversely, information which does not get loaded up into a mental program is typically unretrievable. Programs are built by applying information in real world settings.

NEW MEME 8: ASSESSMENT MUST BE REALITY-BASED

Demonstration of mastery of curriculum should be through application of relevant knowledge, skills, attitudes and values, situations and settings in accordance with standards typical of adult living or the work place. Focus should be placed on real life problem-solving and/or on producing a product which has real life usefulness and standards. Paper and pencil testing should be used sparingly, and only when no other means of assessment are possible. (See Chapter IX for a discussion of assessment and evaluation.)

From our perspective, the current authentic assessment and outcome based assessment movements have bogged down and gone off track (see Chapter IX). Some common sense is needed. Renata and Geoffrey Caine suggest that there are at least four relevant indicators which should guide evaluation:

- the ability to use the language of the discipline or subject in complex situations and in social interaction
- the ability to perform appropriately in unanticipated situations
- the ability to solve real problems using the skills and concepts
- the ability to show, explain, or teach the idea or skill to another person who has a real need to know[36]

The key to authentic, reality-based assessment is that the curriculum it measures must also be reality-based.

93

TOWARD A NEW MEME-BASED CURRICULUM: THE CURRICULUM OF HERE AND NOW

It is one thing to criticize the old; it is quite another to provide a sufficiently clear picture of the new that pioneers can hitch up their wagons, strike out with a destination in mind, and be amply outfitted for the journey. The purpose of the remaining pages of this chapter is to describe the destination of a new meme-based curriculum. The following four chapters, Chapters IV—VII, provide the map and how-tos for arriving at the new destination, a discussion of what to pack in your wagon, and, perhaps most importantly, hints about what to leave behind.

CURRICULUM OF THE HERE AND NOW

Webster's dictionary defines "the here and now" as: "this place and this time; the present." What a recipe for making the school experience relevant for students! And what a recipe for ensuring that students will be successful after they leave school.

To base curriculum in "this place, this time, and in the present" marks a radical departure from disciplines-based curriculum. Conceptually, the contrast is as follows:

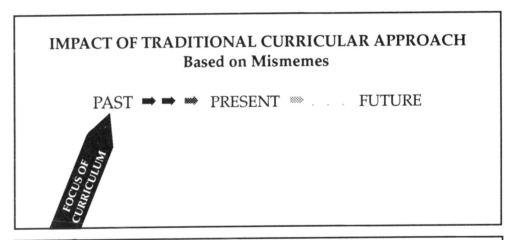

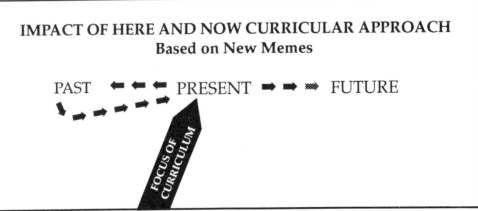

A key feature of here and now curriculum is that it is immediately recognized (by the student) as being relevant* and meaningful, a prerequisite condition for a brain-compatible learning environment. Content which is here and now also activates at least 14 of the 19 senses, thereby enhancing taking in, processing, storing, and retrieving learning (see Chapter II). Furthermore, it purports to teach our young about their world and the skills necessary to act within and upon it, so that students can better anticipate the future, and thus prepare themselves for living the fast-paced changes of the 1990's and beyond.

Here and now curriculum is sourced not in subject areas but in two areas:

1) **a physical location**(s) in the locale of the school community, accessible for study and frequent visiting by students

2) **a human issue**(s) that students are experiencing or can experience

Physical Locations As Source for Curriculum

Obviously, the location or locations vary from school to school. Examples of locations include those designed by Mother Nature, such as mountains, lakes, rivers, meadows, and those which are manmade, such as the school itself, shopping malls, museums, transportation systems, families, churches, city governments, the world of work (the slice represented by the community surrounding the school), and so forth.

All curriculum should be sourced in or given a context in a physical location. Real life is lived somewhere, some place. A real life location is an essential element of a here and now curriculum.

Choose a location which students can visit frequently enough to make it a part of their real world, integration is virtually automatic; subject areas and their lines of demarcation melt away. For example, it is impossible to study only the life science of a location; the story falls woefully short of explaining what the eyes see, the feet feel, the ears hear, and the future will become. There are no dividing lines between life, earth, and physical sciences and technology. For example, a visit to the ocean's tidepools and their marine flora and fauna cannot be understood without knowing about what makes

---

*Please note that such a curriculum is no relative to "consumer math" or "everyday communication skills"—watered down courses for the chronically despondent learner. To the contrary, we are talking about a highly challenging curriculum that would stun most adults. We are talking here about the how and why of the "hard" technologies of mathematics and science behind the mundane, as well as the astonishing, in every day life; we are talking about the application of the "soft" technologies from the fields of psychology, sociology, of human communication, and global interrelationships, etc. We are talking about applications that many teachers have not yet experienced but which will be the daily fare for their students in the early years of the 21st century.

tides and their effect on the food chain which in turn leads into how the tide-pools were formed. Related food chain issues inevitably lead to man, to what machines he uses to harvest the oceans, the source and effect of pollution at this location, who monitors the pollution, which levels of government are responsible for what, what should our class do about the problem, how do we communicate our concerns, and to whom, etc. Learning is much more powerful because students begin with the concrete and then move to the symbolic and abstract.

Although physical locations obviously lend themselves to study of the sciences (life, earth, and physical and technology) and mathematics, human studies—social studies, history, fine arts, and language arts—are all easily integrated. When integrated as in real life, there is no area of "classical" education that will be left out. Also, selection of a physical location as a source for curriculum leads to a greater variety of instructional materials and processes than remaining locked in the classroom.

Human Issues As Source for Curriculum

The intellectual, psychological, physical, and social characteristics of the early adolescent provide valuable tips for the curriculum builder who wishes to focus on human issues. In addition, two authors—Beane and Brady—provide useful models.

Human Issues As Viewed by James Beane—Human issues identified by Beane as particularly appropriate to the middle school student are illustrated below.[37]

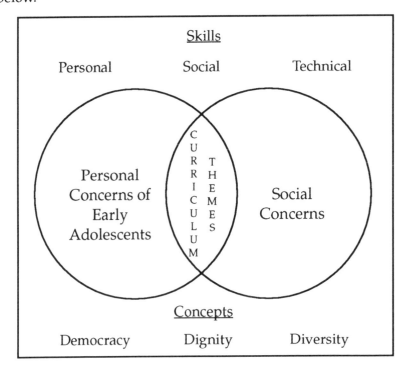

NEW MEMES FOR CURRICULUM

The chart below provides examples of curriculum themes which could be used to integrate these issues. These graphics are taken from his book, *A Middle School Curriculum: From Rhetoric to Reality,* published by the National Middle School Association.[38]

PERSONAL CONCERNS	**CURRICULUM THEMES**	**SOCIAL CONCERNS**
Understanding personal changes	TRANSITIONS	Living in a changing world
Developing a personal identity	IDENTITIES	Cultural diversity
Finding a place in the group	INTERDEPENDENCE	Global interdependence
Personal fitness	WELLNESS	Environmental protection
Social Status	SOCIAL STRUCTURES	Class systems
Dealing with adults	INDEPENDENCE	Human rights
Peer conflict and gangs	CONFLICT RESOLUTION	Global conflict
Commercial pressures	COMMERCIALISM	Effects of media
Questioning authority	JUSTICE	Laws and social customs
Personal friendships	CARING	Social welfare
Living in the school	INSTITUTIONS	Social institutions

THE STUFF OF
CURRICULUM

A yearlong theme based on Beane's suggested themes might look like the mindmap shown below. It would be particularly useful for the first year of middle school attendance (sixth or seventh grades).

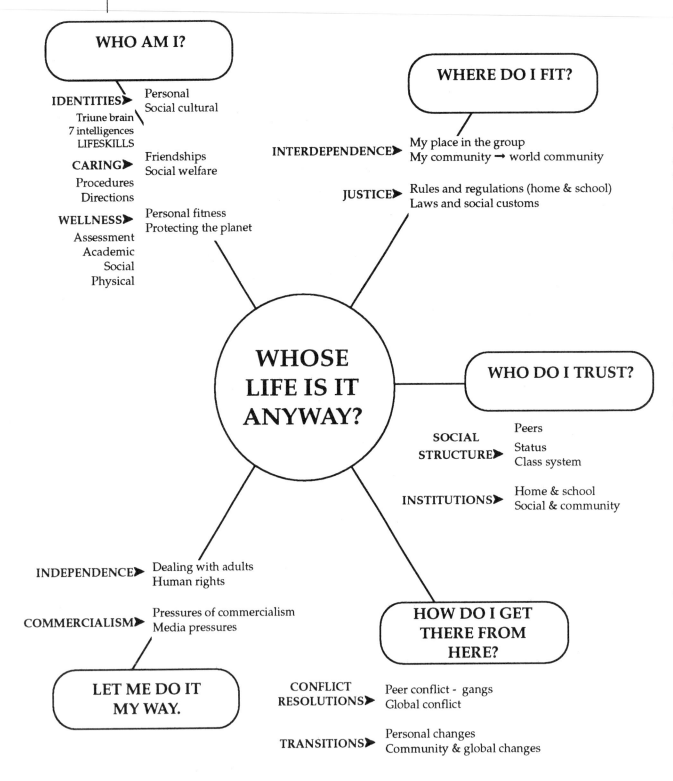

"Whose Life Is It Anyway?" was developed using the student-based themes recommended by James Beane.

Human Issues As Viewed by Marion Brady—His work, *What's Worth Teaching? Selecting, Organizing, and Integrating Knowledge,* makes escape from the old shackles of "disciplines" quite easy because he gives us a lens through which we can perceive and analyze the real world before us. In effect, he asks the questions for us; our answers to those questions, based upon the locale(s) or social issue(s) we select, lead us naturally into developing here and now curriculum.

Brady argues for reality as the basis for curriculum design with a simple, yet powerful logic: "The necessity for understanding self cannot be realized independently of a comprehensive study of the sociocultural systems which structure the self's actions and thoughts"[39] and because "sociocultural systems are the entities that structure our daily lives."[40] Furthermore, he says, "Most personal needs are met, most problems solved, most public goals are attained by organized, collective action."[41]

Because growing up in different societies causes us to see reality differently (or even not at all) and because ours is such a pluralistic society, Brady argues that the appropriate focus of study is societies—the reality-makers. His rationale is:

- If we want to study reality, we must study those things which "design" reality. We must study societies

- If we accept the ancient injunction, "know thyself," as an important goal of general education, we have no alternative but to study the entities most responsible for making us who we are: societies.

- To understand our own society, we need to study societies with contrasting assumptions, premises, and values; this is the simplest, most direct way for us to become aware of our own.

- Humans value freedom, alternatives, choices. Since we can't choose options we've never thought of, the study of other societies expands our freedom by providing us with alternative ideas and ways of acting.

- Our academic disciplines are culture bound. Looking at the phenomena with which each of them deals from the perspective of other societies can expand understanding and strengthen our disciplines.

- Societies are the largest internally consistent units of human organization. They also exercise the greatest control over human affairs

- New knowledge is generated by logically relating ideas. Because the concept "society" can encompass and logically relate every idea appropriate for general education, it is the most powerful of all concepts.[42]

Brady's framework is extremely valuable for several reasons. It allows one to leave the old pictures of subject-based "disciplines" behind it; provides a seamless yet comprehensive way of viewing human issues as they present themselves; and it provides a way of analyzing real life, not just to identify issues or topics of study, but also for building a complete curriculum, i.e. identifying key points and developing inquiries (see Chapters V and VI).

Consistent with Hart's notion of the brain as pattern-seeker, Brady focuses upon patterns and the relationship among patterns—always keeping his eye on the real world. These then become the building blocks of curriculum.

According to Brady, when studying human societies, there are five kinds of information which are useful:[43]

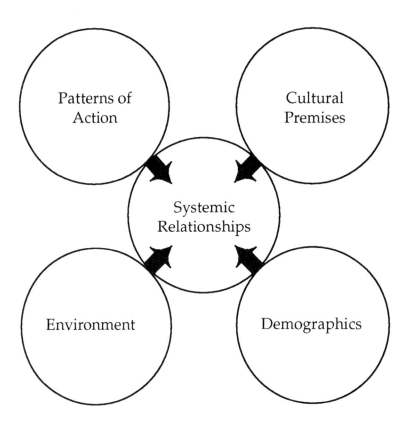

- Descriptions of the actual physical behavior of the members of the system, **the patterns of action**[44] and **interaction** which structure daily activity

- Identification and clarification of the major beliefs, assumptions, **premises**,[45] and values held by the members of the system and underlying most action and interaction, particularly those shared ideas so taken for granted that they tend to be unstated and unexamined

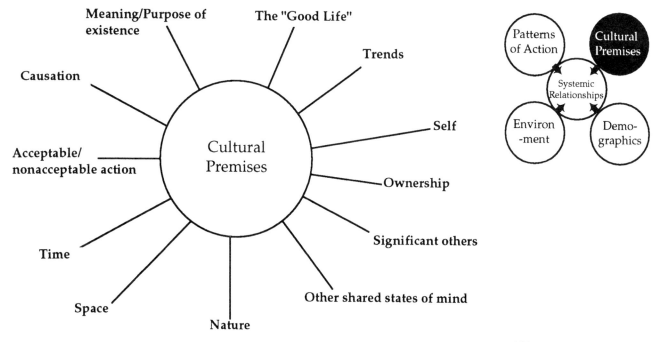

- Information about the **physical environment**[46] within which the system functions

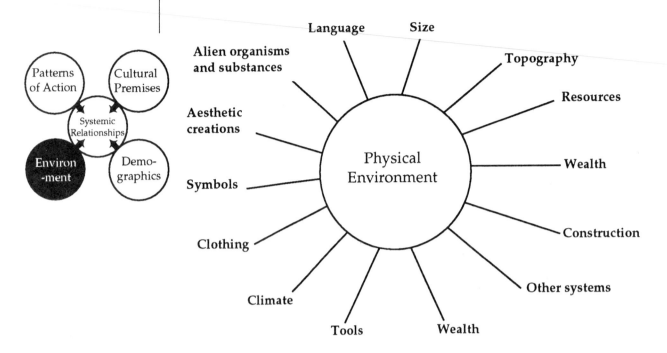

- **Demographic**[47] data, primarily statistical, abut the system's members—their number, age, and so forth

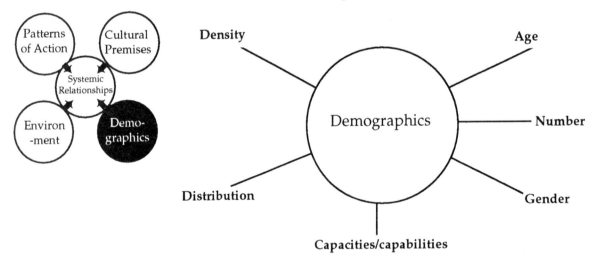

- Description and analysis of the **relationships**[48] between these four—the system's patterned action, cognitive structure, demographics,and environments—with particular emphasis on the processes by means of which changes in various system components affect other components and the functioning of the total system

Viewing Brady's model as a drama[49] is a useful metaphor because it suggests a kind of verve and interest-grabbing capacity which good curriculum, like good theater, needs. Further, dramas are, in a sense, "compressed" models of human behavior. Just as a playwright skips from scene to scene, leaving out hours or even decades and facts not essential to the story, so good curriculum should stick with powerful concepts and avoid non-essential, powerless facts, what we call "factoids."

"A collection of individuals . . .	(actors)	DEMOGRAPHICS
. . .occupying the same general area . . .	(stage)	ENVIRONMENT
. . .acting in similar ways. . .	(action)	PATTERNS OF ACTION
. . .sharing important states of mind	(plot)	PERCEPTIONS OF REALITY
The interaction of actors, stage, movement and plot is. . .	(the play)	SYSTEMIC RELATIONSHIPS
set in time	(setting)	

THE GAP

Admittedly, what this chapter proposes must appear heretical, shockingly radical, and, for many, simply not within the realm of the politically possible. To the extent that you say Yes, may we share several homilies that have attached themselves to one of the authors, gifts from her mentors:

- If school reform were easy, it would have been done long ago

- We have tried everything else—changing structures, instructional strategies, etc.—but those elements haven't produced significant change. It is the hard stuff that is left to do . . . the curriculum and its content.

- Doing the easy stuff rarely solves the hard problems; therefore, gather up your courage and go for the gold!

- If you understand, you are responsible

This last homily has always been the hardest one to live with. It prompts the following discussion about how to bridge the kamikazi gap between what is and what can be. Once you have a vision of how we can be, we can no longer be content with the way we were. Each of us who understands must become a leader in the quest to transform our curriculum. Our students are waiting!

THE PROBLEMS

There are two problems to fix. First, there is already too much stuff to be learned in our curricula; racing through the year to "cover the material" results in little long term learning. And yet the curriculum needed to address the unique characteristics of adolescents is still missing. Second, our traditional curriculum is held to be sacrosanct; it is virtually "unthinkable" to most parents and members of the wider community, not to mention fellow staff (teachers and administrators), to "not do" what our state and district curriculum frameworks have identified as the proper curriculum for grades 6—9.

THE FIX

Problem 1

To solve the first problem, we must put our rhetoric into action. Either there are unique characteristics of adolescents (see Appendix A) and those uniquenesses should be addressed, or not. If so, yes, we must begin to identify what content would best assist an adolescent to understand themselves, their future roles (assumed and potential), and how to move from dependence to interdependence. Hints at that curriculum are illustrated in "Inside the Mind of a Teacher" in Chapter IV.

Problem 2

The second problem, dealing with the old stuff, is clearly more stubborn. The best fix is to gain the political permission to rewrite current state and district curriculum frameworks. For example, in our opinion, the study of ancient history in the sixth grade is wrong-headed. It flies in the face of what we know is age-appropriate at a conceptual, understandability level given the physiological development of the brain (see Chapter 1); it is the most difficult frame in which to try to address the unique characteristics of adolescents, particularly in the sense of trying to assist them in understanding what is going on with them now and to anticipate and prepare for the future; and, it is about as far away from a source for here and now curriculum as one can get.

If you cannot get political permission to rewrite your school's curriculum framework/scope and sequence, stay within the general parameters of the topics of your traditional, discipline-based curriculum but reinvent it.

Reinventing means that you must tease out the answers to two fundamental questions:

- What is worth knowing here?
  The answer must explain how the knowledge, skill, attitudes/values will help students understand their circumstances today and provide a useful framework for the future?

- Why do I think so?
  The answers to this question must tie to the unique characteristics of adolescents.

The best frameworks for analyzing a traditional, discipline-based curriculum in order to determine what's worth knowing are, of course, those by Beane and Brady (see Chapter III).

Limit yourself to a single piece of 8 1/2" x 11" piece of paper per traditional subject for the entire school, e.g. grades 6-8, or 7-9. This will require that all teachers of social studies at all grade levels sit together to create a single one-page statement of what's worth knowing from their subject area. Hint: do not lower the size of the font! Force yourself to limit the statement to one page or less. Keep notes on your discussions of "Why do we think so?" to share with your students, colleagues (teacher and administrator), parents, and community, including school board. As Michael Kirst has pointed out, "Although such a change does not require large sums of money, it calls for other valuable assets—will and imagination."[50] And plenty of courage and political savvy.

CURRICULUM DEVELOPMENT —
CREATING A YEARLONG THEME

Creating a yearlong theme first requires that you have reconceptualized your curriculum *(see Chapter III)* and have chosen a framework for day-to-day working *(see Chapter VII for a discussion of how teachers may team together and about which implementation model may best fit your situation given the students and staff with whom you will be working)*. Only when these decisions have been made can you create a yearlong theme as a context for integrating content and curriculum building.

The stages in developing integrated curriculum are:

Stage 1 **Creating a yearlong theme with monthly components and weekly topics**

Stage 2 **Identifying key points which all students are to learn**

Stage 3 **Developing inquiries and activities which allow students to understand and apply the concepts/skills of the key points**

This chapter describes the how-to steps to complete Stage 1 — Creating a Yearlong Theme. Stages 2 and 3, Identifying Key Points and Developing Inquiries, are described in Chapters V and VI.

Included in this chapter is a discussion of the steps in Stage 1:

Step A: Rethink WHAT students are to learn; finalize your decisions as a school staff (see Chapter III)

Step B: Select the physical locations which will provide *being there* experiences for students and the human issues which best exemplify, or most powerfully convey, what you want students to learn

Step C: Identify your organizing concept and rationale

Step D: Select monthly components and weekly topics

Step E: Dream a theme title that fires up the students (and teacher) with enthusiasm and imagination and provides a cognitive hook for the organizing concept and entire year's content and skills

---

The yearlong theme is a cognitive structure which facilitates pattern identification and recognition of interrelationships among ideas, theories, events, objects. It serves several important functions:

- for students, it is a powerful tool enhancing their capacity to more effectively process, store, and retrieve what is learned and to be able to anticipate what comes next and generalize to other situations

- for the teacher, it serves as an organizer for curriculum building and material gathering throughout the year, providing a thread that connects one month to the next as well as relating to the central organizer for the entire year

- for both teacher and students, it establishes the game plan for the year

A yearlong theme consists of three organizing structures: the yearlong theme, monthly components, and weekly topics.

**YEARLONG
THEME**

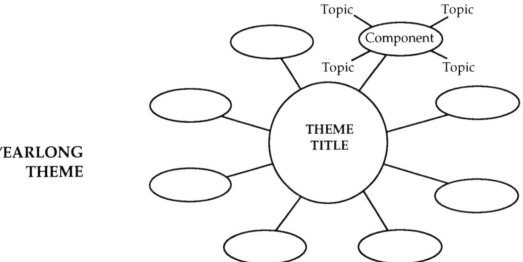

Please note that although we shall be referring to a "yearlong" theme throughout the book, we are aware that such long-term planning may not be possible in the early stages of implementation, especially when only a few teachers are using the ITI model and there are no schoolwide agreements to change the existing structure. In such cases, substitute the term "semester-long" for "yearlong." Also note that the descriptions of components and topics as "monthly" and "weekly" are only an approximate time designation. *Here and now* curriculum has a way of taking on a life of its own and will often dictate its own timeline. Thus, some "monthly" components will last three weeks, others six. Likewise with "weekly" topics.

Creating a yearlong theme is not a linear, sequential thinking task nor is it a process of arranging a set number of given pieces. You will find yourself working on several steps simultaneously, circling back, changing direction, etc. There are, however, three prerequisites: 1) you must have scouted your school's environment for powerful teaching locations and identified the best alternatives, 2) you must have reached most general agreements with yourself and fellow teachers regarding what your students are to learn (see Chapter III), and 3) you must know who you will be working with in terms of both colleagues and students (see Chapter VII). With this in mind, you are ready to begin creating your yearlong theme.

Construction Terminology
for Building an ITI Theme

THEME: A yearlong organizational structure consisting of theme title, monthly components, and weekly topics.

COMPONENTS: The physical locations and human issues experienceable by students

TOPICS: Aspects of the location or human issues to be studied

THEME TITLE: A kid-grabbing vehicle that will lead teacher and students to study of *here and now* curriculum

KEY POINTS: Essential concepts, skills, knowledge, attitudes/ values all students are to learn about the weekly topics (and components and theme title)

INQUIRIES: Applications of the knowledge, skills, values/ attitudes of the key point(s) being taught/learned.

STEP A: RETHINK WHAT STUDENTS ARE TO LEARN

The content and structure of the curriculum is critical in creating a brain-compatible learning environment. You must be clear about what you want student to learn. "Less is more," conceptual vs. factoid, *here and now* are essential guidelines (see Chapter III).

When decisions are finalized and you have your one-page summary in hand, you are ready for Step B.

STEP B: SELECT PHYSICAL LOCATIONS AND HUMAN ISSUES

The most *here and now* physical location, and the one most accessible, is the classroom and school. Whether your primary focus involves human issues or a mathematics or science slant, the school campus and its immediate environs (10-20 minute walk, bike, or bus ride) will usually provide the real world application needed to kick-off your study. Once you have provided a *being there* experience and students have internalized and applied the concrete experience (including building a mental program for using the information), **you can then move to symbolic and abstract levels or backward or forward in time.**

All events occur in time and space, including human issues. Context is half of the story and a powerful shaper of thoughts and actions. Select those human issues which are both central to what you want students to know and which can be powerfully framed by your available physical locations. Remember, there is no one "right way" to orchestrate curriculum; choose that which seems most effective and powerful for your students and you today, given what is happening within your classroom, the school, the community, and the world. Human events and issues, and their teachable moments, resemble a bat on the wing; they flit with speed and ever shifting direction throughout our lives, from day to day.

STEP C: IDENTIFY YOUR ORGANIZING CONCEPT AND RATIONALE

This step in theme building is the most conceptual and abstract but also the most important, especially given the nature of the brain as a pattern-seeking device (see Chapter 1) and the unique characteristics of adolescents. This is also the step that builds power into your curriculum and ensures that it "hangs together" and is worthy of the time and effort that both you and your students will invest in it.

The organizing concept of the theme is the universally recognized big idea that is worthy of middle school students' attention, something that you believe is critical to understanding and participating in life in the United States of America, a critical understanding for adulthood, a notion that is big enough and conceptually powerful enough that it can hold and organize a welter of ideas and thoughts, not to mention a barrel of facts.

The rationale is your explanation why the organizing concept is of such importance to your students. For example, in the theme, "We, the People," the organizing concept is "Structure of Relationships"—from friend, family, and classmates to federal government. The rationale is that democracy can not be sustained if its people do not understand, support, and exercise the philosophy, values, and practices of democracy on a daily basis. (See "Inside the Mind of a Teacher" later in this chapter.)

Do remember that the steps in creating a theme are not linear and sequential. This step is one that you will come back to repeatedly, a touchstone to assess your work. It is a question at the heart of of the question "What's worth knowing? What is most important for me to teach my students?"

STEP D: SELECTING MONTHLY COMPONENTS AND WEEKLY TOPICS

Selection of monthly components and their weekly topics is driven by the physical locations and the human issues you select as a result to Steps A and B. Given the richness of real life settings and the keen interest of adolescents in the issues unique to this stage of their life. it is obvious that possibilities are unlimited. Thus, while brainstorming will uncover the possibilities, a clear statement of your organizing concept and rationale will provide the criteria for selecting among the ideas generated.

THINKING IT THROUGH:
TIPS ON DEVELOPING COMPONENTS AND TOPICS

To guide your brainstorming of components and topics, use the Alfie test: What's it all about? Why did I select this location and this human issue? What is urgent for my students to understand about this location/issue? What does this location/issue illustrate about other locations/issues they will face? You are looking for patterns or hooks that students can carry with them for the rest of their lives.

Look at the location/issue afresh. Remember, leave the old subject area boundaries behind. What is important to know about this now, in the year 1992, 1995, 2001?

For patterns amid human issues, see both Beane's themes and Brady's conceptual framework in Chapter III. For additional mind joggers, consider possible pattern shapers such as: systems, habitats, evolution, form and function, varied uses for an item, comparisons, current or future occupations, a happening or major event, from—to (size, distance such as backyard to universe), structures, etc. There are many ways to view the real world, selecting from it and ordering those selections.

SO, WHAT'S NEW?

For those of you who have been teaching for awhile, this discussion of components and topics may sound familiar. The pre-brain research discussions of thematic curriculum mentioned "units" and "interdisciplinary" study. So, what's the difference here? How do yearlong themes differ?

The two major differences are:

- the theme is yearlong and there is a clear connection between the theme and each of the components and from component to component. Knowing that the brain is a pattern-seeking device, there must be a single web spinning out through the year that makes patterns as real as those of the real world and as memorable

- the environment—all aspects of curriculum and instruction—is brain-compatible

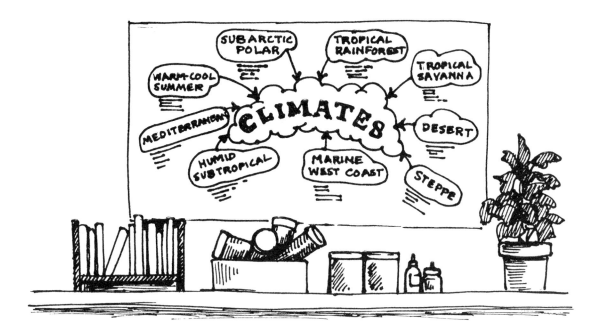

STEP E: DREAM A THEME TITLE

The theme title is an organizational tool, one which drives the entire year, hooks into students' imagination and their prior experience. Be sure you settle on something that fires your enthusiasm as well as that of the students'. You cannot model being an active learner if the theme doesn't speak to you, if it does not elicit your genuine enthusiasm.

While your expectations for learning are high, you are not selecting a theme to guide college-level content. Your theme and the content it weaves together must be appropriate to the developmental level of your students. While students are far more capable than we give them credit for, brain research makes it clear that the brain's organization of itself is not complete until after high school and its stage of organization and development determines the complexity of what it can process (compare, organize, relate, infer, and apply) as distinguished from memorize-and-parrot-back.*

The point here is that the theme must speak to the students at the beginning of the year, not years later when they finally can "get it" or even at the end of the year after you've spent the year teaching about it. It should speak to the student the first day of school. Understanding should not depend on prior experience—many of our students are not so lucky to have rich backgrounds. The themes must already be a part of their experience and understanding and be at the center of a surge of curiosity and interest.

A kid-grabbing theme title is a notion which students—through ample experience or intuition—**already understand and are motivated** by. It is a kid-grabbing twist representing the organizing concept or big idea that you want students to walk away with. It provides the Christmas tree on which the ornaments—concepts and skills—can be hung. Such a cognitive structure greatly facilitates the *pattern-seeking* and *program-building* functions of the brain (see Chapter I).

Examples of theme titles:

- Quest for Power
- We, the People
- You Can't Fool Mother Nature
- It's All in Your Head!
- What Makes It Tick

---

*A valuable resource for gaining an understanding of developmental levels and age-appropriateness is Larry Lowery's book, *Thinking and Learning: Matching Developmental Stages with Curriculum and Instruction.*

CRITERIA FOR EVALUATING YOUR THEME

If your experience in putting together your first theme is at all typical, you will not be satisfied nor feel that things "click" for you until draft number eight or twelve. Curriculum is both highly personal and very intellectually challenging. You will know you are on the right track when your theme and monthly components (as expanded by the weekly topics) meet the following criteria:

- you're excited about it! and so are your students
- it has substance and application to the real world
- the conceptual idea underlying the theme and related content is meaningful (from the students' point of view)
- the rationale behind the theme is truly compelling for you and for students
- the content is age-appropriate
- it is worthy of time to create and implement
- there are readily available materials plus physical locations that can be visited frequently

INSIDE THE MIND OF A TEACHER

The following pages, 116 through 122, are a stream of consciousness visit inside a teacher's head as he/she thinks through developing a yearlong theme, its monthly components, and weekly topics. This internal dialogue will familiarize you with various tools and thought processes for developing curriculum. It's a paddle trip you might enjoy. More than anything else, it conveys the no-boundaries approach to curriculum development for ITI. Go with the real world! And above all, unfurl your wings. This is your chance to truly fly! Bon voyage!

SAMPLE THEME: *WE, THE PEOPLE*

Given the diversity of our nation and my school and what I perceived to be a crisis in democracy in this country, I want to focus on how to structure relationship between people: one-to-one, friends, family, classroom, school, neighborhood, city, county, state, nation. What makes democracy work, one's own life work?

Because we have been successful in getting agreement to move toward a *here and now* curriculum, my three colleagues, the regular staff for our house of 100-110 students (called a college at our campus), are preparing to fly high! We believe the most longterm, powerful real life concept we can give our students is how relationships are structured—from the informal (unwritten agreements among friends and family) to the formal (written legal contracts and government), from two people interactions to structures for a nation of 250 million.

Step A: Rethink What Students Are to Learn

We are agreed that we must and will ensure that the basic survival skills of reading, writing, oral presentation, listening, and mathematics will be mastered at necessary levels of citizenship and success (financial and personal). Two locations which will provide a sense of those standards are a construction site, a high tech manufacturing company, or the district's accounting office.

We will teach to those levels of mastery demonstrated at middle entry jobs in our community. It is also agreed that high levels of science "literacy" are a citizenship must; we will study science as it really exists within our community (the locations and specific issues of our community). Locations which will provide a context for such study are the local landfill or a manufacturing plant.

Step B: Select Physical Locations and Human Issues

Our possibilities for physical locations are excellent as are human issues given the diversity of our community and school. For the first component, it will be inside one's own brain, moving out in subsequent components to classroom, school, and city. City locations will include ethnic social clubs, the courthouse, police department (we have obtained permission for students to spend a shift in a patrol car), shelter for battered wives and children, national guard armory, etc.

Step C: Identify Your Organizing Concept and Rationale

I've been thinking about this a great deal. I want students to understand that most of our wants and needs are met through group situations. I want them to be adept at structuring those group situations which will assist them to get their needs and wishes met best. The research is clear: "Children with high levels of social competence are more likely to be able to elicit positive responses from others and find alternative ways of looking at problems and their position in them; thus, they are more likely to be successful in satisfying personal and social needs. To the contrary, individuals already experiencing problems with crime, delinquency, alcohol and other drug abuse , and mental illness consistently lack the qualities of responsiveness, flexibility, empathy and caring, communication skills, sense of humor, and other prosocial behavior.[1] Thus, my organizing concept will be "Structure for Interaction."We the people of the United States, in order to . . .

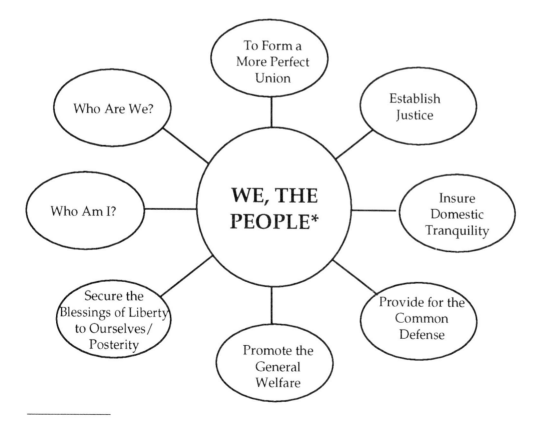

*Use of the first sentence of the U.S. Constitution for a theme organizer is credited to
  Debra Bellon, Lower Lake High School, California

Step D: Selecting Monthly Components and Weekly Topics

I want to start with the students themselves—Who am I? They must first understand themselves, their needs and wants before they can begin to structure relationships that work and thus begin to understand the complexities at governmental levels.

So . . . I will start with what they should know about themselves from the brain research base I am using. My first component, therefore, will be Who Am I? Physical location: one's own brain and body.

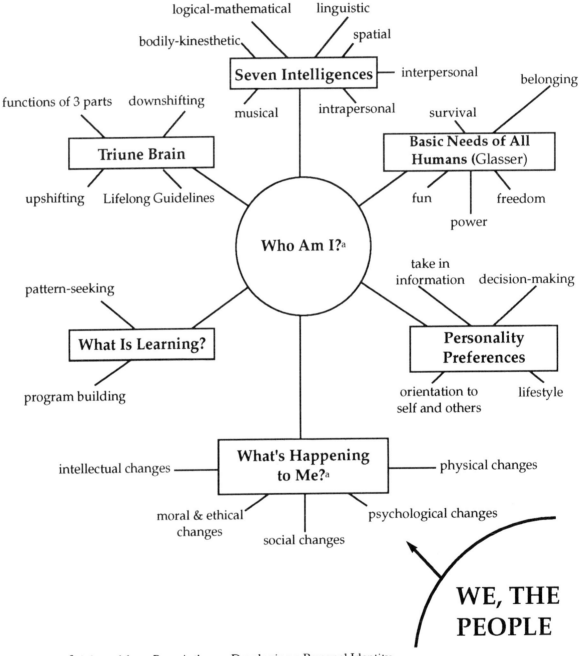

a Adapted from Beane's theme: Developing a Personal Identity

Starting with **"Who Am I?"** will allow me a chance to start with where the students are and provide a cognitive base for understanding "the family of man" in preparation for the next component, "Who Are We?" It is also a perfect vehicle for sharing with students how learning takes place and explains the "cultural premises" of this classroom as a society of learners and the basis for "patterns of action" which are different than the traditional classroom with which they are accustomed to. It also will put them in the driver's seat for becoming a lifelong learner.

Hmm, I'll start with first things first—downshifting. As part of downshifting I'll introduce the effects of group membership (or lack of) on downshifting and immediately begin the TRIBES process for social development and cooperative learning. Then differences in problem-solving (seven intelligences), then basic needs, then personality. These last three will be a good basis for looking at diversity and pluralism later on.

How long this component will last and how deeply we go will depend on my students. However, I know that a good basis cannot be laid in less than five weeks, perhaps as many as seven. The time will be well spent, however. Although I sometimes begin to panic about "not getting to the real stuff," I know from experience that haste makes waste. So much more can be done throughout the year if time is taken to really create a close knit group with good working relationships.

"Who Are We?" has two major goals: transitioning from the personal to the outer world and introducing Brady's conceptual framework in a setting that students both know about and can readily observe—the classroom and school.

The notion of "society" or community is complex, especially when viewed at a national level. So . . . let's see. Looking at the "glue" that holds or structures small, familiar groups or societies together will provide the conceptual basis to move to governmental level issues.

The search for cultural premises and patterns of action in our school and especially in the city will give students a view of the issues they themselves must identify and answer as they formulate who they are.

Because government is, on a simplistic level, a set of agreements of the governed to be governed and the government to govern, the nature of agreement building and maintaining is an essential idea. This is true at the family level, with peers, and in the classroom. This is a key concept given the emergence of adolescents from dependence to independence (and finally to interdependence).

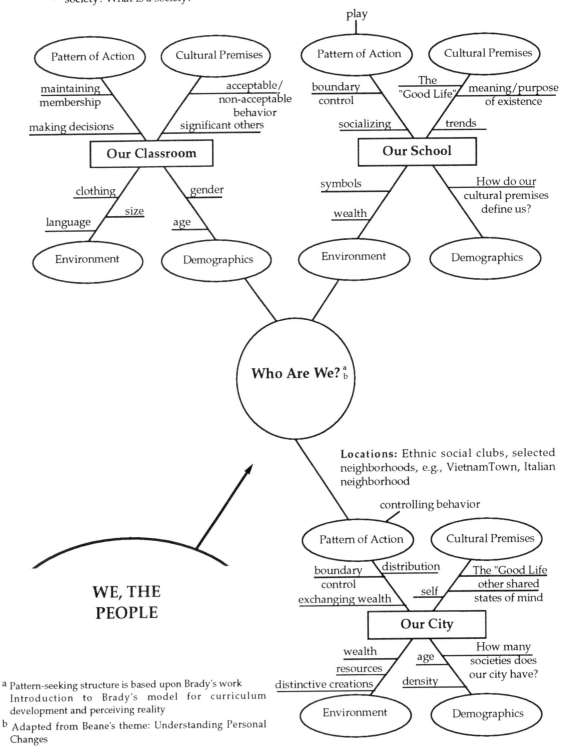

Location: Classroom
Human issue: What makes us a group or society? What is the structure of our classroom society? What is a society?

Location: School
Human issue: What are the agreements which structure our school society?

play

Pattern of Action   Cultural Premises

maintaining membership   acceptable/ non-acceptable behavior
making decisions   significant others

Our Classroom

clothing   gender
language   size   age

Environment   Demographics

Pattern of Action   Cultural Premises

boundary control   The "Good Life"   meaning/purpose of existence
socializing   trends

Our School

symbols   How do our cultural premises define us?
wealth

Environment   Demographics

Who Are We? [a] [b]

Locations: Ethnic social clubs, selected neighborhoods, e.g., VietnamTown, Italian neighborhood

controlling behavior

Pattern of Action   Cultural Premises

boundary   distribution   The "Good Life"
control   other shared
exchanging wealth   self   states of mind

Our City

wealth   age   How many
resources   societies does
distinctive creations   density   our city have?

Environment   Demographics

WE, THE PEOPLE

[a] Pattern-seeking structure is based upon Brady's work Introduction to Brady's model for curriculum development and perceiving reality

[b] Adapted from Beane's theme: Understanding Personal Changes

"To Form a More Perfect Union" takes the building blocks of understanding me (and thus others) and us (and what structures our interactions) and applies it to formulating formal agreements and government structures. To make sure that I'm not jumping too fast, "What's the Glue?" will allow students to work individually, in pairs, or in triads to examine the issue of agreements within interactions which they experience on a daily basis. Working alone in a very small group will stretch and test each individual's understanding of and ability to apply Brady's framework.

Once this groundwork is in place, students will be prepared to examine, for example, today's definitions of the "Good Life" as it affects our visions of democracy and then compare that to the notions held by Americans of the mid 1770's. I expect "study of history" to really bloom at this point.

The Articles of Confederation are interesting for two main reasons: they represent a first attempt at putting the idea of democracy to work, i.e., structuring agreements; and, it was a failure—there was much that it did not address adequately or at all. Knowing that our constitution was based on the lessons of that failure (and successes), what additional insights into our constitution come to light?

Hmmm...as I look at this component, my second panic button gets pushed: that I likely have too much curriculum (I always seem to over plan!). I will reduce and refine it when I have a better sense of my students' prior experiences, learning to learn skills, and basic language skills.

This component will end with two projects: 1) having the class adapt our federal constitution to the needs and visions of Americans in 1992, and 2) having the class adapt the constitution to our school district and school.

Curriculum bulding for **"To Establish Justice"** and future components will be framed in detail after I have a better sense of the skills and experience of my students and after they have experience with the ITI curriculum planning tools. I want them to begin to learn how to direct their own learning.

Location: Chosen by students

Human issue: Application of Brady's framework to our experience

Location: America of 1993 (our community)

Human issue: Applying what we know about issues of *here and now* to historical time periods

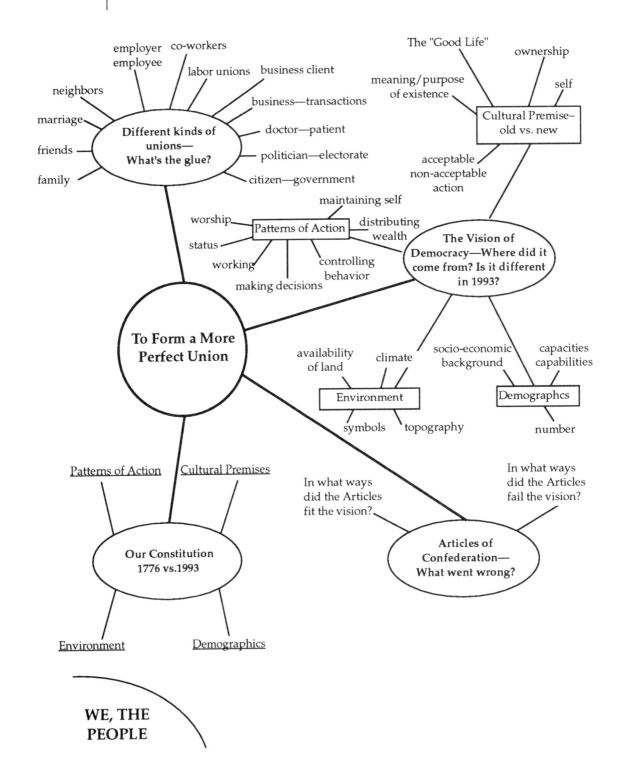

employer   co-workers
employee
labor unions   business client
neighbors
business—transactions
marriage
Different kinds of unions— What's the glue?
doctor—patient
friends
politician—electorate
family
citizen—government

The "Good Life"
ownership
meaning/purpose of existence
self
Cultural Premise— old vs. new
acceptable non-acceptable action

maintaining self
worship
distributing wealth
Patterns of Action
status
The Vision of Democracy—Where did it come from? Is it different in 1993?
working
controlling behavior
making decisions

To Form a More Perfect Union

availability of land   climate
socio-economic background
capacities capabilities
Environment
Demographcs
symbols   topography
number

Patterns of Action   Cultural Premises

In what ways did the Articles fit the vision?

In what ways did the Articles fail the vision?

Our Constitution 1776 vs.1993

Articles of Confederation— What went wrong?

Environment   Demographics

WE, THE PEOPLE

CURRICULUM DEVELOPMENT —
IDENTIFYING KEY POINTS

Once the yearlong theme, monthly components, and weekly topics are established, the next step is to refine your decisions about what's most essential for students to know and be able to do *given your selection of physical locations and their human issues*. What is the *essential core of knowledge and skills* all students are to master each week, month, and year? Not as defined by textbook publishers but rather as framed by your selection of physical locations and human issues? The elements of this essential core are your "key points"—clear, concise statements of the content and skills every student needs to learn *and be able to apply*.

As discussed in Chapter III, the answer to this question is not a completely solo decision. Use of the ITI model is not a return to the 1960's and do your own thing. A significant portion of the answer must be framed and agreed to by groups of teachers so that—from the students' point of view—there are no unintentional gaps or repetition of topics as they move through the school. From prior experience on curriculum committees, we know that this task is not as easy as it seems. Conceptually it seems quit simple. Just answer the questions: "What's worth knowing?" "What must the citizen of the 21st century know and be able to do in order to survive in a high tech society and to participate in/contribute to a democratic way of life?" In practice, however, the task is a difficult one because of the power of our traditions regarding subject area disciplines and our old pictures of the way "it's supposta' be."

Identifying key points is the second step in developing curriculum for Integrated Thematic Instruction. To assist you in doing so, this chapter provides a discussion of the following:

- **developing key points**
- **characteristics of good key points**
- **examples of key points**
- **using key points**
- **importance of using real world and multiple resources**

So what are the stumbling blocks to overcome? The answer, and this comes straight from the mouth of the fiddler on the roof, "Tradition!" Tradition established long ago and reinforced yearly by textbooks.

"Traditions" to overcome include:

- "covering" vs. learning to the level of application

- factoid or surface-level information which stops short of having relevance to the learner's world and which constitutes little more than an introduction to vocabulary and terms

- important sounding but age-inappropriate content

- "telling" about a concept rather than creating the *being there* and *immersion* environments in which students discover and apply what is to be learned

- many personal traditions contained in our own lesson plans of the past and those file drawers of resource materials accumulated over the years

DEVELOPING KEY POINTS

We must take seriously our obligation to students, our duty to give them the best possible preparation for life. Preparation for life is a very different goal than preparation for the traditional high school.

To prepare students for succeeding in the 1990's—The Age of Information—requires considerable soul searching. The questions cannot be answered from one's current bank of information. To do so is to look backward to the past, not forward to the future, thus perpetuating the old traditions. Instead, one must stretch to pull out conceptual understandings that will survive over time. Factoid information, on the other hand, gets rewritten at an astonishing rate. Another failing of factoid key points is that they are powerless to assist a learner in dealing with the real complexity and interrelatedness of the world and its ever-evolving situations.

Key point defined: a key point is a clear, concise statement of a concept, skill, or essential knowledge that will unlock meaning needed to understand and thrive in today's world. For too long we have accepted the assumption that a classical education (study of the artifacts of the past), considered "good" for college preparation and fitting our pictures of deferred gratification, helps us understand and live in the present. It does not.

Recommended thinking steps for developing key points are:

- brainstorm what you believe are the essential concepts for students to know regarding the physical locations and human issues you have selected

- visit your physical locations and
  —interview people to determine what are the most critical concepts and skills needed to function there from their perspective

—apply Brady's conceptual frame to tease out what unlocks meaning in this slice of life—concepts are generalizable to other situations and tools to unlock meaning in other, even dissimilar, environments
—put yourself in your students' shoes, see the location afresh

- hit your library and begin serious research to gain another perspective on what is essential from expert points of view

- begin to identify what *being there* and *immersion* experiences and resources you will be able to provide

- recycle back through steps 1 – 4 (not necessarily in orderly sequence)

BRAINSTORMING

Brainstorming, based on what we currently know, is useful in two ways. First, it helps us to uncover what we know and know how to apply (and don't know) about an area; this gives us an inkling of how much onsite and library research we must do to prepare ourselves to *here and now* curriculum.

Second, brainstorming helps us test the depth of understanding we hold. A long list of factoid information with few conceptual statements alerts us to the need to explore the "whys" behind the areas of study and to search for real world applications for students. Before we can expect to teach students, we must ourselves have answered the question "Why is this information or skill important? How can I use this information in my life today and in the foreseeable future?"

If at all possible, get together with an ITI buddy—one at your grade level if possible but, if not, someone who understands your search for more conceptual rather than fact-oriented key points. Use him/her as a sounding board. "What is essential?" is the most important question you can ask yourself; the quality of its answer will determine the power of your key points.

Note: If you are still tied to a traditional district scope and sequence and your school and district have not yet addressed the fundamental issues of our centuries-old, disciplines-based subject area curriculum, be a realist. If your district's scope and sequence is old and few teachers actually use it, or if it is merely an outline of previous or current textbooks, it might be best to ignore it. If, however, it has been recently done, is age-appropriate, and there are high expectations that it be implemented, look through it carefully and be selective. **A fatal flaw in virtually every scope and sequence is that it contains too much stuff!** Remembering that less is more, distill out those essential understandings and skills that best tie in with your physical locations and human issues—limit your summary to one page, maximum.

VISIT YOUR PHYSICAL LOCATIONS

Interview from a Workplace Perspective

For your interviews, make sure you interview a cross section of people. Your key questions is: "What skills, knowledge, and attitudes/values allow you to be successful at this job? What are the top five in priority order?" Also ask what the prerequisites were for getting the job. What skills, knowledge, and attitudes/values would allow them to do better at their job or to acquire a job that would give them more satisfaction.

Apply Brady's Conceptual Framework

After your interviews and your own on-site inspection of and introspection about the location, sit down with Brady's framework. What concepts (those about patterns of action, cultural premises, environment, and demographics) would enable students to extract the greatest meaning and understanding from their study of this slice of life.

Also allow room for students to build the curriculum with you after they have visited the site.

Put Yourself in Your Students' Shoes

When visiting your physical location, to determine what is most significant to know, step out of your shoes as a teacher and look at the location afresh. In addition to interviewing people on site, picture it from your students' perspectives. What is their prior knowledge, what kind of patterns would they perceive, how would they go about "figuring it out"? If they asked themselves the questions, "Why am I here? Why is this important to me?", what would their answers be? If your curriculum planning can build upon the brain's natural exploration of why, it will allow students to use their brain as it works naturally and thus most powerfully.

The following why questions will assist you to analyze the location from the students' perspective. The answer to these questions will build in meaningfulness and elicit curiosity.

"What are you doing?" A great majority of the skills and knowledge important to the functioning of our lives have been learned in the process of living life and through "on-the job" training, not in a classroom. We learned by watching someone do the task. Because mimicking others is such an extremely powerful learning tool, we recommend that your initial stages of instruction and inquiries provide students with a view of the world from the level of application—watching someone applying what they know in real-life settings, solving real-life problems. For example, isolating and fixing a leaky pipe, flying a plane, planting a garden, building a house.

126

In fact, Frank Smith, in *Insult to Intelligence,* makes a fascinating observation: information at the knowledge and comprehension levels is harder to learn than information at the higher levels because "meaningfulness" is apparent only when knowledge is put to work in real-life contexts.

"Why are you doing this? Is your 'why' important to me, too?" This is the stage of searching for meaning, i.e., is this meaningful/useful to me? (This is always determined from the learner's perspective, not the teacher's.) Typical questions asked at this stage are:

> How and why do you do this? What makes this happen?
> Why do you do what you're doing?
> What's the purpose of this?
> Why did this happen?
> What's the reason/rationale for this?

The answer to "Is your 'why' important to me, too?" is answered more by the quality of the interrelationships than by the brilliance of the directed instruction or the lure of the content itself—those in class between teacher and students and among students and those between the real world expert and the students. Remember the nature of early adolescents. It is essential to establish an environment in which, on behalf of each student, there is inclusion, influence, and affection—an environment in which the message is "You are one of us . . . you belong." In response to this message, the learner then responds, "I want to learn to become like you—what you do and what you know. Doing so will become an important part of my life."

"May I join you?" I want to join your "club."[1] I like and value what you are doing and want this to be an important part of my life.

"What do members of this club do and know and how do they go about it?" Many of Smith's views support the above progression (see *Insult to Intelligence: The Bureaucratic Invasion of Our Classrooms* and *to think*). Here is just a brief synopsis of his discussion of learning and "learning clubs": "We underrate our brains and our intelligence. . . . Learning is the brain's primary function, its constant concern, and we become restless and frustrated if there is no learning to be done. We are capable of huge and unsuspected learning accomplishments without effort."[2] In attempting to de-myth learning, he states, "Learning is not the occasional and difficult thing it is often thought to be. That learning requires effort is another myth. The stress and strain comes from **trying to learn and failing**. When learning is successful, it is totally inconspicuous."[3] "The struggle to learn is usually a struggle to comprehend. The moment of comprehension is the moment of learning. Learning is a smooth, continuous flow from one understanding to another, not a series of sporadic lurches from confusion to confusion."[4]

The key to Smith's definition of learning is this statement: "We learn every time we make sense of something; we learn in the act of making sense of the world around us. Understanding takes care of learning."[5] It is impossible, he contends, to memorize what confuses us; all we remember is our confusion (and perhaps despair). Harkening back to our discussion of an expert, new learnings—when understood—needn't be memorized. Once understood, it snaps into perspective among things we already know. Perhaps the important message here is that our "covering" material never allows students sufficient in-depth learning to establish a basis or context to which new learnings can stick. Everything is a "learn from scratch" effort which requires tremendous effort, doubtful probability of success, and little payoff.

Smith points out that the bulk of life's learning occurs in "clubs"—the language club from which we learned our native language, our high school peer club from which we learned a wide range of values and goals and modes of operating in the world, the learning club established in class by your favorite teacher, etc. The advantages of membership in a club,[6] according to Smith, are: 1) more experienced members show newcomers what activities are carried out by members of the club; 2) more experienced members help newcomers to engage in whatever club activities the newcomers find interesting (they don't teach, they help; learning is always collaborative); and 3) there is no coercion; members are neither forced to engage in activities nor denied participation and differences in ability and in experience, and interests are expected and taken for granted.

Very importantly, the message a club member constantly receives is: "You're one of us. We take it for granted that you will become just like us."

In summary, Smith stipulates that:

- all children learn constantly
- children learn what others do
- children learn what makes sense to them. (Smith points out that, prior to school, children's natural tendency is to ignore nonsense. Understanding this could help us make better judgments about the adequacy and appropriateness of our curriculum.)[7]

HIT YOUR LIBRARY

The world around us is so rich, knowledge explodes so exponentially (especially in areas of science and technology), and our memories from our early schooling are so inadequate, we simply must accept that **research is essential**—even if we teach the lowest ability students. In fact, the lower the achievement levels of students, the harder we should work at framing their curriculum to ensure that we don't overestimate developmental capacity or prior knowledge, nor underestimate interest and the need for the student to connect to the real world, not the pages of a textbook.

Use the mindmap of your yearlong theme to communicate with your public and school librarians. Give them a copy along with the dates you will need resources to plan each component. Our experience is that librarians are thrilled to be presented with a research request whose materials will be studied with care.

Key points, developed after the teacher has secured a knowledge base about the subject area, are statements of what students should know and be able to do when the topic is completed—the essential core of knowledge students will have at the end of the component or topic studied. They are *concise, straightforward statements which capture concepts, skills, and/or significant knowledge which the teacher considers most important.*

RECYCLE BACK THROUGH STEPS 1 – 4

The thinking processes needed to identify effective key points are neither linear nor sequential. Jump around from one step to another. You cannot complete the job by using one mental frame at a time.

CHARACTERISTICS OF GOOD KEY POINTS

Key points which are powerful for teacher planning and useful for enhancing student learning are key points which:

- clearly and concisely describe what is essential to know and be able to apply or use
- are meaty enough to warrant the time that will be spent on them (by both teacher and student)
- say something important enough to warrant 11-16 minutes of direct instruction or an hour+ "discovery process"
- apply to the real world and the students' world (now and in the future as foreseen by the learner)
- are age-appropriate
- can be studied using "firsthand" sources
- are more conceptual than factoid
- are specific enough to guide both teacher and students in their planning and working
- are specific enough to serve as the basis for authentic assessment tools and processes for both short- and long-term purposes

EXAMPLES OF KEY POINTS

Key points are not tricky to write but they require thinking, analyzing, and decision-making. Use common sense! Their purpose is to provide clear focus on what is to be accomplished by both the teacher and students. Powerful key points lead toward conceptual understanding rather than mere listing of factual data.

The primary consideration in stating a key point is that it will enhance the learner's ability to detect patterns and make meaning of what is being learned (see "pattern-seeking" in Chapter I). Each statement represents content which warrants, and can sustain, 11-16 minutes of direct instruction or one hour or more of a discovery process.

Examples of key points appropriate to the theme "We, the People" include the following.

FOR CONTENT

Examples of key points for the component "Who Am I?"

- Intelligence is a function of experience. The more experiences we have, the more able we are to make sense out of and apply new learnings. Experience is enhanced when all 19 senses are activated.

- Intelligence is a problem-solving or product producing capability. Each of us have at least seven ways to problem-solve, each operating from a different part of the brain. Our culture, experience, and our personal inclinations result in our developing some intelligences more than others.

- All human beings have the same basic needs. If these needs are not satisfied, the individual will initiate and maintain efforts to meet those needs. Basic needs, according to William Glasser, are: belonging, freedom, power, and fun as well as survival.

- Our personality preferences, or temperament, strongly influences how we learn and behave. Significant areas of behavior are how we take in information, make decisions, our lifestyle, and our orientation to self, others, and things.

- You will go through more changes during your adolescent years than at any other time in your life. Expect change in these areas: intellectual, physical, psychological, social, moral and ethical.

- Learning is a two-step process: identifying patterns and building a mental program to apply what you learn (knowledge or skills). Definition: learning is the acquisition of useful programs.

Examples of key points for the component "Who Are We?"

- A society is a collection of individuals occupying the same general area, acting in similar ways, and sharing important states of mind. Political boundaries (boundaries of nations) are not the same as boundaries delineating societies. Most nations have many societies within them.

Examples of key points for the component "To Form a More Perfect Union"

- The United States is a political boundary that contains many societies, some the size of a nation-within-a-nation.

- The basis for any union, large or small (two people or a nation), is shared agreements—agreement to act in similar ways. Agreement to consistently act in similar ways usually stems from sharing important states of mind, particularly such beliefs as the "good life," meaning/purpose of existence, and acceptable/non-acceptable action. When these fundamental beliefs change, they usually force change in the agreements of the union.

- The structure of agreements vary with the nature of the entities involved in the agreement. Agreements tend to be informal, unwritten, and often even unverbalized when the group is small and there is a high degree of shared beliefs and common patterns of action; conversely, agreements tend to be formal, written, and very explicit when the group is large and there is a low or unknown degree of shared beliefs and common patterns of action.

FOR SKILLS

- The current format for a business letter is as follows: address blocks for both receiver and sender, date, salutation, and signature closing are all blocked on the left margin, all separated by a double spaced address to the sender and the date of the letter first, followed by two spaces. The content should explain clearly and concisely who you are, why you are wriiting, and what you are requesting.

- An oral presentation must include three main points you want your audience to consider, graphics to support those points, and a call to action.

- Footnotes acknowledge the source of information you use. The first time an author is referenced, give the author's name and title of the book, then, in parenthesis, the state where published, publisher, and date of publication; the page number follows the parenthesis. When an author is referenced a second time, give only the author's surname and page number.

USING KEY POINTS

Keep in mind that key points have a dual audience. *For the teacher* they are a guide for short- and long-term planning and the basis for built-in assessment instrument (daily, weekly, monthly, end-of-the-year). *For the students*, they are a guide to daily work and long-term adventure. Key points constitute the centripetal force that pulls meaning from the real world into the shared space of learner and teacher.

Key points provide the gist for lesson planning—both for direct instruction presentations and for discovery lessons.

When the teacher believes that the *discovery process* would be the most powerful instructional approach, key points focus the teacher's material gathering and planning efforts, guide lesson design, and help frame clear questions for the students to pursue. They also can serve as a means for students to do self-checking.

When the teacher thinks that *direct instruction* would be the most appropriate instructional format, key points provide the goal and content for the teacher's presentation. Information is presented in ways that are *creative, useful*, and have an *emotional* bridge (CUE).The teacher then presents the information in a way students can mindmap the material. The presentation should be rich enough to start the brain's detection of the pattern contained in the key point. Real life artifacts and situations, overhead projector, 3-D models, poetry, rhyme, etc.

Once the key points are determined, the next step in developing curriculum is creating inquiries—activities using firsthand sources through which students can engage all the senses in making meaning within a real world context.

IMPORTANCE OF MULTIPLE RESOURCES

Obviously, the depth of information needed to develop key points is not available in school textbooks. Textbooks are but generic guides. Textbook publishers admit their books are to be a resource, a general guide, not a comprehensive program. In truth, they are primarily an outline of a list of factoids. When used as the only resource they severely limit the knowledge base for all—students and teachers. Thus we must free ourselves of our dependency on textbooks, using them only if they support what we have orchestrated for the students. Imagine how much money is spent on textbooks, books which provide little breadth and depth and often aren't even used. Imagine the "real" resources you could purchase with that money! In contrast, one set of a current *Encyclopedia* on a CD-ROM is an incredible all-purpose resource to begin with.

Only the teacher is in the unique position to evaluate the full range of resources needed in his/her classroom. The teacher, through planning and sleuthing, can amass a great variety of materials, including current writings, resource books, magazines, pamphlets, and, whenever possible, resource people. In some cases the textbook may provide the sequence for the unfolding of events—but always, it is the teacher who creates a rich learning environment.

Therefore, when implementing the ITI model, it is essential for teachers to provide a variety of resources for the students to use during each monthly component. The librarian at the public library could be your closest ally. Don't be shy. Ask your librarian. Provide him/her with a copy of your key points about two–three weeks before the start of your next component. Be sure to specify the range of reading levels in your classroom (and make sure you stretch the top level). You will likely receive anywhere from 40 to 60 resource books for each component.

A librarian can also provide other types of resources for teachers to use when writing their curriculum. Some of the most valuable resources available from the public library are contact information for the local, state, and federal governmental agencies; state and federal senators and representatives; local, state, and national groups concerned with the environment and conservation of natural resources; chancellors of foreign embassies with diplomatic relations with the United States, etc. Needless to say, the professional dedication of the librarian and his/her expertise make it easier for teachers to implement the ITI model.

Excellent resource books to take you beyond the usual confines of written material from a library are:

National Trade & Professional Associations of the U.S.
Columbia Books Inc. Publishers
1350 New York Ave. N. W., Suite 207
Washington, D. C. 20005

Encyclopedia of Associations
Burek, Koek, Novallo, Editors
Gale Research Inc.
Detroit, MI 48226

The Corporate Address Book
by Michael Levine
A Perigree Book published by Putnam Publishers Group
200 Madison Ave.
New York, NY 10016

Directory of Toll-Free Numbers
by Rudolf F. Graf
A Pocket Book published by Simon & Schuster
1230 Avenue of the Americas
New York, NY 10020

Educators Progress Service, Inc.
Dept. DZ
214 Center Street
Randolph, WI 53956-9989

The Timetables of History
by Bernard Grun
A Touchstone Book published by Simon & Schuster
1230 Avenue of the Americas
New York, NY 10020

The Timetables of Science
Alexander Hellemans and Bryan Bunch
Simon & Schuster
1230 Avenue of the Americas
New York, NY 10020

Science & Environmental Resource Guide
California State Department of Education
Office of State Printing
P. O. Box 271
Sacramento, CA 95802-0271

The Timetables of Inventions and Discoveries
Kevin Desmond
M. Evans & Company, Inc.
216 East 49 Street
New York, NY 10017

Consumer Information Catalogue
Consumer Information Center
Dept. TD.
Pueblo, CO 81009

The beauty of most of the the above resources is that, as in real life, students must seek out the information. Have students write letters weekly in search of information that is closer to the source, less pre-digested. Writing to a real audience also strengthens student communications skills and makes the point that there are unlimited resources available for the asking. As they write their letters,

- insist that "perfect" letters are sent (form, spelling, etc.); teach students to proofread each other's letters

- have students type letters on a computer whenever possible

- when appropriate, include a cover letter written by the teacher explaining the ITI model and the purpose of having students involved in the letter writing process

If we are to create an enriched classroom where students have access to a varied and comprehensive range of resource materials, we would expect teachers to collect between 25-100 books, magazines, and other material from libraries, swapmeets, friends, and district offices to support their particular topic of study each month. In an ITI classroom, students begin to gather resources for their own study. It is not unusual for students to become so proficient in identifying resources by the end of the year that they will bring hundreds of magazines, and other materials for one month of study!

The issue is meaningfulness! Critical thinking and higher level decision-making are moot if students don't have the opportunity to look at issues through multiple resources—from all vantage points, i.e., from the eyes of different authors with differing points of view and with the goal of actually doing something now and here with what is learned.

CONCLUDING COMMENTS

Now that you have identified what all students are to learn, you must turn to the heartbeat of the ITI classroom—inquiries, those activities that make learning an active, highly participatory adventure, activities which provide students opportunities to understand and apply the content and skills of the key points to the real world. Now the fun begins!

CURRICULUM DEVELOPMENT —
DEVELOPING INQUIRIES

 Inquiries are the footbridge between the "what" and "how" of curriculum—the what is to be learned (key points) and how students will go about learning and applying/using that information and skill. Webster's definition for "inquiry" is useful here: "the act or an instance of seeking truth, information, of knowledge about something; examination into facts or principles; research, investigation." *(Webster's Third International Dictionary, Unabridged.)*

Inquiries make learning active and memorable and, for that reason, they are the heart and soul of your curriculum-building efforts. They are the point at which words become realities, the talked about becomes one's own experience, where "talking about science" melts into "doing science," where reading about historical figures becomes experiencing their problems and dilemmas. Inquiries frame the real-life opportunities which allow students to apply/use their learnings and, in doing so, build programs (see Chapter 1 for discussion of the importance of pattern-seeking and program-building to the learning process).

Inquiries are also the point in curriculum development at which you begin to involve students in directing and assuming responsibility for their own learning, the point at which you invite students to join you in the driver's seat, to learn to take an active role in shaping the stuff and processes of their day-to-day learning. Unlike the development of textbooks and workbooks, the development of inquiries is not a one-way street, an adult only activity.

This chapter describes how to develop inquires and how to use them as a guide for selecting instructional strategies and designing lessons; Chapter VII explores the use of inquiries in assessing competence/mastery.

> Included here are discussions regarding:
>
> - **refining the essential content to be learned**
> - **how to write inquiries**
> - **example inquiries**
> - **criteria for evaluating inquiries**
> - **how to use inquiries**

REFINING THE ESSENTIAL CONTENT TO BE LEARNED

The process of writing inquiries is an extension of the thinking processes begun with re-thinking the curriculum and identifying key points. That is, as you continue your exploration of what *being there* experiences/resources you can provide, you will want to: continue refining your statements of what are essential concepts for students to know; revisit your library (this time with a more focused perspective); interview people on-site regarding the reality of the workplace; and begin to anticipate instructional strategy issues.

FOCUS ON HERE AND NOW, NOT THERE AND THEN

The most important consideration when developing inquiries is to stay within the realm of here and now—firsthand experiences which students can absorb through all 19 senses. Avoid the "over there" and events which happened in the past (prior to students' immediate experiences of self, family, grandparents) because none are "experienceable" and do not result in the same degree of dendritic growth.

FOCUS ON DOING VS. TALKING ABOUT

The writing of inquiries puts the action into the students' day. Thus, the more "daring do" that you can build in, the better. Go for the gusto! Go for the real life, the firsthand, the tangible product. When writing inquiries, let the creative juices flow! Above all do involve your students in writing inquiries. Students as young as third grade delight in writing them and they write some stupendous ones—insightful, challenging, and fun—some of the best we've ever seen. Each inquiry should be perceived as a meaningful event (from the students' perspectives, of course), worthy of time and energy; if possible, it should be something that students can use at home or in class during further learning.

HOW TO WRITE INQUIRIES

Always keep in mind that the purpose of inquiries is to allow students to **apply** and **expand** the key points. Inquiries are not "activities" for the sake of activities but rather carefully crafted assignments that give students an opportunity to discover, understand and apply the content of the key points they are learning. Because inquiries put action into the students' day, go for the real life, the *being there*, the tangible product. The more "daring do" that you can build in, the better. Go for the gusto!

When writing inquiries, let the creative juices flow! Above all, do involve your students in writing inquiries. Students as young as third grade delight in writing them and they write some stupendous ones—insightful, challenging, and fun—some of the best I've ever seen.

There are two important kinds of tools for writing inquiries: content tools and structural tools to help with the writing of inquiries.

CONTENT TOOLS

Tips From Brain Research

Three elements from brain research essential to developing inquiries are the notion of pattern-seeking, the seven intelligences, and choice. The best inquiries are those which lead students to see the pattern in that which they are learning and that allow each student to work in the problem-solving intelligence of their choice. (See Chapter II for a discussion of these brain-compatible elements and the Inquiry Wheel on page 142 of this chapter.)

Lenses Upon the World From Brady's Framework

Brady's socio-cultural framework is perhaps the best inquiry prompter we know of. Examining the systemic relationships between patterns of action, cultural premises, environment, and demographics is a never ending wellspring of questions which lead to ever more questions to pursue. His framework is the powerful tool for providing a cognitive structure for analyzing that which appears so common, so taken for granted that it has never been thought deeply about.

Thoughts From John Gatto

John Gatto, many times a recipient of Teacher of the Year awards, developed seven themes for teaching his classes of junior high students. They throw open the boundaries for inquiries. His seven themes as he describes them are:[1]

- **Community Service** — The real kind where you go to work with the *paid* employees, and go home when they do. This is opposed to the community service under the tutelage of "nice" people, with milk and cookies, the kind that "decorates" some alternative programs. I expected the kids to shoulder an adult load of responsibility and prove their usefulness to others. All did.

- **Independent Study** — The real kind. One boy took 180 days to get a part on "General Hospital" but in the course of doing so he studied acting, directing, lighting, scripting, advertising, the history of theater, the relationship of theater and the academic disciplines of psychology, sociology, history, etc. And, he got paid! One girl analyzed the public swimming pools of Manhattan and the Outer Boroughs from a professional swimmer's perspective and rated each on the basis of a checklist she had devised, writing "A Swimmer's Guide to Swimming Pools in the New York Metropolitan Area."

- **Apprenticeships** — Either "The One Day Apprenticeship" or long-term. The idea: to learn how someone thinks and makes decisions. The purchase price: trading personal services for the right to shadow a person at work.

- **Field Curriculum** — In which various parts of the community are studied as living texts and contexts in projects which are semi-independent (although designed by myself) and usually lead to a product of immediate utility. To have a kid furnish a two-and-a-half room Manhattan apartment down to the toothpicks and toilet paper by sallying out for days with a clipboard, and tallying the cost of his selections with tax computations, tabulations and the whole package including architect's drawings, placement, symbolic graphics, etc., is a wildly successful example; analyzing the commercial community of a 50-block area of the West Side in order to direct a part-time job search is another.

- **Parent Partnerships** — At any time and for any family-determined motive, kid and mother, kid and father, kid and grandad, kid and aunt, etc. have the right to "write" a piece of family curriculum and substitute it for the school-authored one. I see now in retrospect that this was my nod to home-schooling and to the absolute centrality (in my own philosophy at least) of the family relation as the basis for a "self," and the values which produce a successful, happy life.

- **Work/Study** — Consider a student design for a street peddling business in the Columbia/Barnard area using one of a kind, handmade items made by old people. One boy buffed restaurant floors, in a service business of his own design; many have done pet-sitting; the most successful kid I ever had in a dollar sense made $600 a day selling homemade cartoon character stationery at Comic Book Conventions. His mother called me and gave me living Hell for teaching her son how to make so much money at 13—but, of course, he taught himself! In a work/study program, school time is exchanged for work time as long as the work is self-initiated, a private business launched by the kid, not a "job" to make spending money.

- **Solitude/Privacy/Self-Reliance** —This is a complicated idea . . . but suffice it to say the theme is designed to counteract the hideous *lack* of private space, private time, private thoughts, private business in a government factory school, or most private schools for that matter. I operate on the theory that the formation of a reliable self requires time spent alone in the wells of spirit—and that it is nobody else's business what you do there, store there, think there. With many children crippled by a total surveillance model of schooling, it's necessary to "show them how," to run exercises that *demand* learning to like your own company, keep your own counsel, make your own decisions. Walking the 10 miles alone from Columbia University to the Staten Island Ferry might be one of these, going fishing another, but the whole area touched here is vast, subtly nuanced, singular, and a constant struggle.

Well articulated, John, and much to think about.

STRUCTURAL TOOLS

Once the content issues are settled and you know precisely what you want students to do, the following "ABC" guidelines and process verbs from Bloom's Taxonomy of Cognitive Objectives make the actual writing of inquiries quite surprisingly straightforward and simple.

The "ABC" Guidelines

When writing inquiries, follow the "ABC" guidelines:

- **A**lways start the sentence with an action verb. This makes it an imperative statement, a directive for action rather than a stimulus for a convergent answer.

- **B**e specific about what the inquiry is asking the students to do. Avoid words like "all," "some," or "as many as you can." If the instructions are clear, you will be spared each student coming to you to ask for clarification of what he/she is supposed to do.

- **S**ee ("C") the outcome or finished product the students are asked to create. Have you stated exactly what you are expecting them to do? Is it feasible with the resources and time available? Don't underestimate!!! Are there choices within the inquiries that entice every student in your class to get excited about learning and to be challenged?

BLOOM'S TAXONOMY OF COGNITIVE OBJECTIVES

Although Bloom's Taxonomy was originally developed as a tool for improving the rigor of college testing, the process verbs associated with each "level" are useful mind joggers. These verbs are shown in the concentric circles on the Inquiry Building Wheel on page 144. They are distributed among the pie slices according to five of the seven intelligences (intra- and interpersonal intelligences are omitted from the wheel because each affect the social context of the inquiry rather than its content).

While Bloom's Taxonomy directs the learner to various kinds of application of concept or skill, the seven intelligences help frame inquiries which call for different problem-solving and/or product-producing approaches. This gives students many and varied opportunities to expand their repertoire of successful problem-solving approaches. In contrast, the traditional school curriculum exercises only two of the seven problem-solving capabilities. An empowering curriculum assists learners to expand their range and power of problem-solving capabilities—our goal ought to be the creation of 21st century Renaissance minds.

Strive for a balance of both as you select verbs with which to write your inquiries. A balance will ensure the widest possible choice for students. A suggested rule of thumb: there should be at least four to five inquiries for each key point: one that requires students to visit the real world, to interview experts; one that requires research from primary documents; one that lends itself to active interaction and participation with peers and the production of a tangible product; and one that requires independent thinking such as writing or an individual project. Doing this provides choices for students and nudges them toward adult participation in the workplace and becoming lifelong learners.

To refresh your memory, Bloom's Levels are:

knowledge—the student recalls or recognizes information

comprehension—the student changes information into a different symbolic form

application—the student solves a problem using the knowledge and appropriate generalizations

analysis—the student separates information into component parts

evaluation—the student makes qualitative and quantitative judgments according to set standards

synthesis—the student solves a problem by putting information together which requires original, creative thinking

INQUIRY BUILDER CHART

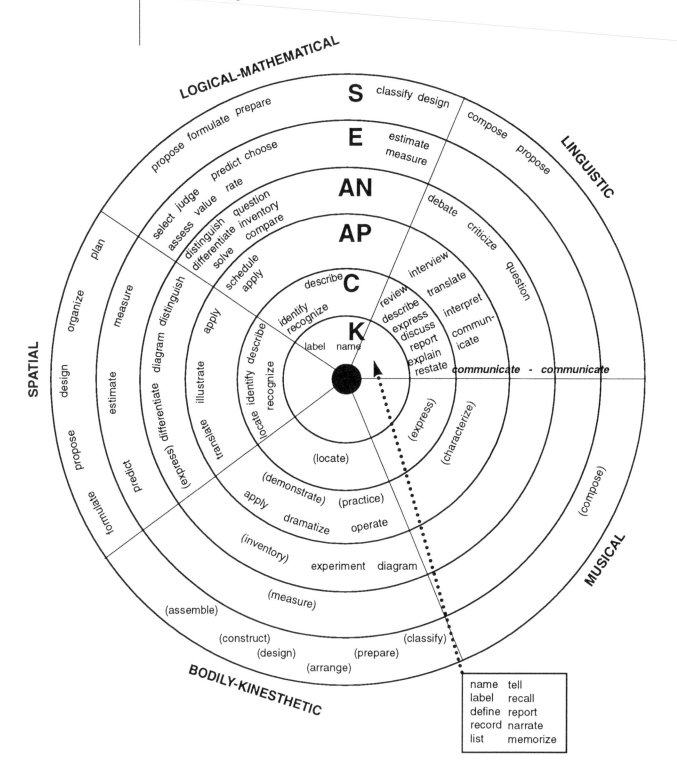

SHAPING INQUIRIES FOR YOUR AUDIENCE

When writing each inquiry, it is helpful to think through how and in what context the inquiry will be used. For example, will this inquiry serve as the whole class activity that follows your direct instruction or will it be your lead discovery process question that will replace a direct instruction presentation. Will it be an assignment for collaboration? Or, would it work best for partners or triads? Accordingly, indicating the intended purpose and size of the group that can select each inquiry might prove to be a very useful classroom management tool. The following code might be helpful.

> **C** = whole class inquiries
> **G** = small group (at least two students)
> **I** = individual or independent

Even though it is important for students to have choice in selecting inquiries, some inquiries can be assigned for all students to develop and research. This allows the teachers uniform feedback about whether students have mastered a particular key point (see Chapter VI).

It is also important to ensure that students have opportunities to problem-solve in all seven intelligences, not just in their strong suit. Keying each inquiry to the seven intelligences helps the teacher keep track of a student's progress in developing a Renaissance mind. For example,

> LM - logical-mathematical
> L - linguistic
> S - spatial
> BK - bodily-kinesthetic
> M - musical
> Ira - intrapersonal
> Ier - interpersonal

The third element of choice is the kind of inquiry based upon Bloom's Taxonomy which also can be easily coded for students when they are choosing an inquiry:

> K - knowledge
> C - comprehension
> AP - application
> AN - analysis
> E - evaluation
> S - synthesis

EXAMPLES OF INQUIRIES

Examples of inquiries for the component "To Form a More Perfect Union" include:

- Select an example union of your choice. Visit two groups—one young and one old—interview the participants and observe their interactions. Based on this information, identify for both groups, in priority order, the four most important cultural premises and the four most significant patterns of action. Are your two sets of lists very similar or do time and age and/or environment seem to change these factors? If so, why? Prepare a four minute oral presentation to your cooperative learning group usingthe C.U.E. guidelines.

- Select an example union of your choice. As a group, visit two groups—one young and one old—interview the participants and observe their interactions. Based on this information, what do you think the structure of each group's agreements is? Is it formal-informal, written-unwritten, explicit-unspoken, etc.? If you were a participant in these groups, what would you do to improve the glue that holds these unions together to make them more workable and satisfying for the participants (consider Glasser's basic needs of all humans)? Based on this information, what recommendations would you make for the structure of agreements in this class, and why? Write a one page essay as a group which includes the following: a description of each group (do not reveal the real names of the group participants); an analysis of the cultural premises and patterns of action of each group, and the structure of agreements, and your recommendations. When you have a perfect paper, share it with another group.

- Based upon the above assignment, select a member of your group to join a discussion panel whose topic is: "How can we improve the structure of agreements in this class?" As a team, prepare a two minute recommendation and prepare to debate the efficacy of your views. Rehearse your group's presentation three times before the panel begins.

Examples of inquiries for the component "Who Am I?" include:

- Create three scenarios that would cause the brain to downshift in the course of a school day and three ways to assist it in upshifting. Dramatize them for the class.

- Construct on an 8 1/2" x 12" sheet of white drawing paper a family tree which traces your family's heritage for at least four generations.

Examples of inquiries for the component "Who Are We?" include:

- Create a poster with at least 10 examples from the entertainment section of a local newspaper which illustrate a view of the "Good Life" which you think is the most common in our community.

- Identify the different cultural communities found in your city by drawing their locations on a city map. Be sure to include a key or legend for identification purposes.

- Using the list below determine which intelligence the following people use most in their daily work.

  - police officer
  - phone operator
  - minister
  - sales clerk
  - carpenter
  - disc jockey
  - truckdrivr
  - cook
  - teacher

Example inquiries for skills include:

- Identify a situation in our community which both you and our local newspaper consider to be a problem because peoples' basic needs are not being met (use Glasser's analysis of basic needs). Write a half page essay describing the problem. Include pertinent information from the newspaper and reference the information using proper footnote form. Also, state what the benefits of footnotes are for the reader, you, as writer, and the original author.

- Divide the classroom by gender and then into groups of four or five. Identify the three most critical problems for the opposite group in today's society. Present the following information in a single page summary to the other "gendered" group for their response:

  - Boys have it more difficult in school/society because:
  - Girls have it more difficult in school/society because:

- Prepare a two-minute appeal to encourage your classmates to do one of the following:
  - end cheating at school
  - establish a dress code for students and teachers

Follow the CUE guidelines for your presentation.

147

CRITERIA FOR EVALUATING INQUIRIES

Does this sound like an incredible amount of work? Initially, yes. But once your awareness of students' capacities and how to meet them expands and you have developed a pattern and program for writing inquiries, you will find that your mind will automatically be searching out activities to carry your curriculum. Also, students as young as third grade are very adept at writing inquiries according to Bloom's Taxonomy once they have learned the application of the seven intelligences and Bloom's six levels. Students love to help write their curriculum— it allows them to develop their sense of independence and control over their lives and lays the foundation for lifelong learning. Try it. Invite them in to the process of their own education. You will find that they can develop inquiries with imagination, great creativity, and surprising challenge. They are often even better than what the teacher comes up with; carefully selected and mixed with those developed by the teacher, they constitute a significant contribution to the teacher's task of developing curriculum. Developing inquiries is also a good thinking exercise because one can't pose a good question or frame a worthwhile learning task without a good understanding of the key point and its application in the real world.

When developing inquiries, there are several criteria to keep in mind. Good inquiries should:

- provide genuine choice for students
- offer firsthand sources in a real-world context
- be clearly related to the key point(s)—they apply/expand the key points and show real-world connections
- be worthy of the time to be spent

When well developed and well orchestrated, inquiries lead to "natural thinking knowledge," a term used by Renate and Geoffrey Caine to describe a combination of "felt meaning" and "deep meaning."

"Felt meaning," is that "aha" response that occurs when something we've been trying to learn suddenly clicks into place and we "get it." It begins as "an unarticulated general sense of relationship and culminates in the 'aha' experience that accompanies insight."[2] According to the Caines, "such insight is much more important in education than is memorization."[3]

The second concept is "deep meaning," defined by the Caines as: "whatever drives us and governs our sense of purpose."[4] It includes all the instincts embedded in our reptilian brains, our needs for social relationships and an emotionally rich life, and our intellectual and spiritual needs.[5] These drives are sources of individual meaning, what people live for, and they are meaningful and drive our inner engines whether they are articulated or not and even whether or not we are conscious of them.[6] The important thing for us here is that "people access passion when deep meanings are engaged";

deep meanings, therefore, "provide a sense of direction because they govern what people look for and what they are willing to do, whether in sports, computing, music, finance, writing poetry, or teaching. And, in part, deep meanings are a source of the energy that people are capable of bringing to bear on a task or activity."[7]

According to the Caines, when information, felt meaning, and deep meaning come together, the result is "natural knowledge," knowledge so much a part of us that we refer to it as "second nature."[8] For example, "I love cars and I've been working on them for so long, figuring out transmission problems is second nature to me." With natural knowledge, "the learner has acquired a felt meaning for the subject or concept or procedure so that new information and procedures fit together. In addition, there is a sufficient connection with the learner's interests or deep meanings so that the information and procedures are personally relevant."[9] Physiologically what occurs in the brain is an increase in the number and quality of connections among neurons already dedicated to the learnings in the area of expertise; starting from scratch with new neurons and fragments of information that have not connected to anything else the learner has already learned is not the way the brain works.

Natural knowledge, then, is perhaps best exemplified by the actions of an expert. Again, the Caines come through beautifully as they describe three noticeable characteristics of experts. Experts: 1) see "larger" patterns and more complex chunks, e.g. the difference between a good chess player and a grand master; 2) have a grasp of context—analysis of the context as well as the characteristics, e.g., what appears to a new teacher to be chaos and disorder in a classroom often has purpose and meaning to the experienced teacher; and 3) store information differently than novices, e.g., novices tend to memorize new information; an expert can read or hear something once and remember it, immediately incorporate it.[10]

The genetic programming of the brain is important here. Again, in the spirit of creating a "brain-compatible" learning environment, we should be working with the natural unfolding process of the brain rather than trying to get it to do things the "school way." In Chapter IV, we referred to Dr. Larry Lowery's descriptions of developmental levels. This description fits the "logical-mathematical" intelligence described by Howard Gardner (see Chapter I) and is the portion of the brain which is heavily used in learning and applying science concepts and skills (the other critical intelligence is spatial). These frameworks are very useful in developing curriculum content.

"Natural knowledge" is arrived at by children—outside of school and without benefit of dittos—through their natural search for meaning to their "why" questions.

Inquiries help the teacher build opportunities for students to arrive at natural knowledge in two ways:

- by giving direction to lesson design, particularly to direct instruction, making it less lecture and more firsthand and experiential

- by structuring student work in ways that encourage students to ask questions and seek their own answers

HOW TO USE INQUIRIES

As the bridge between curriculum development and instructional strategies, inquiries serve important functions for both teachers and students:

For the teacher, inquiries are:

- the ultimate extension of the discussion of "what's worth knowing?"

- a building block for lesson design and selecting instructional strategies when planning to ensure that students learn and develop *programs* for applying the key points

- the vehicle to follow-up on direct instruction or to bypass direct instruction in favor of a discovery approach

For the students, inquiries:

- give structure to their work when they are learning (seeking patterns) and when applying, in real world settings, the knowledge, skills, attitudes/values identified in the key points (building programs)

- are the vehicle for allowing significant choice for students in the classroom while staying on target for what's most important to learn and be able to do

- provide structure for authentic assessment, not only reflective of the real world but in the real world

CLASSROOM MANAGEMENT REQUIREMENTS FOR INQUIRIES

Using action-packed inquiries, providing choice, coming and going to the real world require effective classroom management strategies. Our preferred approach to classroom management is that developed by Pat Belvel, Training and Consulting Institute, San Jose, California. Her approach is practical, powerful, and respectful of both students and teachers. Teachers leave the workshop with tools which immediately allow for better classroom organization and more effective learning through inquiries.

Belvel's "Five P's of Classroom Management"[11] are:

- **powerful**—has to do with whether on not the curriculum being taught is meaningful and real to the student

- **personal**—has to do with the belief systems and experiences the teacher brings to the classroom

- **prerequisites**—are the academic and social level assessments the teacher does before the class ever begins the present school year

- **parameters**—are the procedures and directions the teacher will use for what goes on in the classroom

- **participation**—refers to students actively taking part in the goings-on of the class

Powerful has been addressed in Chapters III through VI. This section on classroom management will only address the area of parameters because it immediately changes what goes on in the classroom.

Typically, explanations and directions are given to students verbally. This can create confusion in the minds of students and inconsistency on the part of the teacher because they are not in writing and cannot be talked about and changed. When teachers take the time to write out the procedures and directions and post them, students are able to begin immediately without asking what they need to do. Teachers need to think about creating a system where all routine procedures are written and posted so students have access to them for quick review. Certainly, taking time out during the first month of school to go over the procedures will allow students to be able to apply them with just a quick review when needed.

Belvel defines procedures as "those strategies and social behaviors which are essential for the activity or routine to happen."[12]

In contrast, directions are "orders for doing assignments which will change with the assignment." The following chart shows some possible directions for doing inquiries.

Examples of procedures are:

PROCEDURES FOR INTRAPERSONAL TIME

- Stay at your own table or desk
- Remain as silent as possible
- Do activities such as: journal writing, reading, drawing, etc.
- When the chime rings there is one minute remaining

PROCEDURES FOR COMING INTO CLASS

- Come into the room with your spiral binder and a pencil
- Go directly to your assigned seat
- Copy the daily agenda and the quote for the day into your spiral binder
- When finished, work intrapersonally on inquiries, journal, or other work

Students entering the classroom can come into the room and immediately begin to be responsible for getting to work without having to ask, "What are we supposed to do?" This provides the teacher with time to work individually with students or to get the next activity ready.

Once students become familiar with these strategies, it might be possible to have them assist in the writing of any new ones. It will give them ownership in the classroom organization.

To provide easier access to procedures have them indexed in a three-ringed notebook so each collaboration team has their own copy. It is then a simple task, once students are familiar with them, to say, "Would you please turn to the procedures for working in skill groups and review them before beginning the next assignment?" Students could take one to two minutes reviewing them and then begin the assignment. The job of the teacher would be to go from group to group checking for understanding or giving immediate feedback.

Examples of directions are:

DIRECTIONS FOR DOING INQUIRIES

- Go to the inquiry board and select the inquiry you wish to complete

- Copy the inquiry, exactly as written, into your spiral binder

- Determine the Bloom level and the intelligence choice and write it after the inquiry

- Using any of the resources in the classroom, completely follow the guidelines of the inquiry when responding

- Answer the inquiry immediately following what you copied from the inquiry board. If you are doing an illustration, follow the directions of the inquiry, fold and staple the paper onto a page in your spiral binder

- Have each member of your group edit your answer and initial at the end of your answer

- Bring your spiral binder to the teacher for confirmation of the job done

Writing and posting procedures and directions is a wonderful tool for teachers, students, and substitute teachers to use. Once they have been established, students will automatically know which procedure or direction they need to use. Inviting students to participate in their development increases understanding of their value.

VII

ASSESSING COMPETENCE VS. GRADING

"I feel that I am learning kind of and kind of not but I don't feel like I'm going to fail, which I hope I don't."

Today's early adolescent[1]

The goal of the ITI model—and the innate drive of the human mind—is mastery. Mastery, not in the sense of "mastery learning" with its 834 discrete skills of reading, but rather mastery as in competence: "capacity, sufficiency, enough to live on with comfort." That is, the learner understands the skill or concept, knows how to apply it in the real world in similar (but varying) circumstances, and has incorporated it into a mental "program" (see Leslie Hart's discussion of programs, Chapter 1). Such mastery or competence is at the heart of positive self-concept, of a sense of empowerment and ability to direct one's life, and it is consistent with the brain's innate search for meaning. In contrast, a teaching standard such as the bell curve is not only highly brain-antagonistic, but is self-defeating for student and teacher.

From a student perspective, grading causes stress, redirects the learner from intrinsic rewards to external rewards, pits student against student instead of assessing all students against a standard of competence. In too many instances, it also creates either low self-esteem or a sense of false assurance. From a teacher perspective, the demands of the system distort what's valuable to know to what's easy to assess and to ensure "alignment" of curriculum with assessment tools.

There is yet another, more fundamental reason why traditional evaluation and grading is brain-antagonistic; it simply ignores how learning takes place. As Hart states: "Learning is the acquisition of useful programs." Using information only to select A, B, C, or D on a multiple choice exam, choosing between true or false, or even writing a short paragraph essay is insufficient to create a program. And, as Hart points out, information that does not become embedded in a program is information that is unretrievable.

Before we go on, check with your own experience. Do you recall your college days? Sitting up studying all hours of the night, the essay exam for your sophomore World Civilizations class? Mountains of data, little or no application of the information, no "program" created. By the time the blue book essays were returned, there was stuff in that essay exam book you had never heard of before! Even the handwriting looked strange! Surely this must be someone else's exam book! But, sadly, the exam book was yours . . . what a waste of time, money, and effort.

Even in more active forms of assessment, doing something once or twice does not a program make. Thus, even an "A" can mean little in terms of long-term memory. And grades of less than an "A" usually mean that the learner, at the time, still harbored uncertainty or misunderstandings. Such tentativeness is a clear indication that an accurate "program" had not been put in place. Thus, a "D" or "F," even a "B" or "C," means that little or nothing will be remembered six weeks later.

In real life outside of the classroom, the difference between mastery and the bell curve is quite stark. In the real world, a "C" or even a "B" is wholly insufficient. Who would want to fly in an airplane that had been serviced by a mechanic who had just passed skill tests with a "C-"? Would you? Certainly not! How about just a little leak left behind by your plumber? Is that OK with you? Of course not!

In real life what really matters is mastery. It is a cruel lie to tell students that a "B" or "C" is OK. The plain and simple but painful truth is that a grade of "B" or "C" represents failure to learn. To come close to mastery ("B+") is, in the long run, no more resultful than an "F" or never having taken the class at all.

All of this may sound unduly harsh, even spiteful. However, we must pay attention to the evidences of student failure to master, to become competent, which lies all about us. Look at the meager learnings with which our high school students depart from our high schools each year. After 3,500 hours of schooling at a cost of roughly $45,000 per student, the United States graduates 1.1 million functionally illiterate graduates. And we haven't begun to mention the tragedy of the millions of students who drop out of school, in many states a figure in the neighborhood of 30 percent.

To persist with the current evaluation and grading system under the guise that we are preparing students for high school is wrong. We must begin to do what is brain-appropriate and reflective of real life rather than copy what the high school does. Our "junior high" days are the way we were . . . we need to get on with the task of remaking the middle school in ways which are brain-compatible and thus powerful . . . the way we can be.

NEW PERSPECTIVES

In reconceptualizing evaluation and grading toward a notion of assessing competence, there are two trends which are two hopeful trends— application of current brain research (the major topic of this book) and authentic assessment, often referred to as performance-based assessment. Both require massive changes in curriculum content and structure as well as the means of assessing student learning and in attitudes—of teachers, students, and the system.

Two key ideas from the authentic assessment movement which are particularly powerful are:

- using real life settings and levels of expectation*
- assessing what's worth assessing rather than assessing what's easy to assess

In short, teachers need to look for alternative ways to assess their students in mastery of those concepts which are meaningful and have real-life application.

This chapter presents several tools for evaluating student learning in ways which are brain-compatible, consistent with goals of the authentic assessment movement, and which can also satisfy district needs for student and teacher assessment and accountability.

---

*Fred Newman, one of the primary leaders of the authentic assessment movement, states, "The idea of authentic achievement requires students to engage in disciplined inquiry to produce knowledge that has value in their lives beyond simply proving their competence in school."

USING THE TOOLS AT HAND

Just as learning should be brain-compatible for students, assessing student learning should be brain-compatible for teachers. In an ITI classroom, there is no need to invent or buy tests or assessment instruments beyond what the teacher has already created in the process of orchestrating learning. Well-crafted key points and inquiries are all that are needed for student (and teacher) assessment and accountability.

It may be useful here to recall the basic structure of successful measurement. Simply put, any assessment procedure must answer the basic question: **Who** will do **what, how well**, as measured by **what, when**.

- **who**—all students (not just the "good" students)
- will do/know and be able to apply **what**—the key points
- **how**—measured by the inquiries
- **how well**—framed by the inquiries and judged according to the "3 C's" of mastery
- **when**—by the end of the semester (not by an arbitrary date such as Friday, quiz day)

Together, key points and inquiries provide the basic assessment tools of what is to be measured, how, and the level and kind of expectations. How to handle the remaining two elements, who and when, is quite clear in a brain-compatible learning environment—all students can achieve mastery of meaningful content when provided with adequate time and given immediate feedback (either by the learning materials/situation itself or by the teacher).

KEY POINTS AS ASSESSMENT TOOLS

Key points **are** the curriculum. They exemplify the notion "less is more." If they have been selected and developed well, i.e., if they are truly what is essential to learn and are conceptual rather than factoid in nature, then they are clearly what's worth assessing. Thus, they are what should be assessed and what students (and teachers) should be accountable for. (For a discussion of how to develop powerful key points, see Chapter 6.)

INQUIRIES AS AN ASSESSMENT TOOL

Inquiries are the engine of the curriculum—they give it power (from the teacher's perspective) and pizzazz (from teacher and student perspectives). They also determine which instructional strategies would be most effective from moment-to-moment, day to day. And, they are ready-made performance-based assessment tools. All that one needs to add is the "three

C's of assessment"—the criteria for making the judgment of "how well" something was learned, whether mastery occurred.

A note of caution: carelessly crafted inquiries, inquiries which reflect only linguistic or logical/mathematical intelligences, inquiries that are busywork or have no real-world application (or for other reasons are just not brain-compatible) are useless as assessment tools. Please re-read the discussion of inquiries, and particularly writing inquiries, using the seven intelligences (seen in Chapter 8).

159

SETTING STANDARDS FOR MASTERY: THE "3 C'S" OF ASSESSMENT

The criteria for determining mastery is threefold: **complete, correct**, and **comprehensive.**

Complete means that the work called for by the inquiry met all the requirements or specifications of the inquiry including timeliness. As when on the job, the task is complete from beginning to end and done within the requested time frame.

Correct means that the work called for by the inquiry contained accurate information or was performed with the requisite job specifications such as a plumber or electrician performing work in accordance with the Universal Code for plumbing or electrical work.

Comprehensive means that the work reflects thoroughness of thought and investigation, not just a one-line response, an opinion forged from a single point of view. What is important and worthwhile about the issue or problem was researched thoroughly, looked at from different points of view (not just one's own opinion or "what it said in the encyclopedia"), and the conclusion supported with the relevant data. On the job, comprehensiveness of response can be as simple (but very valued and valuable) as a secretary researching pricing of office supply items from several mail order catalogs as well as nearby stores before placing the order.

Although students may balk at such criteria and complain about "changing the rules of the game," the notion of completeness and correctness will not be new to them. However, comprehensiveness is a concept that the teacher will have to teach because it is the antithesis of "study" done out of the textbook (with emphasis on "the"). It may take some weeks to shift students from the viewpoint and habits attendant with such notions as quantity is quality, piling up points equals learning. More about this later.

TRANSITIONING TO MASTERY:

Burying the bell curve and instituting expectation and assessment of mastery/competence is not a minor event for students or for the teacher. Most students have lost their childhood sense of wonder and curiosity, their joy in exploring, and learning just for the sake of learning. Instead, school is a place where you wait to grow up so you can begin real life. The major motivator is how many points are needed to get a grade of "___" or how many pages, exactly, does the paper have to be? The notion of learning for the fun of it, doing one's personal best when mediocre will pull the desired grade . . . well, skepticism will be high, snickering widespread. Why, imagine a class with only two grades, mastery or no credit with the criteria for mastery being a very demanding one!

So, be prepared. Think through concrete steps for transitioning students. Here are some tried and true possibilities.

A "HALF-WAY HOUSE"

The "3 C's" criteria of complete-correct-comprehensive are enormously shocking to many students. Unthinkable, even. Also, teachers usually need some kind of immediate way of showing student accountability which will work in the existing system, a system dependent upon "grading" students using letter grades. If so, be aware; it may take some weeks or even months to complete the transition to truly brain-compatible assessment processes and tools. Consider the following as you transition yourself and your students from brain-antagonistic evaluation and grading systems to brain-compatible assessment methods.

Assessing Student Work on Inquiries

After ensuring that your key points and inquiries are well crafted, the first elements of brain-compatible assessment to institute the criterion is "correct." Any assignment that does not meet this criterion is returned to the student, repeatedly if necessary, until the work is acceptable, and correct. After several weeks, and with some forewarning, add the criterion of "complete"—but only after you have taught the notion to students with plenty of clear examples and numerous illustrations. Beginning with the second semester with most classes, but earlier if a class is ready, add the final criterion of "comprehensive." Once again it is imperative to take students through the process with plenty of examples. From this point on, all assignments will be assessed on three of the criteria: correct, complete, and comprehensive.

During this transition to inquiries demanding real life application and real life standards of workmanship, you may feel that adapting your old "points for grades" system is needed. If so, just don't forget that it is a transition stage. Truly brain-compatible assessment is much further down the road.

In the spirit of making learning brain-compatible, it is recommended that the teacher give each student a similar chart which lists every key point (an abbreviated version of the key points listed on the bulletin board or illustrated in the mindmap) for each component. This should be a permanent part of each student's notebook. It is only fair that the teacher share the game plan for the semester (or year) with the students.

If using the point system during your transition from bell curve to assessment of competence, you could attach a point value to each inquiry. During my first year using the ITI model, I chose to vary the points, giving more points to those inquiries which generated the best learning—those at the higher levels of Bloom's Taxonomy (see the Inquiry Building chart on page 144). For example:

> Knowledge .... 1 point
> Comprehension ..... 2 points
> Application .... 4 points
> Analysis .... 5 points
> Evaluation .... 6 points
> Synthesis .... 7 points

Next, establish the number of points necessary to earn a grade of A, B, etc. In establishing the point system, keep in mind that the object is mastery for all students, not a sorting based on speed. In fact, in a brain-compatible classroom, if the teacher has orchestrated learning well, all students should earn an "A"—mastery of the skills and concepts of the curriculum.

It doesn't take students long to figure out that, if their goal is to earn 100 points, they will get there "faster" if they choose the more involved and demanding inquiries. As this looks like a short cut, most students will take it. Before long, they will discover that these "higher" level inquiries are also the most interesting and rewarding. In fact, it was amazing to see how few students chose the levels of knowledge and comprehension from mid-year to the end of school. And the nature of the student body—Black inner city, non-English speaking, White suburban, rural, poor, affluent, etc. does not affect this response. A drive to learn is inherent in the make-up and chemistry of the human brain. Boredom and lethargy are unnatural states.

Another transitional issue you must face is that of individual vs. group cooperation, competition vs. collaboration. As some inquiries are individual and others designed for cooperative group work, students may initially resist the idea of getting the same number of points as what the group as a whole (or proportionately) earned. The better students will complain that their grades will be pulled down, that other students will "cheat" or copy from their work. Such students may in fact hog the task. Low achieving students may be intimidated and withdraw from participation, etc.

Thus, when allowing for choice of inquiries, you might, in the beginning, provide inquiries which are designed primarily for individual work and slowly increase the number of inquiries requiring group work. (The time to introduce cooperative learning is as a format for work that the entire class is simultaneously involved in, such as follow-up to direct instruction.)

A third area of transition for students (and teacher) is a shift away from the teacher as the authority for right answers to the individual learner being responsible for "figuring things out." In real life, there is no 30 hour-a-week person who follows us about shouldering the responsibility for ensuring that the information we encounter is trustworthy or not or pointing out to us that we really didn't quite "get it" when our boss explained a new procedure to us. A hallmark of the lifelong learner is assumption of responsibility for determining what information is reliable, valid, trustworthy and for whether or not we truly "got it."

Accordingly, you will want to shift students to develop their own resources for making such determinations. One useful classroom rule which handles the spontaneous, short-term questions, is that the student may not ask the teacher a question until he/she has first asked three other students.

Another approach, which handles the need for immediate feedback during long-term, somewhat involved tasks, is to teach students an editing process. A simple process might go something like this: When a student has finished an inquiry, each member of the group reads his/her work, applying the "3 C's" of assessment and checks for misspelled words, incomplete sentences, wrong or incomplete answers, etc. Each member then initials the inquiry and returns it to the student asking for editing assistance.

The student then reworks the inquiry, making all necessary corrections. Only then is it brought to the teacher for feedback. It is easy for the teacher to quickly look at the student's binder and determine if the inquiry satisfies the "3 C's." If not, no points are given and a note is written next to the inquiry asking the student to "rethink" or "redo" the inquiry. Students have the option of either redoing the inquiry or selecting a different one to do. Again this is their choice. But the message is clear, what matters in real life is mastery, competence.

Initially student frustration will be high. They may wallow in disbelief or even anger. Teachers will need to be patient and maintain their high expectations. Yet, by the start of the second semester, almost all students will be used to the process and accept it as "that's the way things are done." Some classes may take longer to adjust to the process but, if you refuse to lower your expectations, all of the students will come to understand the editing process and the importance of mastery.

As shifts in these attitudes begin to occur, the door will open to yet more brain-compatible assessment practices, e.g., no points for inquiries completed, only a check-off on key points mastered. Eventually, the internal student motivator becomes the satisfaction of mastery itself, the confidence of knowing one is a competent problem-solver, and love of learning—all necessary ingredients for lifelong learning.

This shift to internal locus of motivation to learn is greatly aided by implementation of the LIFESKILLS, especially Personal Best (see Chapter II, page 47). Again, the goal of the ITI classroom is mastery—all students performing at the level of "A" and beyond.

Keeping Track

The mechanics of "keeping track" of progress toward mastery has a tendency to take on a life of its own. The result is a far less brain-compatible atmosphere than we had intended and we begin to have that cheerless feeling that goes along with being embedded in bureaucratic red tape, even if it is of our own making.

To help counteract the bureaucratic tug of the system, keep in mind the eight elements of brain-compatibility. For example, traditionally when a grading period has ended, teachers wrap up the grading. Nothing is accepted late. However, adequate time demands that, just because study of a component has ended and a new component has started, there is no reason a teacher should "close the book" on students. The teacher should still work with those individuals during the next component to guarantee they eventually master the key points from the last component. *Again*, the expectation of the teacher and the clear message to students is MASTERY! If students are involved in keeping track of their progress of mastery against the key points and in daily work on inquiries, they can keep their eye on the ball; the teacher needn't nag.

Assessing What's Important

The mechanics of using key points as the main assessment tool in the classroom are surprisingly easy. The teacher simply converts his/her grade book into a record of mastery of key points. Key points are listed across the top, students' names along the left. A simple check can suffice or a teacher may choose to record the date and the number of the inquiry used as the assessment tool. The discussions that will ensue around what it means to "know that you know" and "know that you don't know" will be invaluable for students as they begin to piece together what it means to become a lifelong learner.

A chart showing that a student has not mastered one or more of the key points, pinpoints which key points the student must review. This can be done through cooperative learning groups or one-to-one contact with the teacher. This process is repeated until every student masters all key points for a component. Students really become interested in how they are progressing and want to master the key points. If the component ends with any student still having key points to master, the teacher should continue to check with individual students until mastery has been achieved. The expectation is for **mastery** by all students.

Having students use a spiral binder in which they keep a record of every key point, the mindmap (their notes) of direct instruction, the inquiries they have completed, and the research they conduct ensures students will have all the things they need under one cover. Be sure they buy the spiral binders that come three-hole punched so they can be stored in a notebook binder. It helps students keep track of their papers or assignments. It can be an easier way for teachers to keep track of student inquiries for correcting purposes. Teachers concerned with handing out papers can have students staple them onto pages in the spiral binder. Students become very proud of their spiral binders and cherish the quality of the work they have mastered.

Note to the reader: Please be clear that this discussion of grading and point systems is only for transitional purposes if you cannot make the full jump from bell curve to assessment of competence/mastery all in one leap. Your ultimate goal—to be reached as soon as possible—is to assess competence based on mastery of the key points as demonstrated through selected inquiries on a pass/no credit (not on a pass/fail) basis.

NON-TRADITIONAL ASSESSMENT TOOLS

PORTFOLIOS

Given the authentic assessment movement, many schools are using portfolios which include selected pieces of student work, most selected by the teacher, some by the student. Unfortunately, all too often staff do not know how to interpret or analyze the contents of the portfolio. Either there is no criteria or rubric for judging "how well" students perform or staff lack sufficient training to "make sense" of the contents of the portfolios. In such instances the portfolio becomes not a means to making better instructional decisions but an end in itself. Care must be given to ensure that staff have sufficient training to "make sense" of the contents, to learn how to make professional judgments based upon the information. However, if teachers select well-crafted inquiries as the basis for their portfolio selections, the contents of the portfolio will be useful to the teacher's instructional planning, and will clearly reflect achievement of what's most important.

The most often omitted element of the portfolio process is the criteria or rubric to judging "how well" the student performed.

To ensure that the portfolio products reflect the seven intelligences, they must go beyond paper and pencil, e.g., photographs of projects (students also do the photography), models, or other products which are not in written form such as a videotape of the most significant achievements each year which follows the student as he or she continues through the system from kindergarten to graduation. What a present to give a graduate!

WHOLE GROUP PRESENTATIONS

A whole group presentation is just that—a presentation involving every member of the group based upon a long-term (three or more weeks) inquiry which the group selects from the list of whole group projects posted at the beginning of the component. They work on this project throughout the component during daily time blocks allocated for this purpose. The students should be responsible for all of the materials necessary to do the project. Using as a guide the CUE model—the presentation should be creative, useful to the listener, and establish an emotional bridge. Each member of the group must be part of the presentation. Videotaping for self-evaluation purposes is encouraged.

Students As Evaluators

Involving students in assessing performance levels of others has many benefits. It solidifies the criteria or standard of excellence that the student himself or herself is attempting to learn, provides practice in providing constructive criticism instead of put-downs, and ensures active listening. A suggested procedure is the following: at the conclusion of a presentation all students would complete a mindmap which includes the name of the group, the name of the project and two evaluation statements for each group member. The statements should be comments that will lead to individuals improving their involvement in the group presentations. Statements such as, "what was good" and "what could be improved" could lead to the kind of improvement that will benefit students. No letter grades should be given. While the class is completing their evaluation mindmaps and answering the inquiries asked by the presenting group, that group could be viewing their presentation and completing the mindmap for its project. One person from each group could then collect the group's evaluations and give them to the presenting group for "immediate feedback."

The evaluation mindmap is tremendously popular with students because they like being involved in the evaluation process. This process helps students focus on multiple presentation strategies, leading to tremendous improvement in communication skills from month-to-month as the year progresses.

Each student's articulation in and contribution to the group's work (final product and presentation) should be assessed and feedback given. If a point system is being used, teachers should provide two sets of points—individual and group.

One final thought, if you have not had your students involved in the evaluation process, consider giving it a try. It allows students to apply the tools and skills they are learning in class. The evaluation mindmap shown previously works very well because students do not have to assign letter grades. They are providing positive statements that will help the other students and themselves improve their skills. This is an essential part of the ITI model for middle school students.

Yearlong Research Projects

A long-standing criticism of middle school curriculum is that students are not engaged in any really meaningful, long-range projects or reports, one which provides students with an opportunity to experience, firsthand, the time, energy, and commitment it takes to do an extended task. One such long-term task is the "yearlong research project."

During the first two weeks of the school year each student selects a topic *from the yearlong theme* to pursue as a yearlong research project, a topic which they will have until the beginning of May to research and prepare their report. They will become the "expert" or the "teacher" of the class. As the year progresses, they collect material for their project from many different resources, such as newspapers, magazines, letters, resource books, interviews, and any other resources they can find. Initial collections can be stored in a manila folder and shoe box. As they begin to organize the most pertinent materials, provide them with a notebook binder with clear plastic sheets so that they can create a professional looking product. This collection folder needs to be brought in and shared periodically in order to get immediate feedback on the kinds of materials being collected. Students may need help in getting the folder organized. The materials they collect will give them plenty of resources to help them prepare for the presentation.

Based upon this yearlong research project, each student develops a seven- to twelve-minute presentation in the area of their expertise. Beginning in May, two presentations are scheduled during each class to have students draw for presentation order so they will know when they should be ready to present. Students are evaluated on the thoroughness of their research, including their collection folders and their presentation, and to the degree they used C-U-E. Again, each student in class could take part in the evaluation process using the evaluation mindmap. Here again teachers could, in the traditional assessment system, select a point total for grading purposes. Points for the folder and the presentation could be awarded separately.

TIPS FOR MAKING TRADITIONAL ASSESSMENT TOOLS MORE BRAIN-COMPATIBLE

Consistent with the seven intelligences, students should be allowed to demonstrate mastery in a variety of ways rather than being limited only to linguistic processes—reading and checking a box, writing, or oral presentations. The issue should be about whether the student understands the key points, can apply them in real life settings, and has created programs for the skills or concepts connected with them. The means of expressing mastery through an inquiry should not also be a simultaneous test of linguistic ability. If the performance meets the "3 C's" of assessment, then mastery is noted. They could present an inquiry in any number of ways depending upon which of the seven intelligences they may choose. Inquiries could be oral, written presentations, rap songs, poems, creative plays, projects, etc. Students could also show mastery by responding to problems posed in class. Once mastery has been demonstrated, a check mark is put under the key point mastered after the student's name.

ORAL PRESENTATIONS

All too often, oral presentations before the class become a nightmare for the presenter and a complete bore for the listeners. Although the "run-of-the-mill" book reports, state reports, country reports, etc., have no place in a brain-compatible classroom, the opportunity for students to present inquiries orally can be a positive tool to use in the evaluation of student mastery for those students whose written skills are as yet poorly developed.

Two important ground rules to consider: the student must completely research and prepare a presentation that is creative, useful, and emotional (CUE); no more than two oral presentations should be presented each day.

Frequently, students present information which relates to key points not yet covered by a direct instruction or which extends the key points beyond what the teacher will address. What a bonus for the teacher to have another "expert" in the room!

Ideally, these presentations would be videotaped and included in the student's portfolio.

WRITTEN TESTS

The time-honored written test will probably always be part of the evaluation and grading process in the middle school. However, it should be looked at as only one way among many to determine mastery. Its use can easily be minimized by selecting well-crafted inquiries as "test" items—inquiries based on the seven intelligences.

Ideally, providing several inquiries—all of which assess mastery of the same key point(s)—allows students to choose their preferred capability for problem-solving or product-producing.

If forced to use written tests, consider allowing students the alternative of using a mindmap structure to organize and present their responses. It might be valuable to have the students write a paragraph or statement explaining the mindmap. Correcting this mindmap test could be as simple as having each student compare the one they generated for the test to the one they have in their notes.

CONCLUDING NOTES

This section has tried to provide several alternative tools for assessing student performance and mastery. Teachers need to keep in mind that, if they are implementing the ITI model, they need to look toward those assessment tools which provide the most authentic assessment and demand student mastery. Teachers should keep open the possibilities of creating their own unique assessment tools which could provide for more authentic means of determining what students have learned—inquiries are a ready-made tool. However, remember that the key to authentic, reality-based assessment is a reality-based curriculum. Thus, change in curriculum should precede efforts to revamp assessment strategies and tools.

TRANSITION

Given the size of the gap between the way we were—a "junior" version of high school—and the way we can be—a brain-compatible, ITI middle school—the degree of change needed is truly enormous. It is unlikely that a school can make the jump in one leap. On the other hand, a clear picture of the landing site is needed before the first step is taken. We hope that this book has supplied some of the needed brush strokes to reveal a landscape for the future.

Our sense of reality and our past experiences suggest that the size of the leaps as well as the beginning point and timelines will vary from school to school. The purpose of this chapter is to explore what those beginning points and leaps might look like and to look at the nature of the transitions required. But first, a word about change and transition.

While the change needed in schooling is huge, the need for personal transition within is even greater. And, as William Bridges has pointed out in his book *Managing Transitions: Making the Most of Change,* "it isn't the changes that do you in, it's the transitions."[1] Change, he says is situational: the new teaming structure, double or triple length instructional periods, expanding one's expertise in other subject areas, converting from textbook to integration based on physical location, a new principal or school board.

On the other hand, *transition* is "the psychological process people go through to come to terms with the new situation."[2] Transitions requires that we change our personal programs for lesson planning and classroom management, that we toss out old lesson plans and assignments, that we be willing to start from zero and be very inexpert indeed about something that we felt quite comfortable about before and for which we received praise and recognition.

"Change is external, transition is internal."[3]

Bridges cautions us that change cannot and will not work unless transition occurs. To understand how profound this comment is, think back to your school's last big change effort that fell flat on its face. The school plan was totally and completely revamped after an extensive needs assessment and faculty and student involvement. The good ideas got written on the page, complete with detailed calendar and who was to do what. Yet, six months later . . . nothing. No behaviors changed, no new actions were taken.

Things remained as before. Why? Because transition—internal shifts—did not occur.

Bridges maintains that transition is very different than change. The starting point for transition is not the outcome to be implemented but the ending that you must make in order to leave the old situation, actions, and attitudes behind. Thus, while situational change hinges on the new thing, psychological transition depends on letting go[4]—letting go of old beliefs, the old reality, and the old identity you had before the change took place. For example, letting go of the disciplines with their familiar and comfortable boundaries and our established place as "expert." Says Bridges, "nothing so undermines organizational change as the failure to think through who will have to let go of what when change occurs."

Thus transition starts with an ending. The "way we can be" must begin with letting go of "the way we were."

Letting go need not be a funeral. Many of the things we must set aside served us well and were successful for their time and use—celebrate them, thank them for the service and then step forward with a sense of adventure and high hopes, not with regret.

Because there is much to let go of about the old "junior high" model and many vested participants, it is unlikely that we will make the transition in one year or even two; three to five years is more likely. Accordingly, this chapter describes a continuum of implementation options, each suggesting the changes needed. The transitions that accompany them are, however, a personal journey.

This chapter describes possible stages in the transition to a fully integrated and brain-compatible ITI program for students. The five transition models are:

1. SINGLE SUBJECT INTEGRATION MODEL (working within the departmentalized model)

2. COORDINATED MODEL

3. INTEGRATED CORE MODEL (two or three periods)

4. INTEGRATED DOUBLE CORE MODEL (two double periods)

5. SELF-CONTAINED CORE MODEL

This chapter discusses each model, its structures and advantages, plus "tips" and "pitfalls" to help teachers implement whichever model is selected.

Variables to consider when selecting from among these five models include the number of teachers willing to implement a brain-compatible approach to curriculum and instruction, the number of class periods in the day, and the number of subjects and class periods to be taught by each implementor. For example, Model 1, the single subject integrated model, is ideal for the teacher flying solo, "doing ITI alone," because it can be implemented by a single teacher or several teachers, each working independently, on a campus with little or no support from administration or colleagues. In contrast, Model 4, the integrated double core model, requires a close partnership with fellow teachers and widespread commitment to restructure the "system."

All the transitional models require establishment of a brain-compatible environment for all students and mastery of the teacher competencies outlined on page 25.

MODEL 1: THE SINGLE SUBJECT INTEGRATION MODEL

This model is a typical beginning point when working within a departmentalized structure and is an essential building block for any and all further integration. It is the first step toward eliminating fragmentation by integrating the parts and pieces of a content area. While it may seem a contradiction in terms to refer to integrating a single subject area, we mean precisely that. The integration occurs at three levels:

- sourcing curriculum in students' lives and experiences rather than in the centuries-old definitions of "disciplines"

- presenting the content as it appears in real life rather than presenting content as a pursuit of the "disciplines" of physics, chemistry, economics, government, business, or technology—e.g., life, earth, and physical sciences and technology as seen out the window of the classroom or integrating history, geography, and the sociology of man relative to a real problem within one's own community

- using this content as the proving ground for applying the basic skills of reading, writing, speaking, mathematics, and problem-solving, thus building meaningfulness back into the curriculum

Mastery of this model by a teacher provides the tools necessary to go about implementing ITI, regardless of subject matter focus, using any of the other models described in this chapter and for restructuring the entire school.

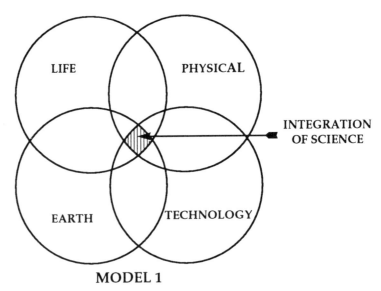

MODEL 1

The Single Subject Integration Model, Model 1, is a typical beginning point on the road to more powerful teaching/learning; it is the basic conceptual and implementation building block for all the other ITI middle school models. It offers the advantage of allowing teachers to begin their ITI journey in the subject area they feel most confident to teach. Many teachers in the Bay Area Middle School project in California* started their ITI odyssey with this model.

An example of a yearlong theme designed for implementation through the Single Subject Integration Model is "Patterns in Nature."

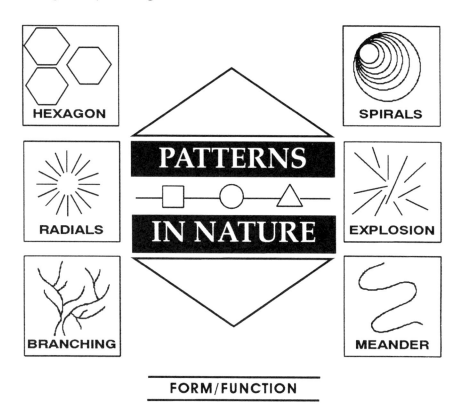

Using "Patterns in Nature" for science study would allow the teacher to integrate life, earth, and physical sciences plus technology quite easily. For a focus on art, this theme would be powerful for study of natural landscapes. For the social studies teacher, the component on branching might include branches of government, cultural roots, family trees, major river systems where ancient as well as modern cities were built, and even hypotheses about the future.

"Patterns in Nature" could also easily be used by a teacher who would like to help students begin to make connections among their classes **even if the other teachers have not yet begun to collaborate across department lines.** In order to assist students in bringing the pieces of their daily fare together into a meaningful whole and applying them to the real world, an ITI teacher can begin to consider including other subject areas whenever

---

*The Bay Area Middle School Project (BAMS), funded by the David and Lucile Packard Foundation includes Mission Hill Junior High (Santa Cruz), Almeria Middle School (Fontana), and Altimira Middle School (Sonoma). The program involves over 70 teachers using all five of the models described in this chapter.

possible. If collaboration among staff across department lines has not yet been established in your school, merely consult the state/district curriculum frameworks to see what the basic ideas are at your grade level. For example, it is possible to include the correct form for writing business letters in language arts classes when students are writing letters to obtain information for their yearlong research project. Math concepts could be included when teaching science because many math skills are needed in order to apply science knowledge. Integrating concepts from other content areas makes what students are studying more whole and more like the real world; it significantly expands the breadth and depth of the course learnings for our students.

Because of the teaming possibilities of this theme, it is a good solo beginning which could then easily lead into teaming with other subject area teachers in the future.

Author Ann Ross's ITI teaching experience was primarily with this type of model. Because she taught two different subject areas, eighth grade science and seventh grade social studies, she had two separate themes—one based in science and one based in social studies. The first theme was entitled "Science Mysteries," and integrated earth and physical science concepts required by the district science continuum. It did, however, omit life science because that was part of the seventh grade science curriculum, thus fragmenting the integrated nature of science in the real world. Yet, it was a beginning toward integrated, thematic curriculum—a beginning which electrified students and enabled Ann, as teacher, to take her first steps toward powerful, brain-compatible learning experiences for her students.

If you have decided to develop a yearlong theme using the single subject integration model, the following "tips" and "possible pitfalls" might be of great assistance as you begin.

Tips for Implementation:

- create a brain-compatible and healthy environment before the school year begins
- make sure your first component is fully developed before the start of the school year
- display your yearlong theme on the classroom wall for continual reference by you, your students, and parents
- make sure your key points are essential and conceptual, not factoid, and that they are expressed as a pattern
- make sure you have plenty of real life sources as well as other resource materials
- display key points and inquiries for the current component on the wall for continual reference
- obtain training in cooperative learning skills and how to use the Lifelong Guidelines and LIFESKILLS for yourself and other ITI teachers

- accept that you can't do everything the first year; a reasonable aim is three components—one to kick off the year, one to end the year, and one in the middle
- decide which content from other subject areas you will include with your content area
- inform parents of your "game plan" the first week of school; don't wait until Back to School Night in October or November
- make sure your department chair and administrators are informed and knowledgeable about what you are doing
- bring your librarian in on your quest for resources for your theme

Possible Pitfalls:

- failure to get administrative support up front
- not keeping your administrator, parents, and colleagues informed on an ongoing basis
- trying to do too much
- doing it "solo" and perhaps creating hostility among staff members if they do not understand what you are doing and why
- not informing parents soon enough about the changes

The graphic below illustrates the potential* of this model to provide a thoroughly brain-compatible learning environment *from the students' point of view* and from the perspective of their *entire day.*

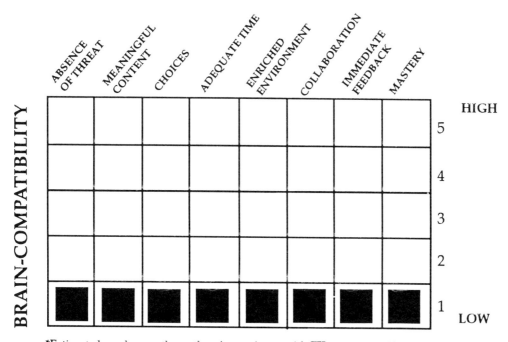

*Estimate based upon the authors' experience with ITI transition efforts.

MODEL 2: COORDINATED MODEL

This model is designed for teachers from different departments who want to team together. Teams may consist of two team members (e.g., science and math), three team members (e.g., science, social studies, and language arts), or four team members (e.g., science, social studies, language arts, and math). It is a popular beginning point for ITI implementation and school restructuring. Like the single subject integration model, its appeal is that it allows each teacher to begin in the subject area of his/her strength while, from the student perspective, things in their day begin to come together. Also, each subject must be integrated within itself before coordination efforts take place.

The coordinated model* can be implemented at two levels, one requiring no change of the departmentalized structure, the other requiring considerable change in departmental structure, registration procedures, and ways of working and communicating together. In either case, the critical feature of this model is that a team works together to plan a common year-long theme, synchronizing their respective content areas to create a closely coordinated curriculum.

Beginning Levels of Implementation — At beginning levels of implementation, teachers choose to team together to plan their curriculum and problem-solve instructional strategy issues. Thus, although each teacher develops his/her own subject area and teaches separately, he/she does so with knowledge of what the other team member(s) is/are doing on a daily/weekly basis.

At the beginning levels of implementation, teachers teach independently to students who are assigned as a result of the regular registration process. This randomness of students precludes one team member building on the daily experiences provided by the other team members. **The result is a synchronization of curriculum but not true integration.**

Higher Levels of Implementation — At higher levels of implementation, teachers not only plan together in teams but they teach as a team and share the same students. Obviously, the school as a whole must be moving toward restructuring and be willing to create some flexibilities for small teams of teachers. Commitment must be made by the school as a whole to begin to break down departmental barriers and to allow flexibilities in curriculum planning, including common planning periods, and to schedule the

---

*In the ITI model, there is a significant difference between coordination and integration. Coordination is used here to mean the synchronizing of separated content topics into a common time frame. Topics which most closely relate in context occur within the same time frame, yet they are traditionally taught in separate classes by different teachers. This is what is commonly called an interdisciplinary approach. In contrast, "integrated" means that the topics of all the content areas being taught are reconceptualized so that the separation of subjects disappears. Coordination at the highest levels of implementation is a significant step toward true integration **but we recommend pursuing integration as one's goal from the very beginning of one's journey.**

coordinating teachers and their students prior to running the regular registration process. Although the team shares the same students and thus can "play off each other," true integration is still hampered by the rigidity of the time schedule of set class periods. This model becomes particularly effective when it is implemented across an entire grade level and when the 40+ period blocks are combined into longer time periods to allow for adequate time.

The following models and sample themes could be implemented at either a beginning level or a high level of implementation, depending upon the degree of structural change made in the school.

TWO SUBJECTS

The first step in teaming is the coordination of two subjects by a team of two teachers planning for students at the same grade level. The two subjects could be language arts and math, science and math, science and fine arts, social studies and math, or social studies and science, etc.

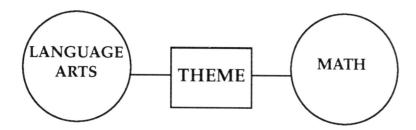

An example of a theme planned for language arts and math is "Making a Difference in the World," developed by Dean Tannewitz and Gail Purtell of Altimira School, Sonoma School District, California. Both teachers use the same yearlong theme and components; what differs are the topics, key points, and inquiries.

LANGUAGE ARTS

paragraph: review to mastery
sun-shadow mandala
synonyms, antonyms
thesaurus use
Call It Courage by Armstrong Sperry
friendly letter
mini-research (one source)
goal setting
free verse poetry
social action: personal goal setting &
    achievement

biography
family tree: people, jobs, interests,
    location
introduce "expert paper" (research)
interview
compare and contrast
Brady overlay: environment
    & cultural premises
debate
social action: letter of appreciation

tales, fables, and myths
the short story
Brady: patterns of action and
    environment
point of view/bias
simile/metaphor
business letter
surveys: creating, compiling,
    presenting
oral presentation
team activity: cultural exchange
    day
social action: surveys on critical
    school issues

MY PEOPLE
(significant others)
Biography
Family Tree: people,
jobs, interests, location

friendship
cooperation
caring

MY WORLD
(independence)
"I am the star of my life!"

**OTHER WORLDS,
OTHER PEOPLE**
(diversity)
"Celebrating our differ-
ences"

organization
effort
fun

flexibility
curiosity
patience

**MAKING A
DIFFERENCE
IN THE
WORLD**

integrity
problem-solving

initiative
perseverance

**ONE WORLD,
ONE PEOPLE**
(unity)

common sense
responsibility

OUR COMMUNITY
(interdependence)

OUR ENVIRONMENT
(the planet)
"One touch of nature makes
the whole world kin."

expert papers
bibliography
biography: people who have
    made a difference in the world
science fiction
speeches: reading, writing,
    presenting
persuasive writing
team project: adoption of
    Sugarloaf State Park
social action: to be determined by
    the students

haiku
magazine articles/essays
debate
expert papers: presentation
myths
natural history writing
observational writing
diary
team activity: "choose your issue
    and tell the world about it" day
social action: consensus, selecting
    an issue we can all support–
    identifying steps toward
    change and beginning the
    journey

newspaper: reading, analyzing,
    creating
The Pearl
report of information
problem-solving
editorial writing
satire/political cartoon interpre-
    tation
"The Good Life"
social action: attend community
    meeting in interest area of
    your choice

MATHEMATICS

MODEL # 2

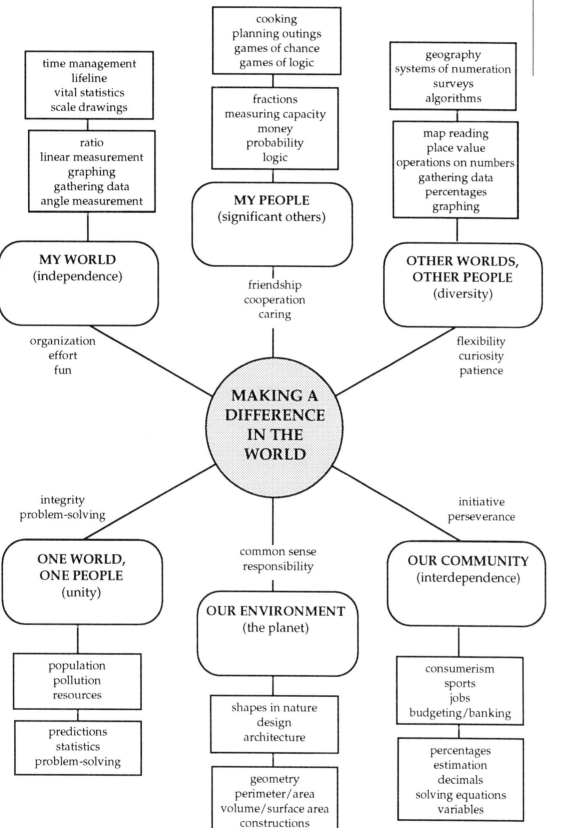

cooking
planning outings
games of chance
games of logic

fractions
measuring capacity
money
probability
logic

MY PEOPLE
(significant others)

time management
lifeline
vital statistics
scale drawings

ratio
linear measurement
graphing
gathering data
angle measurement

MY WORLD
(independence)

geography
systems of numeration
surveys
algorithms

map reading
place value
operations on numbers
gathering data
percentages
graphing

**OTHER WORLDS,
OTHER PEOPLE**
(diversity)

organization
effort
fun

friendship
cooperation
caring

flexibility
curiosity
patience

**MAKING A
DIFFERENCE
IN THE
WORLD**

integrity
problem-solving

common sense
responsibility

initiative
perseverance

**ONE WORLD,
ONE PEOPLE**
(unity)

OUR ENVIRONMENT
(the planet)

OUR COMMUNITY
(interdependence)

population
pollution
resources

predictions
statistics
problem-solving

shapes in nature
design
architecture

geometry
perimeter/area
volume/surface area
constructions

consumerism
sports
jobs
budgeting/banking

percentages
estimation
decimals
solving equations
variables

THREE SUBJECTS

Coordination of three subjects requires a larger teaming effort—three teachers across three different subject areas such as science, math, and social studies.

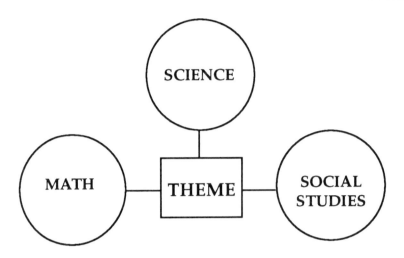

A theme with excellent potential for use in coordinating three subjects is "What Makes It Tick?" As the flow of the components follows the process of getting up in the morning and getting through one's day, application to real life is obvious to students; so, too, is the integration of content into real life.

This is a theme which cries out for structural change in the school and especially the registration process. To take advantage of field trips to the mall and make the most of follow-up in the classroom, this theme would be much more powerful at a high level of implementation with all three teachers having the same students.

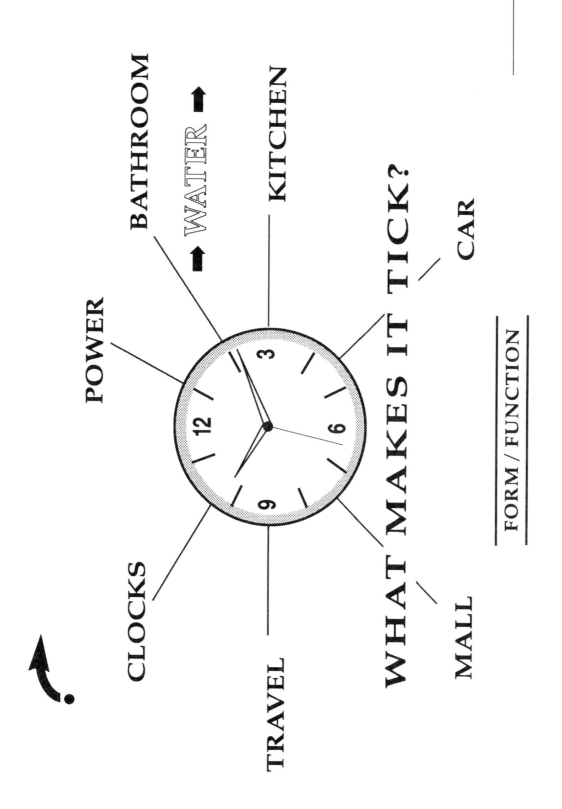

FORM / FUNCTION

FOUR SUBJECTS

Coordination of four subjects by a team representing four subject areas provides a strong basis for initiating structural change. From the team's point of view, it is essential to have the same group of students; thus, the registration process must change even if for these four teachers only. Such a change is easier than it seems: all that is needed is to "set aside" the schedule for these four teachers into a clump of four periods with a joint planning period and allow them to recruit the number of students which fit the school's teacher–student ratio. These students are then also "set aside" for these subject areas. This four-subject block is then entered as a given before the regular registration process runs its course.

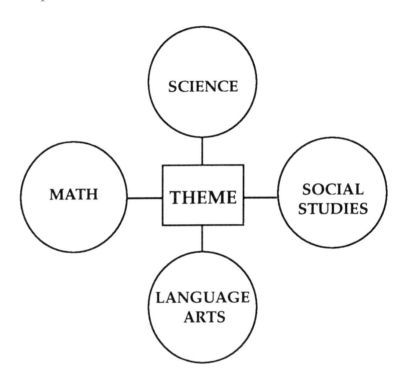

The coordinated model is a challenging model to implement because of the rigidity of the middle school structure. To succeed, administrators and teachers need to look at subject areas in totally new ways, constantly searching for the answers to questions such as, Where do we begin? What connections can we make? How can we make those connections? What should our goals be for implementation? How much of the ITI model can we realistically implement in our first attempt? These are but a few of the questions which need to be asked on a regular basis.

Working with different groups of middle school teachers from around the United States has demonstrated to the authors the importance of a theme that is driven by the content of science or social studies rather than skill areas such as reading, writing, and computation. For example, language arts—even with a whole language approach—does not provide enough "being there" experiences to activate all 19 senses and give students something to sink their teeth into. Similarly, when a skill is overemphasized, it becomes an end in itself, not a means for understanding and acting upon the world. Most students, especially high risk students, learn best when the content of their real world is addressed through *"being there"* experiences. We believe the evidence is quite persuasive: it has proven easier for teams attempting to coordinate all four content areas and show connections among them if science or social studies is used to drive the theme rather than the more skill-based and abstract areas of language arts and mathematics.

When teachers share the same group of students, it enables greater coordination among the teachers. If the four classrooms could be located adjacent to each other, then the four periods of time could be manipulated by the teachers. It would be easy to schedule guest speakers because all of the classes could meet together. It would be easy to provide an audience for inquiries which ask students to do speeches, skits, plays, and music. This coordination among the four subject areas could lead to an even more powerful model for students: the integrated model where teachers are working to totally integrate all of the subject areas. Moving from one class to the next would be an extension of the previous class, subjects would not be separate but would flow together as four water tributaries meeting and forming a beautiful, wide river flowing as one to its final destination.

When all members of the team know where the others are in relation to the theme, the possibilities for application and mastery are greatly expanded. For example, if students could write a science research paper in their science class and have it analyzed for science concepts, then take it to math class for analysis of math concepts, then to social studies class for analysis of history or geography concepts, and, finally, into language arts class for assessment of communication skills and writing mechanics, their sense of standards in the workplace would be greatly enhanced.

Teachers in the coordinated model need to share the responsibilities of putting together and orchestrating the parent orientation and parent closure nights. These forms of outreach to the community are vital.

Tips for Implementation:

- refer to the *Tips for Implementation* under Model 1—they are the building blocks for this model
- train all members of the team in the ITI model so that they share a common vision and vocabulary for working together
- train all staff at the school on ITI—at least the brain-base and overview of ITI
- form teams taking into account personality and temperament types (see Keirsey and Bates, *Please Understand Me: Character and Temperament Types)*

- ensure there is adequate time (team and personal) to plan and coordinate
- train in cooperative learning skills
- understand that choosing the coordinated model is tantamount to having the camel put his nose into the tent—more structural change must follow and flexibility of students, teachers, administrators, and parents is essential
- assign space to team members so that they have adjoining classrooms, or are at least in close proximity to one another
- alter the schedule to ensure that the team has the same students

Possible Pitfalls:

- see *Possible Pitfalls* under Model 1
- team members do not share the same philosophy and theory about learning based on current brain research and the ITI model
- teams were formed by the administrator without considering teacher personalities, talents, and interests
- ideas about implementing differ among the team members and/or between the team and the school as a whole and the district office
- students move back and forth among team and non-team classrooms
- planning time to coordinate what is being taught in each subject area is insufficient to the task
- flexibility within the existing middle school structure to create connections among all four subject areas doesn't exist
- cooperation/collaboration strategies are not in place; insufficient training
- running out of curriculum because sufficient time was not allotted for curriculum development
- resistance of students and parents to "something new"

The graphics below illustrate the potential of this model to provide a thoroughly brain-compatible learning environment *from the students' point of view* and from the perspective of their *entire day*.

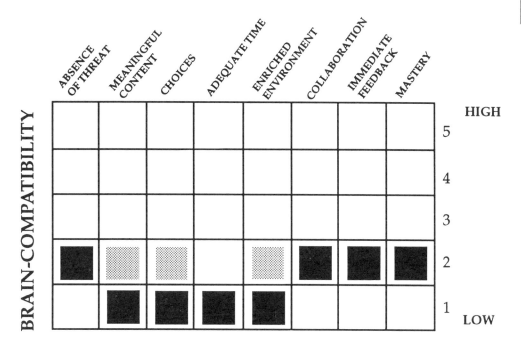

MODEL 2 — Beginning Levels of Implementation

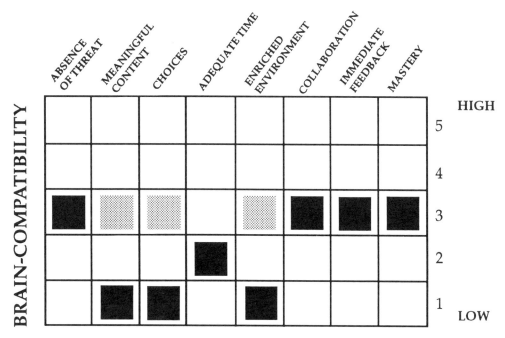

MODEL 2 — Higher Levels of Implementation

Grey area = potential if curriculum is significantly revised and based upon *here and now*

187

MODEL 3: INTEGRATED CORE MODEL
(two or three periods)

This model incorporates the elements of the first two models, i.e., the integration within a single subject to reflect real life and the coordination among subjects. However, it takes a giant leap toward true integration—one teacher, one mind integrating and synthesizing what is worth learning and how it is to be learned across subject areas—first in the teacher's mind, and then in the students'.

This model assumes willingness of the school to begin to create pockets of flexibility for teachers willing to take on not just coordination with others through a common theme but full integration of two or more subjects. In this model, one teacher remains with the same students for a two- or three-period block of time. The teacher orchestrates the content areas for which he or she is responsible around a common theme.

A significant strength of this model is adequate time. The artificiality of the 40+ minute class period is minimized. Teachers using this model often comment on how wonderful it is to have sufficient time with their students to allow genuine in-depth exploration of complex, rich, real-world topics/situations which connect two or three subject areas in unique and meaningful ways. Examples include totally integrating the teaching of language skills into science or social studies through long-term projects and through extensive, in-depth explanation of real life issues and concerns. This allows students to readily see the importance of correctly written sentences, paragraphs, and reports when using content that has a purpose and is for a real audience.

The core model is a very powerful ITI model for middle school and can be implemented one core team at a time by altering the registration process so that the cores—the teachers and students—are scheduled first before letting the regular registration process run its course for remaining teachers and students.

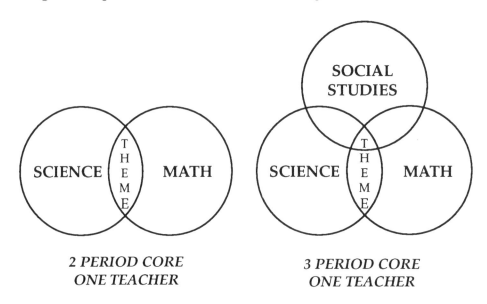

2 PERIOD CORE
ONE TEACHER

3 PERIOD CORE
ONE TEACHER

An example of a theme for a two period core in a school whose curriculum is in transition is "Light and Dark," developed by Peggy Chute, Sherry Hamilton, Maxine McElroy, and Nancie Noyer for seventh grade, Almeria Middle School, Fontana, California. Each classroom has created an *"immersion"* environment in the specific culture being studied.

MODEL 3

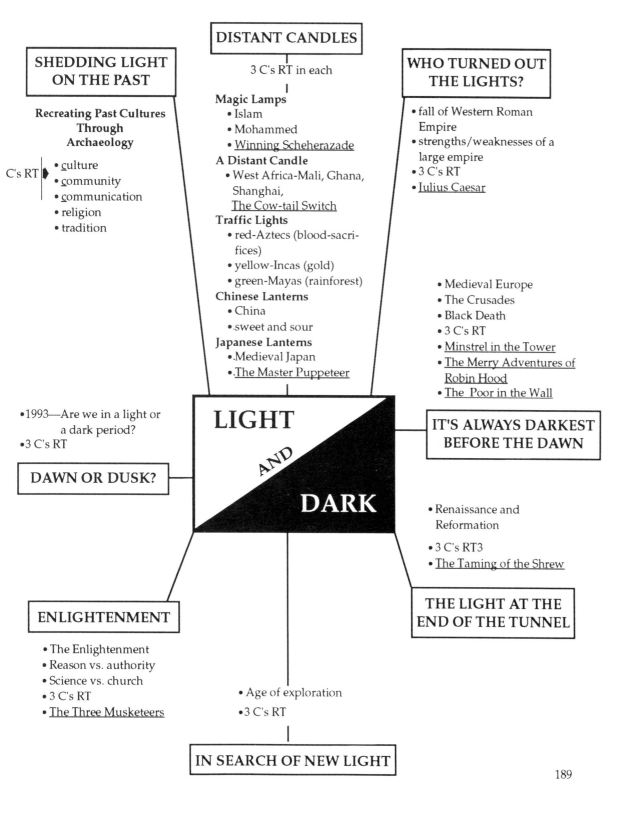

DISTANT CANDLES

3 C's RT in each

Magic Lamps
- Islam
- Mohammed
- <u>Winning Scheherazade</u>

A Distant Candle
- West Africa-Mali, Ghana, Shanghai, <u>The Cow-tail Switch</u>

Traffic Lights
- red-Aztecs (blood-sacrifices)
- yellow-Incas (gold)
- green-Mayas (rainforest)

Chinese Lanterns
- China
- sweet and sour

Japanese Lanterns
- Medieval Japan
- <u>The Master Puppeteer</u>

SHEDDING LIGHT ON THE PAST

Recreating Past Cultures Through Archaeology

C's RT
- culture
- community
- communication
- religion
- tradition

WHO TURNED OUT THE LIGHTS?

- fall of Western Roman Empire
- strengths/weaknesses of a large empire
- 3 C's RT
- <u>Julius Caesar</u>

- Medieval Europe
- The Crusades
- Black Death
- 3 C's RT
- <u>Minstrel in the Tower</u>
- <u>The Merry Adventures of Robin Hood</u>
- <u>The Poor in the Wall</u>

LIGHT AND DARK

- 1993—Are we in a light or a dark period?
- 3 C's RT

DAWN OR DUSK?

IT'S ALWAYS DARKEST BEFORE THE DAWN

- Renaissance and Reformation
- 3 C's RT3
- <u>The Taming of the Shrew</u>

THE LIGHT AT THE END OF THE TUNNEL

ENLIGHTENMENT

- The Enlightenment
- Reason vs. authority
- Science vs. church
- 3 C's RT
- <u>The Three Musketeers</u>

- Age of exploration
- 3 C's RT

IN SEARCH OF NEW LIGHT

189

Tips for Implementation:

- refer to the *Tips for Implementation* for Models 1 and 2
- collaborate with colleagues in other departments to identify the concepts in each subject area that are to be learned
- ensure adequate time to plan—more time will be needed in the second and third subject areas (if it has been some time since teaching those areas, research time needs to be built in)
- ensure all team members are proficient in cooperative learning skills, a requisite skill for creating a brain-compatible environment
- draft a theme which serves as a powerful umbrella over the subject areas to be taught
- inform parents of your plan as well as how the goals of each subject area will be met
- keep a visual in your room which illustrates the relationship of the theme and key points to the district course of study for each of the subjects integrated into your core

Possible Pitfalls:

- see *Possible Pitfalls* for Models 1 and 2
- attempting to do too many concepts in each area
- getting bogged down and doing more of one subject than another
- parents not recognizing that the concepts of each subject area are being addressed and mastered
- credentialing problems—waivers may be necessary

The graphic below illustrates the potential of this model to provide a thoroughly brain-compatible learning environment *from the students' point of view* and from the perspective of their *entire day*.

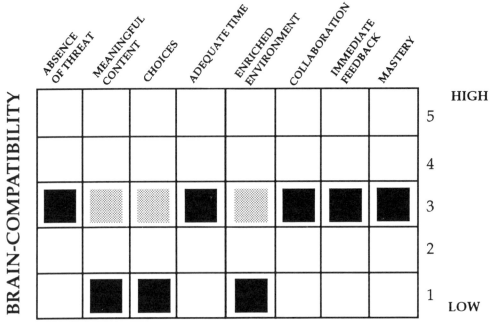

Grey area = potential if curriculum is significantly revised and based upon *here and now*

MODEL 4: INTEGRATED DOUBLE CORE MODEL

As its name implies, this model consists of two integrated cores joined together so that two teachers share the same 60+ students who receive instruction in all four (or more) content areas organized through the same yearlong theme.

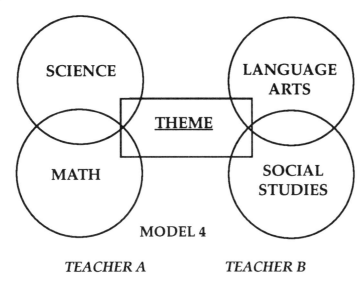

MODEL 4

TEACHER A   *TEACHER B*

In this model, it is imperative that each teacher be aware of what the other is teaching on a daily basis if integration is to be accomplished to the fullest extent possible. Thus, common prep time on a daily basis is essential. Teachers also need to work out the details of the parent orientation and parent closures to present this information together. Planning and coordination are essential in the use of yearlong research projects, group projects as closures to a unit, and assessment for reporting progress and proficiencies.

Among the many advantages of this powerful model is the creation of a sense of connection and family for students and a school-within-a-school buffer for teachers. Bureaucracy is brought down to livable size so that teachers have the necessary flexibility to craft curriculum and learning experiences which allow students to see the connections which make learning exciting, alive, meaningful, reflective of real life, and fun.

Extensive implementation of this model will require massive restructuring of the school on a schoolwide basis, a complete break from a departmentalized mode with its focus on "disciplines." (See discussion of curriculum in Chapter IV.)

Tips for Implementation:

- refer to *Tips for Implementation* for Models 1, 2, and 3; remember they are your building blocks
- schedule the two cores back-to-back

- locate classrooms close to each other, preferably adjacent and with a moveable wall to create one large classroom
- schedule 60+ students on the same schedule
- eliminate bells for class exchanges; instead, let the content dictate the clock; balance of time among subjects should be figured on a yearly/semester basis, not daily or even weekly
- provide daily, joint planning time
- select teachers with a willingness to become/be learners, to research and become knowledgeable (depth and breadth) across multiple curricular areas

Possible Pitfalls:

- see *Possible Pitfalls* for Models 1, 2, and 3
- curriculum still sourced in disciplines rather than real life events and situations
- inadequate preparation or inappropriate instructional strategies for the lengthened time periods
- inflexible scheduling of classes not enabling the double cores to meet back-to-back with the same students
- teachers being assigned to a team by an administrator rather than mutual self-selection
- no training in how to team

The graphic below illustrates the potential of this model to provide a thoroughly brain-compatible learning environment *from the students' point of view* and from the perspective of their *entire day.*

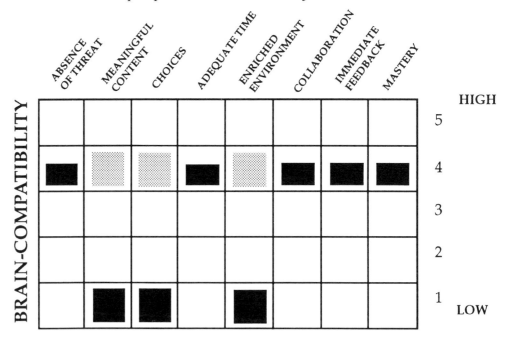

The grey areas reflect the degree of brain-compatibility possible if students' classes outside the four+ subject core are also taught in a brain-compatible way.

MODEL 5: SELF-CONTAINED CORE MODEL

Although common for sixth grade, the self-contained core model* at seventh and eighth grade is a rarity. Often described as the "Renaissance Man" model because of the content expertise demands on teachers, this model, when well executed, has the most potential for being truly brain-compatible. It affords opportunity for the greatest sense of belonging and group development, eliminates inconsistencies in classroom management expectations and communication gap problems, and, above all, it provides maximum flexibility in terms of usage of time, concentration on long-term projects, allowing the flow of the topic to dictate the amount of time spent on any one "subject" during a particular day, etc.

However, and this is a big however, few teachers have the academic background to bring the necessary breadth and depth of knowledge to the multiple subjects contained in the core of four or more subjects. It also requires extensive restructuring of the school and a complete break from the current departmentalized mode with its pictures of "disciplines" as content. The four (or more) subject areas can vary, e.g., social studies, fine arts, science, and language arts, or physical education, math, science, and social studies, etc.

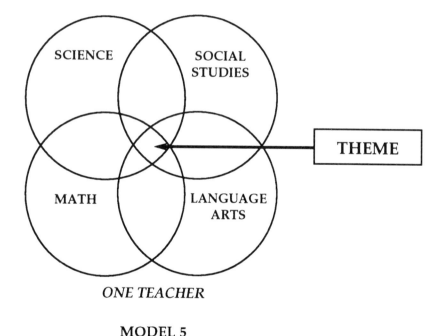

ONE TEACHER

MODEL 5

---

*Do note that the self-contained core model has little in common with the isolated state of the typical self-contained elementary classroom. In the ITI self-contained core, there is great movement and interchange among students—out to the real world, resource people into the classroom, cross-age activities and electives provided by other staff and community members, etc.

Tips for Implementation:

- refer to the *Tips for Implementation* for Models 1, 2, 3, and 4
- schedule blocks of time which will provide four (or more) contiguous class periods
- select teachers who are knowledgeable in all core subjects
- identify a schoolwide/grade level-wide definition of the skills and concepts which need to be taught in all four subject areas
- provide adequate planning/curriculum writing time for networking with other teachers in order to receive necessary content support

Possible Pitfalls:

- see *Possible Pitfalls* for Models 1, 2, 3, and 4
- need for a multiple subject credential
- not enough time in the schedule for networking or planning
- four periods not scheduled together in a single block

The graphic below illustrates the potential of this model to provide a thoroughly brain-compatible learning environment *from the students' point of view* and from the perspective of their *entire day.*

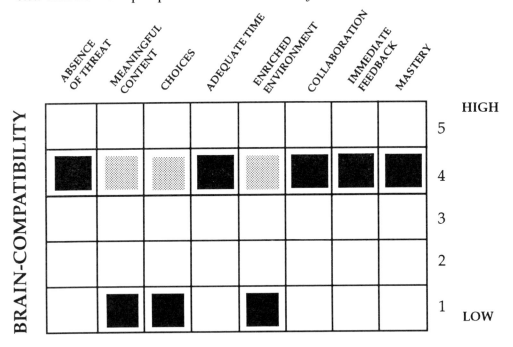

Grey area = potential if curriculum is significantly revised and based upon *here and now*

Comments—These five models are not the only vehicles for transitioning into a fully brain-compatible ITI school; however they provide teachers with some starting points.

APPENDIX A
CHARACTERISTICS
OF MIDDLE GRADE STUDENTS[1]

A. INTELLECTUAL DEVELOPMENT

Middle Grade Students:

1 Display a wide range of individual intellectual development as their minds experience transition from the concrete-manipulatory stage to the capacity for abstract thought. This transition ultimately makes possible:

- Propositional thought
- Consideration of ideas contrary to fact
- Reasoning with hypotheses involving two or more variables
- Appreciation for the elegance of mathematical logic expressed in symbols
- Insight into the nuances of poetic metaphor and musical notation
- Analysis of the power of a political ideology
- Ability to project thought into the future, to anticipate, and to formulate goals
- Insight into the sources of previously unquestioned attitudes, behaviors, and values
- Interpretation of larger concepts and generalizations of traditional wisdom expressed through sayings, axioms, and aphorisms

2 Are intensely curious;

3 Prefer active over passive learning experiences; favor interaction with peers during learning activities;

4 Exhibit a strong willingness to learn things they consider to be useful; enjoy using skills to solve real life problems;

5 Are egocentric; argue to convince others; exhibit independent, critical thought;

6 Consider academic goals as a secondary level of priority; personal-social concerns dominate thoughts and activities;

7 Experience the phenomenon of metacognition—the ability to know what one knows and does not know;

8 Are intellectually at-risk; face decisions that have the potential to affect major academic values with lifelong consequences.

B. Physical Development

Middle Grade Students:

1 Experience accelerated physical development marked by increases in weight, height, heart size, lung capacity, and muscular strength;

2 Mature at varying rates of speed. Girls tend to be taller than boys for the first two years of early adolescence and are ordinarily more physically developed than boys;

3 Experience bone growth faster than muscle development; uneven muscle/bone development results in lack of coordination and awkwardness; bones may lack protection of covering muscles and supporting tendons;

4 Reflect a wide range of individual differences which begin to appear in prepubertal and pubertal stages of development. Boys tend to lag behind girls. There are marked individual differences in physical development for boys and girls. The greatest variability in physiological development and size occurs at about age thirteen;

5 Experience biological development five years sooner than adolescents of the last century; the average age of menarche has dropped from seventeen to twelve years of age;

6 Face responsibility for sexual behavior before full emotional and social maturity has occurred;

7 Show changes in body contour including temporarily large noses, protruding ears, long arms; have posture problems;

8 Are often disturbed by body changes:

  • Girls are anxious about physical changes that accompany sexual maturation;
  • Boys are anxious about receding chins, cowlicks, dimples, and changes in their voices;

9 Experience fluctuations in basal metabolism which can cause extreme restlessness at times and equally extreme listlessness at other moments;

10 Have ravenous appetites and peculiar tastes; may overtax digestive system with large quantities of improper foods;

11 Lack physical health; have poor levels of endurance, strength, and flexibility; as a group are fatter and unhealthier;

12 Are physically at-risk; major causes of death are homicide, suicide, accident, and leukemia.

C. Psychological Development

Middle Grade Students:

1 Are often erratic and inconsistent in their behavior; anxiety and fear are contrasted with periods of bravado; feelings shift between superiority and inferiority;

2 Have chemical and hormonal imbalances which often trigger emotions that are frightening and poorly understood; may regress to more childish behavior patterns at this point;

3 Are easily offended and are sensitive to criticism of personal shortcomings;

4 Tend to exaggerate simple occurrences and believe that personal problems, experiences, and feelings are unique to themselves;

5 Are moody, restless; often feel self-conscious and alienated; lack self-esteem; are introspective;

6 Are searching for adult identity and acceptance even in the midst of intense peer group relationships;

7 Are vulnerable to naive opinions, one-sided arguments;

8 Are searching to form a conscious sense of individual uniqueness— "Who am I?";

9 Have emerging sense of humor based on increased intellectual ability to see abstract relationships; appreciate the "double entendre";

10 Are basically optimistic, hopeful;

11 Are psychologically at-risk; at no other point in human development is an individual likely to encounter so much diversity in relation to oneself and others.

D. Social Development

Middle Grade Students:

1 Experience often traumatic conflicts due to conflicting loyalties to peer groups and family;

2 Refer to peers as sources for standards and models of behavior; media heroes and heroines are also singularly important in shaping both behavior and fashion;

3 May be rebellious towards parents but still strongly dependent on parental values; want to make own choices, but the authority of the family is a critical factor in ultimate decisions;

4 Are impacted by high level of mobility in society; may become anxious and disoriented when peer group ties are broken because of family relocation to other communities;

5 Are often confused and frightened by new school settings which are large and impersonal;

6 Act out unusual or drastic behavior at times; may be aggressive, daring, boisterous, argumentative;

7 Are fiercely loyal to peer group values; sometimes cruel or insensitive to those outside the peer group;

8 Want to know and feel that significant adults, including parents and teachers, love and accept them; need frequent affirmation;

9 Sense negative impact of adolescent behaviors on parents and teachers; realize thin edge between tolerance and rejection; feelings of adult rejection drive the adolescent into the relatively secure social environment of the peer group;

10 Strive to define sex role characteristics; search to establish positive social relationships with members of the same and opposite sex;

11 Experience low risk-trust relationships with adults who show lack of sensitivity to adolescent characteristics and needs;

12 Challenge authority figures; test limits of acceptable behavior;

13 Are socially at-risk; adult values are largely shaped conceptually during adolescence; negative interactions with peers, parents, and teachers may compromise ideals and commitments.

E. Moral and Ethical Development

Middle Grade Students:

1 Are essentially idealistic; have a strong sense of fairness in human relationships;

2 Experience thoughts and feelings of awe and wonder related to their expanding intellectual and emotional awareness;

3 Ask large, unanswerable questions about the meaning of life; do not expect absolute answers but are turned off by trivial adult responses;

4 Are reflective, analytical, and introspective about their thoughts and feelings;

5 Confront hard moral and ethical questions for which they are unprepared to cope;

6 Are at-risk in the development of moral and ethical choices and behaviors; primary dependency on the influences of home and church for moral and ethical development seriously compromises adolescents for whom these resources are absent; adolescents want to explore the moral and ethical issues which are confronted in the curriculum, in the media, and in the daily interactions they experience in their families and peer groups.

[1] Reprinted, by permission, from *Caught in the Middle: Educational Reform for Young Adolescents in California Public Schools*, copyright 1987, California Department of Education, P. O. Box 271, Sacramento, CA 95812-0271.

APPENDIX A

APPENDIX B
THE CHEMISTRY
OF NURTURING INTELLIGENCE

Recent research regarding poor nutrition and drugs on the neurons in the brain has special interest for middle school students and parents. In spite of all the data about nutrition today, the brain may be the most undernourished and abused organ in the human body.

The human brain weighs about three pounds, about two percent of our total body weight. The brain cannot store or borrow energy from any other part of the body; it must be produced in the neurons of the brain. The brain is totally dependent upon the blood system to provide a continuous supply of glucose and oxygen. Brain cells burn 50 percent of all the glucose carried by the blood system.

Scientists believe that over 100,000 chemical reactions take place each second in the brain, requiring incredible amounts of energy. If you have been exhausted after periods of intense concentration, it might have been due to your brain using as many calories during this activity as it would have used during an exhausting physical workout! One-third of the calories we consume are used by the brain.

Junk food eaten by teenagers today is high in fat and low in protein. This loads the bloodstream with glucose. To counteract (clean up) this overload, the body produces insulin, a blood sugar-lowering hormone. Insulin tells the organs to take glucose out of the blood, which they do, leaving very little for the brain. Thus, the brain cannot generate and maintain neurotransmitters to carry on their functions at the optimal level.

What impact might this have on learning? Try to remember the last time you consumed a large quantity of foods high in fat and low in protein (pizza, milkshake, french fries, candy bars, cheeseburger). Think back to how you felt later in the day—sleepy, lethargic, not able to concentrate. Consider what teenagers eat and also what they don't eat. Girls, especially concerned about weight, severely restrict their intake of protein and carbohydrates.

Neurotransmitters, which are generated and maintained by the brain, are powerful chemicals which affect memory, intelligence, alertness, and aggression. The brain produces about 50 different neurotransmitters. Ten of the more influential are:

- Endorphin—the brain's painkiller, released during times of extreme stress and joy!
- Dopamine—sexual arousal, initiating and coordinating movement

- Adrenaline—mood elevating, assertiveness, and mental alertness
- Noradrenalin—mood elevating, assertiveness, and mental alertness
- Acetylcholine—memory enhancing and helps control movement
- Serotonin—induces sleep and calms and counter-balances adrenaline and noradrenalin
- GABA (Gamma Amino Butyric Acid)—inhibitor for chronic anxiety, helps concentrate mental focus
- Glycine—inhibitor for preventing epilepsy
- Histamine—sensory integration in the thalamus of the brain
- Glutamic acid—mental activity and learning

All neurotransmitters are produced from amino acids found in protein. Knowing this may deter individuals from seriously thinking about attempting to diet using a plan that is low in protein. Some signs of not having enough amino acids in the diet include: apathy, lethargy, loss of concentration, depression, and insomnia. Brain researchers have found that brain neurotransmitter levels can be influenced by a single meal.

The production of neurotransmitters is also seriously affected by the use of any drugs, legal or illegal. Using drugs causes the levels of neurotransmitters to rise in the synaptic gaps of neurotransmitter-using neurons. For example, researchers think the use of cocaine creates an increase in the levels of dopamine being released into the synaptic gaps of dopamine-using neurons. Marijuana is thought to cause an increase in the serotonin in the synaptic gaps of serotonin-using neurons, which accounts for its sedative effects. Amphetamines cause increased production of noradrenalin in the noradrenalin-using neurons. The use of drugs only temporarily causes the release of the neurotransmitters. This explains why using these drugs over a long period of time causes the drugs to seemingly lose their effects. When drug users talk about "coming down" or "crashing," it is because the neurotransmitter reserves have been exhausted and are unable to be further stimulated.

The long-term result of all this is that the brain needs large quantities of amino acids, vitamins, and minerals in order to counteract the inadequate neurotransmitter levels. The junk food diets of American teenagers are not capable of providing these increased amounts to insure the brain of operating at its highest capabilities. If the diets of America's teenagers were adequate, perhaps it would be unnecessary for individuals to turn to the use of anti-depressants, anti-anxiety, and recreational drugs to make up for low neurotransmitter levels.[1]

GLOSSARY

Authentic Assessment—focus of a nationwide movement in education which advocates using assessment tools and processes which require students to apply what they have learned to real world situations and which apply standards of performance from the adult world

Bay Area Middle School Project (BAMS)—a project using the ITI middle school model which consists of three model middle schools plus an informal network of schools also seeking to become middle school models. The project is privately funded by the David and Lucile Packard Foundation

Being There - the most powerful input to the brain is being in a real world location; activates all 19 senses thereby significantly increasing learning (pattern identification and program-building)

Bloom's Taxonomy—a model developed by Benjamin Bloom, et al, used in developing questioning strategies. The process verbs characterizing each level are used to develop inquiries

Brain stem/reptilian brain— one of the three levels of the triune brain as described by Dr. Paul MacLean. This level is responsible for survival during life-threatening situations. There is no language or visual memory associated with this level of the brain

Brain-compatible learning environment—coined by Leslie A. Hart in his book, *Human Brain and Human Learning,* it is a key concept in the Kovalik Integrated Thematic Instruction (ITI) model. A brain-compatible environment is one which allows the brain to work as it naturally, and thus most powerfully, works

Brain-compatible components—are eight conditions that enhance and support lifelong learning. They are: Absence of Threat, Meaningful Content, Choices, Adequate Time, Enriched Environment, Collaboration, Immediate Feedback, Mastery/Application

"3 C's" of Assessment - a process by which student achievement is assessed in an ITI classroom. The expectation is for mastery of key points by all students on an "A/no credit" basis; demonstration of mastery is through performance completing inquiries

"C-U-E"—an acronym describing the three ways information can be presented in order for the learner to readily retrieve it. The "C" stands for creative, the "U" for useful and the "E" for emotional bridge

Cerebral cortex—one of the three levels of the triune brain described by Dr. Paul MacLean. This is the part of the brain where cognitive learning takes place, e.g., reading, writing, mathematics, geography

Classroom leadership—consists of those strategies necessary for the adequate maintenance of a classroom where students can learn, free from threat and disruptions by other students

Collaboration—one of the eight brain-compatible elements of the ITI model which stresses the importance of allowing students not only to work in groups but to be involved in processing of information in collaborative ways

Common core of knowledge—redefined in the ITI model to mean those concepts, skills, knowledge, and attitudes/values essential to participate in a democracy and our high-tech society

Component—an integral structure of the ITI model; the framework for one month (approximately) of the yearlong theme

Coordinated model—one of the middle school ITI transition models. It involves four content teachers working together using the same central yearlong theme. The teachers meet to coordinate units or topics to show curriculum connections for students

Core class—a class which meets for at least two class periods with the same teacher to study different content areas

Curriculum frameworks—curriculum guidelines for each subject area drawn up by state departments of education for use in local districts

Dendrites—structures found on the neurons which are responsible for transmitting messages from one neuron to the next. One dendrite has the capability of communicating with at least 600,000 other dendrites

Developmentally appropriate—concepts and/or facts which are understandable (versus memorizable) by students given the current degree of development of the brain. Dr. Larry Lowery discusses the biological stages of thinking and learning in his book, *Thinking and Learning: Matching Developmental Stages with Curriculum and Instruction*

Direct instruction—the 11 to 16 minutes of teacher presentation of a key point which provides the focus of the classroom activities; direct instruction is only one way of providing such a focus for student work

Downshifting—shifting out of the cerebral cortex where cognitive learning takes place in response to a highly emotional situation (positive or negative) or in response to a life threatening situation

Evaluation mindmap—a mindmap used whenever students are involved in the evaluation of presentations, reports or any other activity. It is a positive, not negative, tool which asks, "What could be improved?" and "What was good about the presentation?"

Hands-on experiences—a term describing two levels of input: of the real thing and hands-on of something that is symbolic or representing a real thing, such as a real frog or a plastic model

Healthful environment—a classroom environment which includes as much of nature as possible. Teachers can create a nature-like environment incorporating the proper combination of plants, colors, music, and light into their classroom

Imaging—refers to the ability to create a visual image in one's mind representing what words mean, i.e., DOG - seeing a big, fluffy Collie, etc. According to brain research, the brain processes and stores images not the sound of words (unless there is a highly emotional event). Students who cannot do this have difficulty comprehending what they read or hear

Immersion—a rich environment that simulates as richly as is possible the real life environment being studied, such as transforming a classroom into wetlands or pond or a period of history to allow students the opportunity to experience or role-play being alive during that period

Input, types of—1. Being there, physically being in the real world environment; 2. Immersion—full simulation of the real world environment, includes many real world things; 3. Hands-on of the real thing e.g., (frog); 4. Hands-on of representation (e.g., plastic model of a frog); 5. Second-hand— pictorial representation, written word (e.g., pictures, videos, or stories about frogs); 6. Symbolic— mathematics, phonics, grammar

Inquiry—a key curriculum development structure in the ITI model--an activity which expands or supports a key point

Integrated Core Model—a middle school ITI model where one teacher will have the same group of students for at least two or three class periods. The teacher will coordinate all subjects he/she is assigned to teach around a central yearlong theme

Integrated Single Subject Model—a middle school ITI model designed for use in a single subject or departmentalized classroom in one curricular area

Integrated Thematic Instruction (ITI)—the name given to a brain-compatible, fully integrated instructional model developed by Susan Kovalik of Susan Kovalik & Associates. The model consists of a central yearlong theme, monthly components, weekly topics, key points, inquiries and political/social action

Key point—essential knowledge, skill, attitude/value all students are expected to master

Learners' Manifesto—developed by Frank Smith in, *Insult to Intelligence: The Bureaucratic Invasion of Our Classrooms*, includes the following maxims: The brain is always learning; Learning does not require coercion or irrelevant reward; Learning must be meaningful; Learning is incidental; Learning is collaborative; The consequences of worthwhile learning are obvious; Learning always involves feelings; Learning must be free of risk

Lifelong Guidelines—the parameters for classroom/schoolwide interactions with other students and staff. They are TRUSTWORTHINESS, TRUTHFULNESS, ACTIVE LISTENING, NO PUT DOWNS and PERSONAL BEST

LIFESKILLS—are 15 personal/social parameters that promote PERSONAL BEST. They include: Integrity, Initiative, Flexibility, Perseverance, Organization, Sense of Humor, Effort, Common Sense, Problem-Solving, Responsibility, Patience, Friendship, Curiosity, Cooperation, Caring

Limbic system—the level of the triune brain described by Dr. Paul MacLean which has to do with emotions. The brain downshifts to this area when confronted by a highly emotional situation--positive or negative. There is little language associated with this level of the brain beyond expletives

Mid-California Science Improvement Program (MCSIP)—funded by the David and Lucile Packard Foundation, which uses the ITI model with a focus on science K-6. Involves 250 teachers from 21 schools in six California counties

Mindmapping—an instructional strategy where information is represented visually usually as a web or cluster around the main idea with symbols and colors rather than in traditional outline form

Neurons—the building block of intelligence. The human brain is thought to have over 100 billion neurons. They cannot repair or reproduce themselves. One neuron has the capability of communicating with at least 600,000 other neurons

Neurotransmitters—the chemicals produced by the brain which enable neurons to communicate with each other. There are at least 50 known neurotransmitters produced by the brain. The 10 major ones are: endorphin, dopamine, adrenaline, noradrenalin, acetylcholine, serotonin, GABA, glycine, histamine, and glutamic acid

Paradigm—a set of rules or boundaries through which we filter incoming information. Rigid, inflexible paradigms can make change almost impossible

Parent closure—an integral part of the ITI model where students invite their parents into school and demonstrate to them their ability to apply the concepts they have been learning

Parent orientation night—an integral part of the ITI model where teachers invite the parents of their students into school one evening during the very first week of school to explain the ITI model and the year theme. Teachers provide a parent packet containing information which explains the brain research behind the ITI model and provides a preview of the upcoming school year

Pattern-seeking—a key concept of brain-compatibility; describes the means by which the brain makes meaning from incoming data bits. Some of the major pattern categories include objects, actions, procedures, situations, relationships, and systems

Political/social action—an integral part of the ITI model which provides students a vehicle for applying what they learn to real world problems. It assists students in becoming contributing citizens with concerns for local as well as global problems

Programs—a key concept of brain-compatibility describing how the brain stores and uses what it learns. It is defined as "a personal goal achieved by a sequence of steps or actions" which becomes stored in the brain for later retrieval when an individual needs it. Every goal we accomplish is due to implementation of a program or programs

Restructuring—a term describing the current reform effort in the nation. Often defined too narrowly as dealing with structure issues only, such as changing the traditional departmentalized structure system

Self-Contained Core Model—the middle school ITI model where one teacher will have a group of students for at least four class periods in which all four major subjects will be integrated around a central yearlong theme

Set up time—the period of at least a month at the beginning of a semester or school year where teachers introduce their students to the ITI model

Seven Intelligences—problem-solving or product-producing capabilities identified by Howard Gardner: logical-mathematical, linguistic, spatial, bodily-kinesthetic, musical, intrapersonal, and interpersonal. We are born with all seven but will develop each according to cultural preference demands and the individual's inclinations and experience

Student handbook—a handbook to explain the ITI model written especially for students who enter an ITI classroom after the beginning of a semester or year

Symbolic input—the most difficult way for the brain to input information such as phonics, grammar, algebra

Theme math—using the content subject areas to frame math problems. To integrate math, all you need are numbers plus events, places, or things for context

Tribes—a book and program for social development and cooperative learning; identifies the steps of group development, such as inclusion, influence and affection. Created by Jeanne Gibbs

Triune brain—refers to the three levels of the brain as developed by Dr. Paul MacLean. The triune brain is one way of looking at the brain as the organ for learning

Upshifting—refers to the brain being able to move from the lower levels of the triune brain (brain stem and limbic system) to the cerebral cortex where cognitive learning takes place

Weekly topics—an integral structure of the ITI model; framework for dividing each monthly component into (approximately) weekly topics or areas

Yearlong research projects—assignments students choose during the first two weeks of school to become the "expert" on for the class. They will research and present their information toward the end of the school year

Yearlong theme—assignments students choose during the first two weeks of school to become the "expert." They research and present their information to the class

FOOTNOTES

Introduction

1 James Beane, *A Middle School Curriculum from Rhetoric to Reality* (Ohio: West-Camp Press, Inc., 1990), p. 2.

2 Beane, p. 64.

Chapter I How the Brain Learns

1 Leslie Hart, *Human Brain and Human Learning* (Arizona: Books for Educators, 1983), p. xiv.

2 Marion Cleeves Diamond, *Enriching Heredity: The Impact of the Environment on the Anatomy of the Brain* (New York: Free Press, 1988), chapter 5.

3 Robert Rivlin and Karen Gravelle, *Deciphering the Senses* (New York: Simon and Schuster, 1984), chapter 1.

4 Leslie Hart, *Human Brain and Human Learning* (Arizona: Books for Educators, 1983), p. 125.

5 Hart, p. 125.

6 Hart, p. 126.

7 Reuven Feuerstein, *Don't Accept Me As I Am* (New York: Plenum Press, 1988), p. 5.

8 Ned Hermann, *The Creative Brain* (No. Carolina: Brain Books, 1989), p. 33.

9 Hermann, p. 34.

10 Howard Gardner, *Frames of Mind* (New York: Basic Books, Inc., 1983), p. x.

11 Gardner, p. xiii.

12 Gardner, p. xi.

13 Gardner, pp. 60-61.

14 Gardner, p. 77.

15 Lawrence F. Lowery, *Thinking and Learning: Matching Developmental Stages with Curriculum and Instuction* (California: Midwest Publications, 1989), p. 2.

16 Gardner, p. 190.

17 Hart, p. 57.

18 Hart, p. 190.

19 Hart, p. 190.

20 Hart, p. 65.

21 Hart, p. 56.

22 Hart, p. 89.

23 Hart, p. 190.

24 Hart, p. 88.

25 Hart, p. 88.

26 Hart, p. 89.

Chapter II Elements of a Brain-Compatible Environment

1 Leslie Hart, *Human Brain and Human Learning* (Arizona: Books for Educators, 1983), p. 44.

2 Pat Belvel, *Peer Coaching Manual* (San Jose: Training & Consulting Institute, 1992), pp. 13-17.

3 Belvel, p. 34.

4 Paul Messier, *The Brain: Research Findings Undergirding Innovative Brain-Based Learning Models*, reprinted by permission in *1990 Summer Institute: Decade of the Brain* by Susan Kovalik and Associates (Arizona, 1990), pp. 1-2.

5 Frank Smith, *Insult to Intelligence: The Bureaucratic Invasion of Our Classrooms* (New York: Arbor House, 1986), p. 62.

6 Susan Kovalik, *Integrated Thematic Instruction: The Model* (Arizona: Susan Kovalik & Associates, 1992), p. 14.

7 Smith, p. 46.

8 Frank Smith, *to think* (New York: Teachers College Press, 1990), pp. 27-28.

9 Smith, p. 27.

10 Richard Wurman, *Information Anxiety* (New York: Doubleday, 1989), cover.

11 Hart, p. 67.

12 Beverly Merz, "The Case of Mystery Epidemic"(*Good Housekeeping,* March 1992) and Claire Safran, "Schools That Make Kids Sick"(*Good Houskeeping,* March 1992).

13 Frank Smith, *Insult to Intelligence, the Bureacratic Invasion of our Classrooms* (New York: Arbor house, 1986), p. 59.

14 Elizabeth Cohen, *Designing Groupwork: Strategies for Heterogeneous Classroom* (New York: Teachers College Press, 1986), p. 10.

15 Brady, p.6.

Chapter III The Stuff of Curriculum—Taking a New Look at an Old Issue

1 James Beane, *A Middle School Curriculum from Rhetoric to Reality* (Ohio: West-Camp Press, Inc., 1990), p. 2.

2 Beane, p. 1.

3 John Taylor Gatto, "Houses, Boats, Families and the Business of Schooling" (The Sun Magazine, 1993), paragraph VI.

4 Barbara Benham Tye, *Multiple Realities* (Maryland: University Press of America, 1985), p. 8.

5 Gatto, paragraph VI.

6 Tye, pp. 8-9.

7 Arthur G. Powell, Eleanor Farrar, David K. Cohen, *The Shopping Mall High School: Winners and Losers in the Educational Marketplace* (Boston: Houghton Mifflin Co.), p. 244.

8 Powell, p. 246.

9 Tye, p. 10.

10. Ken Tye, *The Junior High: School in Search of a Mission* (Maryland: University of America Press, Inc., 1985), p. 35.

11 Tye, p. 37.

12 Tye, p. 36.

13 Tye, p. 35.

14 Harvey A. Averch and others, *How Effective is Schooling?* (California: The Rand Corporation, 1972), pp. x, xiii.

15 Christopher Jencks and others, *Inequality* (New York: Basic Books, 1972), p. 95.

16 Beane, p. 5.

17 Richard Dawkins, *The Selfish Gene* (England: Oxford University Press, 1976), p. 13.

18 Richard Bergland, *Fabric of Mind* (New York Oxford Press, 1985) p. 7.

19 Bergland, pp. 26-27.

20 Bergland, p. 26.

21 Bergland, p. 27.

22 Al Shanker, quoted during an AFT address.

23 Pat Roy, "Revisiting Cooperative Learning," Outcomes-Based Education Conference, Phoenix, Arizona, November 17, 1992.

24 Marion Brady, *What's Worth Teaching? Selecting, Organizing, and Integrating Knowledge* (State University of New York Press, 1989) p. 122.

25 Brady, p. 122.

26 Brady, p. 122.

27 Brady, p. 123.

28 Brady, p. 123.

29 Brady, p. 125.

30 Heidi Jacobs, editor, *Interdisciplinary Curriculum: Design and Implementation* (Virginia: ASCD, 1989) p. 14.

31 Marion Brady, *Curriculum: The Basics,* pp., 7-8.

32 Hart, p. 75.

33 Carl Glickman, "Revisiting Site-Based Management", Outcomes-Based Education Conference, Phoenix, Arizona, November 16, 1992.

34 Mihaly Csikszentmihalyi, *Flow: The Psychology of Optimal Experience* (New York: Harper and Row, 1990), pp. 74-75.

35 Renate and Geoffrey Caine, *Making Connections: Teaching and the Human Brain* (Virginia: ASCD, 1991), p. 156.

36 Beane, pp.4- 6.

37 Beane, p. 41.

38 Marion Brady, *What's Worth Teaching? Selecting, Organizing and Integrating Knowledge* (New York, 1989), p. 14.

39 Brady, p. 20.

40 Brady, p. 6.

41 Brady, pp. 26-28.

42 Brady, pp. 35-43.

43 Brady, pp. 43-53.

44 Brady, pp. 56-64.

45 Brady, pp. 53-56.

46 Brady, p. 53.

47 Brady, p. 56.

48 Brady, p. 65.

49 Brady, p. 33.

50 Michael W. Kirst, *Who Controls Our Schools? American Values in Conflict* (Stanford Alumni Association, 1984), p. 160.

Chapter V Identifying Key Points

1 Frank Smith, *Insult to Intelligence: The Bureaucratic Invasion of our Classrooms* (New York, 1986), pp. 29.

2 Smith, p. 18.

3 Smith, p. 27.

4 Smith, p. 29.

5 Smith, p. 28.

6 Smith, pp. 29-30.

7 Smith, pp. 32

Chapter VI Developing Inquiries

1 John Taylor Gatto, The Exhausted School (The Oxford Village Press ,1993) p. 16.

2. Renate and Geoffrey Caine, *Making Connections: Teaching and the Human Brain* (Virginia: ASCD, 1991), p. 95

3 Caine, p. 95.

4 Caine, p. 97

5 Caine, p. 97.

6 Caine, ;. 97

7 Caine, p. 97.

8 Caine, p. 99.

9 Caine, p. 99.

10 Caine p. 101.

11 Pat Belvel, *Peer Coaching Manual* (San Jose: Training & Consulting Institute, 1992), pp. 13-17

12 Belvel, p. 14

Chapter VIII Transition

1 William Bridges, *Managing Transitions: Making the Most of Change* (Addison-Wesley Publishing Company, Inc.,1991), p. 3

2 Bridges, p. 3.

3 Bridges, p. 4.

4 Bridges, p. 5.

PRACTICAL APPLICATIONS OF RESEARCH
INTO HOW THE HUMAN BRAIN LEARNS

HUMAN BRAIN AND HUMAN LEARNING
by Leslie A. Hart . . . . $ 17.95

This is a truly revolutionary book, one sorely needed if we are to design classrooms to meet the challenges of life in the 21st century. Hart describes a "brain-compatible environment" and how to open the doorway to quantum leaps in student outcomes. The human brain operates most powerfully when it is allowed to function consistently with its natural processes. *(Published by Books for Educators, 1983.)*

"ANCHOR" MATH: The Brain-Compatible Approach to Learning
by Leslie A. Hart . . . . $ 16.95

This is a book written for teachers who find that students respond to math as if it were of another world and had nothing to do with them. An informal book for all who teach elementary math and want to greatly increase student achievement, it explores the ways of "anchoring" math to the real world as perceived and processed by a student's mind. A follow-up book to *Human Brain and Human Learning*, it discusses how to teach math in a brain-compatible way. Perceptive, fresh, challenging. Just the tool needed to breathe real life into math and significantly increase student learning. *(Published by Books for Educators, 1992.)*

IN THEIR OWN WAY by Thomas Armstrong . . . . $ 8.95

Practical advice for parents on how to develop children's strengths by encouraging preferred learning styles. Never labeling students "gifted" or "learning disabled," Thomas Armstrong identifies the various learning styles that make independent success possible. Examples of how to assist children to develop their latent abilities both inside and outside the classroom are provided. *(Published by Tarcher Press, 1987.)*

FRAMES OF MIND: Theory of Multiple Intelligences
by Howard Gardner . . . . $ 16.00

This book explodes the notion of a "generic" intelligence. Instead we have at least seven major problem-solving capacities, each of which operates from a different area of our brain. Of the seven, the typical school curriculum addresses only two. Yet the other five intelligences are essential for success in life. This information is vital for anyone involved in curriculum development. *(Published by Basic Books, Inc., 1983.)*

VISUALIZING & VERBALIZING FOR LANGUAGE COMPREHENSION &
THINKING (A Teacher's Manual) by Nanci Bell . . . . $ 29.95

For every teacher and parent with a child who decodes at grade level but struggles to comprehend, this book will open doors for you. Metaphorically speaking, the mind's link to language is through pictures. Those who cannot or do not make pictures (visualize) in their head to capture the content as they listen or read will not be able to comprehend. This is a "how to" manual for helping students (child or adult) create the "hardwiring" in their brains necessary to visualize and thus capture meaning from incoming language. *(Published by Academy of Reading, 1991.)*

MAKING CONNECTIONS: Teaching and the Human Brain
by Renate and Geoffrey Caine . . . . $ 15.95

A flagship book by ASCD (Association for Supervision and Curriculum Development) marking a new era in their leadership in curriculum and instruction. Provides a comprehensive synthesis of current brain research — readable and useful. *(Published by ASCD, 1991.)*

ENDANGERED MINDS: Why Our Children Don't Think
by Jane Healy, Ph.D. . . . . $ 11.00

Recipient of the 1991 Susan Kovalik Gold Medal Award for the best teacher resource book, Dr. Healy examines the reasons why our children are less able to concentrate, less able to absorb and analyze information, and less able literally to THINK than the generations that preceded them. Her in-depth exploration of the impact of extensive TV and video experience on the left hemisphere and language processing is sobering and suggestive of the need for massive restructuring of our curriculum and classrooms. *(Published by Simon & Schuster, 1990.)*

YOUR CHILD'S GROWING MIND: A Guide to Learning and Brain Development From Birth to Adolescence by Jane Healy, Ph.D. . . . . . . $ 9.95

A clear, laymen's translation of the most current scientific theories on brain and nervous system development into practical information for parents (and teachers). Provides a detailed explanation of how children develop language and memory and addresses academic learning—reading, writing, spelling, mathematics. *(Published by Doubleday, 1987.)*

THE ABSORBENT MIND by Maria Montessori . . . . $ 9.95

Designed initially for the indigent of Italy's slums and now made available primarily for the children of the affluent in private schools, Maria Montessori's educational methods and the observations and theories upon which they are based have stood the test of time and recent brain research. An important handbook for parents and teachers alike. *(Published by Delta Press, 1967.)*

INSULT TO INTELLIGENCE by Frank Smith . . . . $ 16.95

Using brain research, Frank Smith outlines the Learner's Manifesto: The brain is always learning; learning must be meaningful; it does not require coercion or irrelevant reward; it is incidental; it is collaborative; the consequences of worthwhile learning are obvious; learning always involves feelings and it must be free of risks. Examine why the basal readers, electronic workbooks and other computer programs don't lead to improved performance and what we can do to improve our schools. *(Published by Arbor House, 1986.)*

THINKING AND LEARNING: Matching Developmental Stages With Curriculum and Instruction by Larry Lowery . . . . $ 10.95

A concise description of the evolving thinking processes of children, this is a handy tool at a school or district level for examining curriculum content and determining what is age-appropriate for our students and thus understandable (rather than memorizable). Our textbooks are wildly inappropriate in many areas! *(Published by Midwest Publications, 1989.)*

2

to think by Frank Smith . . . . $ 18.95

This is a book to fascinate you and challenge you. Is there such a thing as "thinking skills"? Does the brain have to be (or can it be) taught to think and problem-solve? According to Frank Smith, "No," but we can and should give children ample opportunities to practice problem-solving — problem-solving real-world, worthwhile problems. Join him for an analysis of the language of thinking and of the common assumptions that many different aspects of thinking represent distinct mental processes. Written from a rare combination of scholarship, research background, respect for the human brain and sympathetic understanding of teaching. *(Published by Teachers College Press, 1990.)*

BRAIN FACTS: A Primer on the Brain and Nervous System
by the Society for Neuroscience . . . . $ 2.50

This 32-page booklet provides a clear, non-technical description of the basic neurological functions including brain development, sensation and perception, learning and memory, and how movement occurs. Superb illustrations. *(1990.)*

RETHINKING THE CLASSROOM

INTEGRATED THEMATIC INSTRUCTION: The Model
by Susan Kovalik (Replaces **TEACHERS MAKE THE DIFFERENCE)**
Second edition, 1993 . . . . $ 24.95

This book is a result of working with teachers in schools which have adopted the ITI model districtwide. It provides a step-by-step discussion of how to implement ITI. What are the readiness factors for the teacher, classroom, school? How are state and district guidelines incorporated into a yearlong theme? What are possible starting points: weeklong themes, monthlong and, finally, yearlong themes where all content and skills are woven together in a meaningful package? Examples abound! *(Published by Susan Kovalik & Associates, 1992.)*

KID'S EYE VIEW OF SCIENCE: A Teacher's Handbook for Implementing an Integrated Thematic Approach to Science, K-6
by Susan Kovalik and Karen Olsen . . . . $ 21.95

Kid's Eye View will change forever how you think about science and about learning. Written to include the latest in brain research and curriculum development, it has suggestions and guidelines for both district level and classroom implementation. This book provides teachers with the tools needed to throw open the doors of natural curiosity and elicit high levels of thinking and problem-solving. Join "Mary Froggins" on her campaign to make science the core of your integrated curriculum. *(Published by the Center for the Future of Public Education, 1991.)*

CLASSROOM OF THE 21ST CENTURY: Integrated Thematic Instruction
by Robert Ellingsen . . . . $ 15.95

How does a high performance, brain-compatible, thematic classroom function? Robert Ellingsen provides a step-by-step description of how to powerfully weave basic components of learning around a year-long theme. Companion book for the videotape listed below. *(Published by Susan Kovalik & Associates, 1989.)*

THE WAY WE WERE - THE WAY WE CAN BE: A Vision for Middle School by Ann Ross, Second Edition, 1993 .... $ 21.95

Interested in restructuring? This second edition reflects the experiences of those readers who used the first edition as their guide to classroom transformation and schoolwide restructuring. The book bubbles with practical ideas that can be implemented immediately in departmentalized, team, and core classroom settings. Plenty of sample themes and processes for developing curriculum in a team setting. *(Published by Susan Kovalik & Associates, 1993.)*

ADVENTURES DOWN THE MISSISSIPPI: A Year's Integrated Thematic Curriculum for Grades K-8 by Karen Kindrick and Cynthia Black .. $ 19.95

This is a recipe book - the first of its kind from Susan Kovalik & Associates! Real curriculum for an entire year developed for a multi-age grouping of students, ages 5-14. It includes key points for all subjects—math, science, social studies, fine arts and language arts—plus inquiries, resources and closures. *(Published by Susan Kovalik & Associates, 1990.)*

VIDEOTAPES ABOUT ITI (VHS 1/2" FORMAT)

CLASSROOM OF THE 21ST CENTURY by Robert Ellingsen ...... $ 175.00

Observe an Integrated Thematic Instruction (ITI) fourth-grade classroom where all curriculum content and skills are orchestrated around a yearlong theme. Listen to the students speak for the power of the model. A detailed 75-page handbook accompanies this video to facilitate replication in all classrooms. Video 30 minutes. *(Produced by Susan Kovalik & Associates, 1989.)*

I CAN DIVIDE AND CONQUER: A Concept in a Day
by Martha Miller Kaufeldt .... $ 155.00

If the learning environment is brain-compatible, allowing the brain to learn naturally (and therefore most powerfully), something as "hard" as long division—concept and computation – can be mastered in a single day. Visit a fourth grade teacher as she takes her 30 students plus 20 more fourth, fifth, and sixth graders through an unforgettable day of conquering long division. Division Day has been replicated throughout the country by individual teachers, whole schools, and even entire districts! What's next? Why multiplication in a week, of course! Winner of the "Gold Apple Award" for the best Teacher Education video of 1987. Video 30 minutes. Handbook included. *(Produced by Susan Kovalik & Associates, 1987.)*

"AT HOME" WITH INTEGRATED THEMATIC INSTRUCTION
by Cynthi Black and Karen Kindrick .... $ 59.95

This video shows the application of the Integrated Thematic Instruction model to a home schooling environment with children ages 3 to 13. It illustrates how to integrate the basic skills of reading, writing and math with science, social studies, art and music. The accompanying handbook provides curriculum for an entire year — a yearlong theme ("Adventure Down the Mississippi"), monthly components, key points, and inquiries. Video 30 minutes, handbook, 175 pages. *(Produced by Susan Kovalik & Associates, 1992.)*

**THE HOW AND WHY OF INTEGRATED THEMATIC INSTRUCTION,
Volumes 1, 2 & 3** by Susan Kovalik . . . . $ 31.95

Susan shares the philosophy and practicality of Integrated Thematic Instruction. This three-tape series presents the steps necessary to create a classroom of the 21st century. Recorded before an enthusiastic live audience. Audiocassette, one hour each volume. *(Produced by Susan Kovalik & Associates, 1989.)*

HOW TO'S IN THE CLASSROOM

WHAT'S WORTH TEACHING? SELECTING, ORGANIZING AND INTEGRATING KNOWLEDGE by Marion Brady . . . . $ 19.95

This book provides a fresh look at curriculum from the perspective of the 1990's; it is not an extension of older frames of reference. Reflective of current brain research and consistent with Leslie Hart's learning theories and the Kovalik Integrated Thematic Instruction model, Brady provides a workable framework for analyzing deficits of traditional curriculum and for creating curriculum appropriate for the 21st century. According to Brady, "the proper subject matter of education is reality" and should be demonstrably applicable to daily experience, universal and equally valid for every student, and integrated and part of a coherent conceptual structure. This is a "must read" book for teachers and administrators. *(New York State University Press, 1989.)*

THE KID'S GUIDE TO SOCIAL ACTION: How to Solve the Social Problems YOU CHOOSE—and Turn Creative Thinking into Positive Action by Barbara A. Lewis . . . . $ 14.95

The 1991 Susan Kovalik Gold Medal Award for the best classroom resource book, the guide is an extraordinary source for exploring life beyond the classroom. It provides step-by-step examples of how to initiate and follow through on social action projects; includes many anecdotal stories of actions by kids across the country which changed their communities. Part II, Power Skills, is a practical guide to the levers by which power is exerted in a democracy. Fabulous integration of the application of language arts skills, social studies, and real life! *(Published by Free Spirit Publishing, 1981.)*

MEGASKILLS: How Families Can Help Children to Succeed in School and Beyond by Dorothy Rich . . . .$ 12.95

This is the bridge for bringing home and school together into a close partnership on behalf of children. According to the author, the megaskills are the values, attitudes, and behaviors that determine a child's achievement. "They are our children's inner engines of learning. While they are reinforced in the classroom, they get their power from the home." The megaskills are: confidence, motivation, effort, responsibility, initiative, perseverance, caring, teamwork, common sense, and problem-solving. Clear, immediately transportable from the page into practice, over two-thirds of the book is devoted to "recipes" – activities that can be done in the everyday world, home or school. Perhaps the best parent-teacher handbook in the past 20 years. *(Published by Houghton-Mifflin, 1988.)*

TRIBES: A Process for Social Development and Cooperative Learning
by Jeanne Gibbs . . . . $ 19.95

Whatever your approach to cooperative learning, you will find this to be a valuable tool for training students to work successfully in a group setting. Practical and hands-on, this book provides many exercises and scenarios that are immediately transferable to your classroom. *(Published by Center Source Publications, 1987.)*

SCIENCE THROUGH CHILDREN'S LITERATURE: An Integrated Approach by Carol Butzow and John Butzow . . . . $ 24.50

This book allows teachers to see the vast possibilities in connecting literature and science in their daily curriculum. It provides step-by-step suggestions for K-3 and good beginning examples for 4-6. Additional references for further study are included. *(Published by Libraries Unlimited, 1989.)*

SOCIAL IMPACT ON STUDENTS

DESIGNING GROUPWORK: Strategies for the Heterogeneous Classroom by Elizabeth Cohen, Foreword by John Goodlad . . . . $ 15.95

A rare combination of useable research and practical how to's, this book provides a theoretical base for using any and all cooperative learning models and provides a convincing rationale for its importance to learning and to our society. Also provides how to's for the bilingual and multi-ability classroom. Readable, practical, this book comes with our highest recommendation. *(Published by Teachers College Press, 1986.)*

ALL GROWN UP AND NO PLACE TO GO: Teenagers in Crisis
by David Elkind . . . . $ 9.95

Teens are expected to confront adult challenges at an early age, without preparation. The normal adolescent rituals have disappeared, their symbols and trappings usurped by younger children, thus leaving teens with no markers for their own passage into adulthood and thus all grown up with no where to go. *(Published by Addison-Wesley Publishing Co., 1984.)*

THE HURRIED CHILD: Growing Up Too Fast Too Soon
by David Elkind . . . . $ 10.95

Often with the very best intentions, parents and the schools expose children to overwhelming pressures by blurring the boundaries of what is age-appropriate, expecting or imposing too much too soon. The effects of such hurrying is crippling. *(Published by Addison-Wesley Publishing Co., 1988.)*

HIGH RISK STUDENTS: Children Without a Conscience
by Ken Magid and Carole McKelvey . . . . $ 9.95

This is a book that will disturb your sleep for many a night. It is a well-researched, compelling account of the almost irreversible damage caused by lack of bonding by infants and the young with a primary care-giver. These are children who cannot trust, who cannot love, who will not be loved. Found on every school playground and most classrooms, they are products of every level of society, even the best-intentioned families. *(Published by Bantam Books, 1987.)*

MISEDUCATION: Preschoolers at Risk by David Elkind . . . . $ 10.95

According to Dr. Elkind, early miseducation can cause permanent damage to a child's self-esteem, the loss of the positive attitude a child needs for learning and the blocking of natural gifts and potential talents. *(Published by Alfred A. Knopf, 1987.)*

LEADERSHIP—SETTING A VISION

WINNING THE BRAIN RACE: A Bold Plan to Make Our Schools Competitive by David Kearns and Dennis P. Doyle . . . . $ 9.95

As Chairman and CEO of Xerox, Kearns sees a clear connection between the quality of education and the ability of business to survive and compete in the world marketplace. But he also sees that the issue is even bigger: the survival of our society as we know it. Building on lessons of the market place, Kearns and Doyle present a six-point program for reform centering around choice, restructuring, professionalism, standards, values, and federal responsibility. As a view "from the other side of the fence," this book shifts our perspective, opening up new avenues of thinking. *(Published by the Institute of Contemporary Studies, 1989.)*

CAUGHT IN THE MIDDLE: Educational Reform for Young Adolescents in California Public Schools
by the California State Department of Education . . . . $ 5.00

A clear and urgent call for action, this book provides a description of the unique needs of the middle school student (grades 6-8) and a comprehensive proposal for change. "Must reading" for anyone involved in restructuring/improvement efforts on behalf of students in grades 6-8. *(Published by the California State Department of Education, 1987.)*

LEADERS: The Strategies for Taking Charge — The Four Keys of Effective Leadership by Warren Bennis and Burt Nanus . . . . $ 10.95

With observations such as "managers do things right, leaders do the right thing," this book provides a penetrating look at leadership — what it is and what it isn't — and advances a new theory of leadership and strategies to go with it. *(Published by Harper and Row, 1985.)*

LEADERSHIP TOOLS

DINOSAUR BRAINS: Dealing with All Those Impossible People At Work
by Albert Bernstein and Sydney Rozen . . . . $ 22.95

Dinosaur Brains is a practical, step-by-step guide to dealing with all kinds of difficult people at work. It will help you understand irrational people and how to avoid becoming one of them. It may also prevent you from making the kinds of mistakes that could lead your career (and you!) to extinction. A humorous, yet serious, application of the triune brain theory. *(Published by John Wiley & Sons, 1989.)*

HOMESCHOOLING FOR EXCELLENCE: How to Take Charge of Your Child's Education—And Why You Absolutely MUST
by David and Micki Colfax . . . . $ 8.95

After 15 years of experience with educating their children at home (and sending them to Harvard University), the Colfaxes provide straight talk for parents. Also valuable for educators . . . a fresh look at the topic of curriculum and how to make it come alive. *(Published by Warner Books, 1988.)*

THE SEVEN HABITS OF EFFECTIVE PEOPLE by Stephen Cove . . $ 12.00

This book represents a significant break with the personal/professional growth/empowerment books over the past 50 years. Covey defines a "habit" as the intersection of knowledge, skill, and desire. Making the distinction between personality ethic and character ethic, the author lays out a powerful agenda for improving one's effectiveness at work and at home. *(Published by Simon and Schuster, 1989.)*

THE MENTOR TEACHER ROLE: Owners' Manual
by Karen Olsen . . . . $ 16.95

This is a "how to" book: how to make your work as a mentor teacher or staff developer more powerful. Included are frameworks for teaching adults, designing and conducting effective in-service and a new coaching model specifically designed to be used by peers with peers. This handbook is a must for those whose responsibilities include teacher training and staff development which builds on teachers teaching teachers. *(Published by Books for Educators, 1989.)*

THE FIFTH DISCIPLINE: The Art and Practice of the Learning Organization by Peter M. Senge . . . . $ 25.00

Question: Does your organization have a learning disability? Applauded by Ed Deming, creator of Japan's zero defect management approach, steeped in common sense and a clear view of our current organizations and future challenges, this is the most unusual book on management to appear in decades. Here are just a few of the sections of the book: How our actions create our reality . . . and how we can change it; the Fifth Discipline: the cornerstone of the learning organization; nature's templates: identifying the patterns that control events; the principle of leverage; the art of seeing the forest *and* the trees; building the learning organization; prototypes, etc. This one is guaranteed to shift your perspective of your bureaucracy and open up doors to new possibilities. *(Published by Doubleday, 1990.)*

UNPLUGGING THE PLUG-IN DRUG: Help Your Children Kick the TV Habit by Marie Winn . . . . $ 7.95

Filled with practical advice from children, parents and teachers, this book explains TV addiction and how to fight it. Includes tips on how to plan ahead, making a week without TV a time for more reading, more play, and a more enjoyable family life. The research into the effects of TV on children will jar you! *(Published by Penquin Books, 1987.)*

PLEASE UNDERSTAND ME: Character & Temperament Types
by David Keirsey and Marilyn Bates . . . . $ 11.95

This is perhaps the most versatile book on our list. It is wonderfully useful and powerful when working with students in the classroom or with adults in staff development, whether in a leadership role or at home in the realm of one's personal life. Described here are qualities that we are born with and which change very little through life. The message here is to learn to live with, and, yes, even appreciate, others. Give up trying to change 'em! Each personality type has strengths and capacities that strengthen a team effort. *(Published by Prometheus Nemesis Book Company, 1978.)*

RESTRUCTURING

GUIDE TO SCHOOL CHANGE by Leslie A. Hart . . . . $ 12.50

This book focuses on the <u>process</u> of change and how to implement it, on student <u>learning</u> rather than on <u>teaching</u>. Refreshing and succinct, excellent for leadership teams and school site council members. Hart discusses change (what it is and isn't), gives options to consider, provides a brief introduction to findings from current brain research, offers some alternatives in effecting school change, and discusses some of the prickly "people" aspects of change. *(Published by Books for Educators, 1985.)*

IMPROVING SCHOOLS FROM WITHIN: Teachers, Parents and Principals Can Make the Difference by Roland S. Barth . . . . $ 14.95

Lasting improvement in public education, argues Barth, must come from within the schools: those closest to students are best qualified to implement and sustain change. Offers a range of innovative ideas on how to reform our schools from within. *(Published by Jossey-Bass, 1990.)*

HOW TO MAKE MEETINGS WORK: The New Interaction Method
by Doyle and Straus . . . . $ 4.95

A wonderfully practical "how to" book—how to stop wasting time and get things done at meetings, give everybody a feeling of greater participation and influence, develop agendas and arrange meeting rooms (and even chairs) in order to make meetings pay off, ways a "facilitator," a "recorder" and a "group memory" help generate more and better solutions to problems, and, when to NOT have meetings! *(Published by Jove Books, 1976.)*

THE PREDICTABLE FAILURE OF EDUCATIONAL REFORM: Can We Change Course Before It's Too Late? by Seymour B. Sarason . . . . $ 23.95

Long-standing educational structures, coupled with the need of various groups to defend their interests and preserve their power, stifles reform efforts—all resulting in failure, predictable failure. Arguing that we need to reevaluate the very aim of educational reforms and come to terms with our past—the lessons of good intentions gone awry. Sarason offers insights into how educators can make significant reforms that produce substantial, long-lasting results. *(Published by Jossey-Bass, 1990.)*

HORACE'S COMPROMISE: The Dilemma of the American High School
by Theodore Sizer. . . . . $ 8.95

With great insight and humor, Sizer outlines the failure of the current high school and offers a blueprint for reform. This book is the text for the Coalition of Essential Schools reform effort. *(Published by Houghton Mifflin, 1984.)*

HORACE'S SCHOOL: Redesigning the American High School
by Theodore Sizer . . . . $ 19.95

This book provides invaluable insights into the process of making change happen—a compendium of the experiences of those involved in the national Coalition for Essential Schools. *(Published by Houghton Mifflin, 1992.)*

20 TEACHERS by Ken Macrorie . . . . $ 9.95

A revealing glimpse into the teaching of 20 teachers whose students consistently do brilliant and meaningful work and how they "enable" learners to learn. Describes 43 commonly held characteristics of these powerful teachers. *(Published by Oxford University Press, 1984.)*

MUSIC TO RENEW AND ENERGIZE

A KID'S EYE VIEW OF THE ENVIRONMENT *(cassette tape)*
by Michael Mish . . . . $ 9.95

An ingenious mix of interviews with young children about environmental problems with solutions set to music and song. Each tune is in a different musical style – Latin rhythms, European folk song, modern hip, etc. Delightful for its professional musicality, lyrics guaranteed to be a smash hit with students. Excellent way to integrate music into science. Have some fun! Good enough to play again and again and *again! (Published by Mish Mash Music, 1989.)*

NEW TITLES

A MIDDLE SCHOOL CURRICULUM FROM RHETORIC TO REALITY by James Beane . . . . $ 12.00

MAPPING INNER SPACE: Learning and Teaching Mind Mapping by Nancy Margulies 21.95

POSITIVE DISCIPLINE by Jane Nelsen 10.00

REDESIGNING EDUCATION by Lynn Stoddar 12.95

SCIENTIFIC AMERICAN: Special Issue—Mind and Brain September, 1992 . . . . 4.95

SEVEN WAYS OF KNOWING by David Lazear 30.00

SEVEN WAYS OF TEACHING by David Lazear 17.95

THE EXHAUSTED SCHOOL by John Taylor Gatto 10.95

FOR THE CLASSROOM

DESK CHIMES —A musical way to reconvene your class. . . .$34.95

NEW RELEASES

INTEGRATED THEMATIC INSTRUCTION: The Model
by Susan Kovalik (Replaces **TEACHERS MAKE THE DIFFERENCE**)
Second edition, 1993 . . . . $ 24.95

This book is a result of working with teachers in schools which have adopted the ITI model districtwide. It provides a step-by-step discussion of how to implement ITI. What are the readiness factors for the teacher, classroom, school? How are state and district guidelines incorporated into a yearlong theme? What are possible starting points: weeklong themes, monthlong and, finally, yearlong themes where all content and skills are woven together in a meaningful package? Examples abound!

"ANCHOR" MATH: The Brain-Compatible Approach to Learning
by Leslie A. Hart . . . . $ 16.95

This is a book written for teachers who find that students respond to math as if it were of another world and had nothing to do with them. An informal book for all who teach elementary math and want to greatly increase student achievement, it explores the ways of "anchoring" math to the real world as perceived and processed by a student's mind. A follow-up book to *Human Brain and Human Learning*, it discusses how to teach math in a brain-compatible way. Perceptive, fresh, challenging. Just the tool needed to breathe real life into math and significantly increase student learning.

THE WAY WE WERE - THE WAY WE CAN BE: A Vision for Middle School by Ann Ross, Second Edition, 1993 . . . . $ 21.95

Interested in restructuring? This second edition reflects the experiences of those readers who used the first edition as their guide to classroom transformation and schoolwide restructuring. The book bubbles with practical ideas that can be implemented immediately in departmentalized, team, and core classroom settings. Plenty of sample themes and processes for developing curriculum in a team setting.

"AT HOME" WITH INTEGRATED THEMATIC INSTRUCTION
by Cynthi Black and Karen Kindrick . . . . $ 59.95

This video shows the application of the Integrated Thematic Instruction model to a home schooling environment with children ages 3 to 13. It illustrates how to integrate the basic skills of reading, writing, and math with science, social studies, art, and music. The accompanying handbook provides curriculum for an entire year—a yearlong theme ("Adventure Down the Mississippi"), monthly components, key points, and inquiries. Video 30 minutes, 1/2 VHS; handbook, 175 pages.

ORDER FORM

Qty	Title / Item	Price	Total

Subtotal	
*Sales tax	
**Shipping	
Total	

* Applies only to Arizona residents, 5%

**Shipping via UPS and handling: 10% of order with a minimum of $3 and maximum of $45 (to Canada, slightly higher, via U.S. mail)

PURCHASE ORDER # _____

Name _____

Shipping Address _____

City_____ State _____ Zip _____

Billing address (if different)_____

City_____ State _____ Zip _____

Phone_____

♦UPS requires a street address to deliver books; please do **not** use a P.O. box number. All orders are U.S. funds.

Prices are subject to change without notice.

Mail order to: BOOKS FOR EDUCATORS
P. O. Box 20525
Village of Oak Creek, AZ 86341
Telephone: (602) 284-2389 / Fax (602) 284-0247

ORDER FORM

Qty	Title / Item	Price	Total

Subtotal	
*Sales tax	
**Shipping	
Total	

* Applies only to Arizona residents, 5%

**Shipping via UPS and handling: 10% of order with a minimum of \$3 and maximum of \$45 (to Canada, slightly higher, via U.S. mail)

PURCHASE ORDER # _____

Name _____

Shipping Address _____

City_____ State _____ Zip _____

Billing address (if different)_____

City_____ State _____ Zip _____

Phone_____

✦UPS requires a street address to deliver books; please do **not** use a P.O. box number. All orders are U.S. funds.

Prices are subject to change without notice.

Mail order to: BOOKS FOR EDUCATORS
P. O. Box 20525
Village of Oak Creek, AZ 86341
Telephone: (602) 284-2389 / Fax (602) 284-0247